P9-DFC-045

THOMAS JEFFERSON

AND THE POLITICS OF NATURE

LOYOLA TOPICS IN POLITICAL PHILOSOPHY

Thomas S. Engeman,
Series Editor

This series originates in the Frank M. Covey, Jr., Lectures in Political Analysis. The Covey Lectures are delivered annually at Loyola University Chicago and published in a series by the University of Notre Dame Press. Frank Covey, a distinguished lawyer and Loyola alumnus, endowed the lectures to promote the study of political philosophy, in the expectation that this enquiry would contribute to human understanding and political justice. The books in the Loyola Topics in Political Philosophy series offer a number of responses of prominent scholars to issues addressed in the Covey Lectures. Each volume contains an introductory essay by the Covey lecturer and a concluding reflection on new issues raised by the contributors. The intention of the series is to offer the best current scholarship to teachers and students, as well as to general readers.

THOMAS JEFFERSON

AND THE POLITICS OF NATURE

THOMAS S. ENGEMAN

Editor

UNIVERSITY OF NOTRE DAME PRESS
Notre Dame, Indiana

© 2000 by
University of Notre Dame Press
Notre Dame, Indiana 46556

All Rights Reserved

Manufactured in the United States of America

The editor and publisher express their gratitude
for permission to publish:

Joyce Appleby, "Commercial Farming and the 'Agrarian Myth' in the
Early Republic," *Journal of American History* 68, no. 4 (March 1982):
833–49. By permission of the *Journal of American History* on behalf of the
Organization of American Historians.

Jean Yarbrough, material from *American Virtues: Thomas Jefferson on the
Character of a Free People* (Lawrence: University Press of Kansas, 1998).
By permission of the University Press of Kansas.

ISBN 0-268-04211-X

A Cataloging-in-Publication record for this book is available
upon request from the Library of Congress

∞ *The paper used in this publication meets the minimum requirements of the
American National Standard for Information Sciences—Permanence of Paper
for Printed Library Materials, ANSI Z39.48-1984.*

AUSTIN COMMUNITY COLLEGE
LEARNING RESOURCE SERVICES

for

Susan
and
Morgan

❖

Contents

❋

Acknowledgments

꘠

The series introduced by this volume has had many contributors and well-wishers. The original proposal was greeted warmly by James P. Langford, the director of the University of Notre Dame Press. At Loyola, Kathleen McCourt, Dean of the College of Arts and Sciences, and John Williams, chair of the Department of Political Science, gave the project their blessing and support.

I am grateful for the aid I have received from all the contributors to this volume, especially Michael P. Zuckert. I also thank the staff of the University of Notre Dame Press for their help. In particular, credit should go to our editor, Rebecca DeBoer, who worked quickly and competently to keep the project on track.

A number of graduate assistants have given of their best to this project, including Scott Yenor, Steven J. Michels, and Douglas Davis. I am likewise grateful to Mary Margaret Kelly, the administrative assistant of my department, for her efforts. I thank Fred D. Miller, Jr., and the staff at the Social Philosophy and Policy Center at Bowling Green State University of Ohio for their aid while I was a scholar in residence. Loyola's Office of Research Services provided financial assistance at opportune moments during the course of this project. Finally, I thank Frank M. Covey, Jr., who has been everything an academic benefactor could be.

Introduction

⁂

Thomas S. Engeman

Today few political heroes remain well known or admired. Indeed, such accomplished statesmen as George Washington, James Madison, and Alexander Hamilton—an American captain general, two presidents, and founders all—no longer capture mass attention or affection. Of course, there are exceptions to our general amnesia. Thomas Jefferson and Abraham Lincoln still seem to fascinate us, as they always have; they stand tall in the American pantheon, the greatest of our Olympians. As Michael Zuckert notes in the afterword: "the outpouring of books on Jefferson continues unabated, the 'shrine' to Jefferson at Monticello attracts record numbers of visitors, movies are made about him." Why is this the case? The public concern reserved for Jefferson and (I would argue) Lincoln transcends a simple weighing of their statesmanship in the actual coin of sacrifice and success. They are beloved at least as much for their great words as for their great deeds; their understanding is more lasting than their actions. Indeed, they have proven our theoretical statesmen, our philosopher presidents. Proclaiming a new, natural equality, Jefferson gained the liberation of the colonies. Lincoln ended chattel slavery under the same Jeffersonian banner of equal liberty. With the Declaration's principles of equality and liberty as their fighting words, Jefferson created, and Lincoln renewed, the theory and practice of American democracy.

Abraham Lincoln understood well Jefferson's exalted place in America's imagination and political soul. For Lincoln, Jefferson's Declaration of Independence served equally as a clarion call announcing the battle for liberty officially joined, and as the proclamation of principles support-

I

ing a wholly new type of political regime. Jefferson's words created the *novus ordo seclorum*, a new (political) order of the ages, as is inscribed on the Great Seal of the United States. For this reason, Lincoln emphatically celebrated Jefferson's authorship of the Declaration of Independence: "Thomas Jefferson . . . the great oracle and expounder of our faith"; "Thomas Jefferson . . . penned the immortal paper"; "the principles of Jefferson are the definitions and axioms of free society"; and, finally:

> all honor to Jefferson—to the man who, in the concrete pressure of a struggle for national independence by a single people, had the coolness, forecast, and capacity to introduce into a merely revolutionary document, an abstract truth, applicable to all men and all times, and so to embalm it there, that to-day, and in all coming days, it shall be a rebuke and a stumbling block to the very harbingers of re-appearing tyranny and oppression.[1]

For Lincoln, Jefferson (not George Washington, or anyone else) "was, is, and perhaps will continue to be, the most distinguished politician of our history." Jefferson was "one of the greatest teachers of freedom and free labor." Altogether, reflecting on the Declaration's influence on him, Lincoln said:

> I have never had a feeling politically that did not spring from the sentiments embodied in the Declaration of Independence . . . I have often inquired of myself, what great principle or idea it was that kept this Confederacy so long together. It . . . was something in the Declaration giving liberty, not alone to the people of this country, but hope to the world for all future time. It was that which gave promise that in due time the weights should be lifted from the shoulders of all men, and that *all* should have an equal chance. This is the sentiment embodied in that Declaration of Independence.[2]

According to Abraham Lincoln, the "essential" Jefferson is the revolutionary author of the Declaration of Independence. The essential Jefferson taught the true principles of democracy, "the definitions and axioms of a free society." The Southern conservative, George Fitzhugh, overstated Lincoln's analysis in a revealing way. Fitzhugh thought Jefferson the ultimate liberal, his liberalism resulting in social anarchy, not lawful freedom: "The true greatness of Mr. Jefferson was his fitness for revolution. He was the genius of innovation, the architect of ruin, the inaugurator of anarchy . . . He thought everything false as well in the physical as in the moral world. He fed his horses on potatoes, and defended harbors with gunboats, because it was contrary to human experience (and) human opinion."[3]

Because of his revolutionary defense of democracy and his subsequent popularity, Jefferson was treated with the utmost respect by Lincoln. Lincoln made Jefferson not only the theoretical "oracle" of the principles and axioms of democratic society, but the greatest practitioner of American practical statecraft as well. Lincoln claimed Jefferson as his political and theoretical mentor. He employed Jefferson's writings, often implausibly, to support his own position in a host of political controversies. At different times Lincoln claimed Jefferson's support for a tariff to encourage domestic manufactures, the presidential veto, the Missouri Compromise, exclusion of slavery in the Northwest territories, judicial review, colonization, and God's wrath at the enslavement of one people by another.[4] In 1860, when an opposition paper claimed Lincoln had defamed Jefferson in an early speech (1844), Lincoln immediately responded to the charge through a friendly paper: "Throughout the whole of his political life, Mr. Lincoln has ever spoken of Mr. Jefferson in the most kindly and respectful manner, holding him up as one of the ablest statesmen of his own or any other age."[5] In *The Federalist* papers, James Madison made a similar appeal to the wisdom of the great democrat. Madison enlisted Jefferson's support for the necessity of separation of powers (while very deferentially condemning Jefferson's insistence on frequent referral to the people to maintain a sufficient separation).[6]

Jefferson certainly understood himself as a "revolutionary" democrat. He called his presidential election in 1800 a greater revolution than that of 1776. Jefferson knew he would "revolutionize" the Federalist commercial elites, stopping the development of their constitutional "monarchy." Three decades later Alexis de Tocqueville still agreed with Jefferson's estimate of the election's import:

In 1801, the Republicans finally got control of the government. Thomas Jefferson was elected President; he brought them the support of a famous name, great talents, and immense popularity . . . When the Republicans came to power, the opposing party seemed to be engulfed by a sudden flood. A huge majority declared itself against it, and suddenly finding itself so small a majority, it at once fell into despair. Thenceforth the Republican, or Democratic, Party has gone on from strength to strength and taken possession of the whole of society.[7]

Jefferson's election confirmed his place as the great American democrat. Not only had he authored the Declaration of Independence, he had also founded the party which successfully championed its principles. As

America's foremost democrat and Democrat, Jefferson led the electoral overthrow of the Federalists' "monarchy" and commercial elitism. Moreover, by encouraging agriculture he solidified the nation economically and socially, fueling massive immigration onto American free soil. The long period of Jeffersonian democracy, extending into the 1830s and 1840s was kindly remembered by the long-lived Ohioan, William Dean Howells, as the "golden age" of American democracy. Howells's agrarian utopia, Altruria, reflects his lifelong appreciation of Jefferson's economic statecraft. In her essay in this volume the historian Joyce Appleby has memorably renewed an appreciation of Jefferson's agrarian economic policies:

> The battle between Jeffersonians and Federalists appears not as a conflict between the patrons of agrarian self-sufficiency and the proponents of modern commerce, but rather as a struggle between two different elaborations of capitalistic development in America. Jefferson becomes, not the heroic loser in a battle against modernity, but the conspicuous winner in a contest over how the government should serve its citizens in the first generation of the nation's territorial expansion.[8]

It almost goes without saying that Jefferson's democratic or egalitarian policies, rooted in such pro-agrarianism, were teamed with a passionate defense of political liberty. While the Declaration of Independence embraces the natural equality of all mankind, it also argues, indeed demands, human liberation: "Men are endowed by their Creator with certain [inherent and] inalienable rights; that to secure these rights, governments are instituted among men, deriving their just powers from the consent of the governed; that whenever any form of government becomes destructive of these ends, it is the right of the people to alter and abolish it and to institute a new government." Jefferson's First Inaugural Address also justifies the new government in terms of liberty:

> What more is necessary to make us a happy and prosperous people? Still one thing more . . . a wise and frugal government, which still restrains men from injuring one another, which shall leave them otherwise free to regulate their own pursuits of industry and improvement, and shall not take from the mouths of labor the bread it has earned. This is the sum of good government.

Enumerating the "essential principles of government" later in his inaugural address, Jefferson concludes with "freedom of religion, freedom of the press, freedom of the person under *habeas corpus*; and a trial by juries impartially selected." In defending Jefferson from the charge he was a strong president who violated laws and rights when in office, Raoul Berger writes: "The charge that Jefferson had no 'respect for law' simply does not square with the facts."[9]

A serious question is how Jefferson, the leading liberal theorist of the nineteenth century, became the hero of the very different liberalism of the twentieth. Robert Booth Fowler addresses this theoretical paradox in his essay in this volume: "As a self-declared Jeffersonian democrat (and Democrat), President Franklin D. Roosevelt dedicated the Jeffersonian Memorial in 1943. There was considerable irony in the event in that FDR by then was no advocate of small government, which was integral to what it meant to be a Jeffersonian and a Jeffersonian democrat." Having discredited the Federalists' "commercial" liberalism, the Progressives and FDR created a new, more democratic or egalitarian patriotic tradition supporting their theoretical refounding of American politics. Herbert Croly believed Jefferson's egalitarianism could be combined with Hamiltonian energy; Franklin Roosevelt argued that the "egalitarian" Jefferson had, himself, laid the groundwork for the modern welfare state:

> He did not deceive himself with outward forms. Government to him was a means to an end, and an end in itself; it might be either a refuge and a help or a threat and a danger, depending on the circumstances. We find him carefully analyzing the society for which he was to organize a Government . . . Jefferson realized that the exercise of the property rights might so interfere with the rights of the individual that the Government, without whose assistance the property rights could not exist, must intervene, not to destroy individualism, but to protect it.[10]

From a nineteenth-century liberal who thought equality was guaranteed by liberty, Roosevelt converted Jefferson into a twentieth-century liberal. In FDR's view, the suppression of some rights, among them property rights, was necessary to protect equal freedom and "true" individualism.

While directly opposed to the kind of society and government Jefferson sought, FDR argued that Jefferson's love of equality and of the common man—especially the farmer (as opposed to the professionals and businessmen, the bourgeois)—indicated his clear preference in the "war" between labor and capital. Moreover, Jefferson's intellectualism, his faith in scientific progress and in the necessity of constant revolutions in both social and political institutions, and his desire for a more secular society than the other founders, were all offered as proof that Jefferson was the "Sage" of Monticello—the true progressive philosopher of the American Founding. As Jeffrey Sedgwick writes: "it was in this century that his [Jefferson's] face was enshrined on Mount Rushmore, his home in Monticello was reopened to the public . . . and the Jefferson Memorial in Washington, D.C., took its place next to the Lincoln Memorial and the Washington Monument. . . . Jefferson could triumph in the twentieth century only to the extent his primary political aims of human liberty and progress could be divorced from his chosen means of limited government."[11]

Moreover, as the embodiment of American sentiment, virtue, taste, and education—American democracy at its peak, its "best and brightest"—Jefferson's personality has always loomed large in the assessment of the man. As the great democrat, Jefferson argued that Americans should avoid the corruption of commercial individualism and live as virtuous men and women. But did he do so himself? If the personal (and moral) is the political, as Jefferson suggested—in firm opposition to the "amoral" rational interestedness of his opponents (like Publius)—each age has had to examine Jefferson's heart as well as his head. Since modern sentiment has made the treatment of the oppressed the touchstone of sincerity, Jefferson's apparent indifference to slavery in his personal life is now widely condemned. For the same reason, his ostentatious, Epicurean (materialistic and aristocratic) life at Monticello raises questions. Some claim his indifference to civil liberties as president is hypocritical. Robert Dawidoff quotes his fellow Virginian John Randolph's dismissal of Jefferson as "St. Thomas of Cantingbury." Booth Fowler highlights faults that modern scholars continue to expose in Jefferson's image as the American sage and virtuous democrat writ large.

But Jefferson's personality and "image" do not dictate *our* interest in him. Jefferson's political thought remains central for a proper understanding of the principles of American democracy. This was Abraham Lincoln's view and still appears to be the popular view. While the essays collected here examine many aspects of Jefferson's life and image in American culture, our primary concern is directed to a serious reconstruction of Jefferson's political thought and an assessment of its continuing significance. A brief introduction to the collected essays is offered in the following section.

Michael Zuckert's Jefferson is the great teacher of the theory and practice of modern natural rights philosophy. Indeed, Zuckert argues that Thomas Jefferson's political thought continues to offer the best theoretical approach to democracy available to us. The Declaration of Independence, in particular, provides the best summary of the principles of liberty, equality, and consent at the heart of modern democracy. The *Notes on the State of Virginia* is Jefferson's most comprehensive statement on the meaning and application of the principles of the Declaration. In this essay, Zuckert, a distinguished Jefferson scholar, offers his comprehensive interpretation of Jefferson's political thought.

If Zuckert moderates ("domesticates," according to Fowler) Jefferson's natural rights philosophy, suggesting natural rights are rationally reciprocal as Kant theorizes, Jean Yarbrough argues that Jefferson incorporates the authors of the Scottish Enlightenment and principles from the Republican tradition, to achieve a similar moderating effect. In Yarbrough's view, both the Republicans and the Scots make Jefferson's liberalism less libertarian and more public-spirited and political than Zuckert suggests. Against Zuckert, Yarbrough argues that Jefferson's fully developed thought is revealed more clearly in the letters, stretching across fifty years, than in the early Declaration of Independence and *Notes on the State of Virginia* upon which Zuckert relies.

Garrett Ward Sheldon looks at the broader cultural influences shaping Jefferson's thought. Sheldon traces Jefferson's republicanism to its "source" in Aristotle, not to later writers usually thought to have been more directly influential on him. In particular, Jefferson's ward system incorporates the republican advantages of active citizenship through direct democracy, as espoused by Aristotle, within a liberal, extended republic governed by elected representatives in large districts. Moreover, unlike Zuckert, Sheldon traces the "Kantian" aspects of Jefferson's thought directly to his support of Christian ethics. For Jefferson, Christianity's effectual truth is not its message of salvation but its universal morality. This morality is capable of providing the basis of a virtuous, self-governing, and humane republic. In Sheldon's reading, Jefferson consciously wove together aspects of the three dominant American traditions—Lockean liberalism, Aristotelian republicanism, and reformed Christianity—to make a truly democratic whole. Jefferson informed the principles of the Declaration with a prudent and pervasive "communitarianism" similar to Alexis de Tocqueville's description of the practice of American liberalism in the 1830s.

Robert Dawidoff supports many of the arguments about Jefferson's thought developed in the essays of Zuckert, Yarbrough, and Fowler. But Dawidoff is more concerned with Jefferson as a writer and literary figure than as a political thinker and actor. In Dawidoff's view, Jefferson was a self-conscious polymath following the fashion of the European aristocracy. The tension between Jefferson's personal conduct and his evocation of democratic virtue is attributable to his embrace of the noble ease, high living, and perhaps, the moral freedom granted the aristocrat. The tension between the moral freedom of the great—and their obedience to general morality—has been a theme of liberal thought since Machiavelli made this an issue for republican politics. Machiavelli argued that the prince who publicly pursued pleasures denied to the populace would weaken his rule and debase public morals. Machiavelli's solution—dissembling on the part of the prince—is perhaps sufficient in a monarchical state. But in a democratic republic, leaders continue to be chosen for moral as well as political ends. In Dawidoff's view, whatever were Jefferson's defects, his great legacies remain: (1) his splendid teaching of natural rights and liberties, (2) the ennobling of democratic possibilities through the greatness of his exemplary life and actions, and (3) the creation of a potent "noble lie" through his image of a romantic, agrarian pastoral society. Jefferson's America is a democratic garden of Eden where virtue and ability find a home in a simple agrarian society of equal freedom.

Booth Fowler describes a Jefferson greatly shrunk in stature as a result of recent critical reexamination. In this case, less *is* more. A shorter, slimmer Jefferson, as it were, is for Fowler a truer and more useful founder for contemporary Americans. While Jefferson *was* a political revolutionary and (secondarily) a political theorist, Fowler does not consider these aspects most characteristic. A committed egalitarian, Jefferson was more pragmatic than principled in his politics. For example, in Fowler's view, Jefferson did not believe that there was a natural right to property. The state had the right to make pragmatic redistributions necessary to guarantee the imperative of social equality. For Fowler, Jefferson was more forthcoming about his Epicurean self than those who romanticize him as the heroic Sage of Monticello and the founder of a new nation. Jefferson was modest enough to know that he was not the stuff from which heroes are made. But Jefferson had unique qualities, and we justly recognize him for them. Above all he loved life: "Thomas Jefferson was an extraordinary but very real human being, in love with life and its endless dimensions, flawed as we all are, and always a restless, pragmatic, reflective, manysided Epicurean." Jefferson is a democratic Everyman, someone we can look to because he is really one of us. Thomas Jefferson is the American for our season.

In considering Jefferson's extraordinary success as a statesman—the greatest democratic leader in history in the view of both Alexis de Tocqueville and Abraham Lincoln—Joyce Appleby turns to the economy. She argues that Jefferson's agrarian policies were less romantic than those of Alexander Hamilton and of the Federalists generally, who sought a British model of industrial development. Faced with an empty continent, a worldwide demand for food (not finished goods), and the desire to make freeholders out of increasing waves of immigrants, Jefferson's policies were brilliantly successful. They created a thriving economy and middle class, particularly in the free-soil states formed in the Northwest Territory. Their success guaranteed a succession of Democratic party victories until the party's inability to solve the slave crisis destroyed Jefferson's political construction. In retrospect, Jefferson's agrarian America escaped the problems of industrialization, urbanization, and class conflict, as Jefferson had fore-cast. These problems did not arise until the end of the nineteenth century, when their development led to massive changes in American political thought and practice. Indeed, the modern "administrative" state was cre-ated by the Progressives to tame the evils of the new industrialization.

Finally, James Ceaser explores a great problem in Thomas Jefferson's thought and democratic statesmanship: the problem of race and of slavery. While defending natural liberties and the right of all to self-government, Jefferson argued that natural differences between the races are such that whites and blacks should be physically separate forever. While insisting that slavery was wrong, and blacks naturally entitled to the Declaration's natural rights, Jefferson felt the differences between them would always cause animosity if they remained within one political community. Ceaser traces Jefferson's belief in racial inferiority to a speculative new natural science prominent among European thinkers of his day. Unfortunately, Jefferson insisted in bringing these putative "facts" into the political realm in spite of the comfort such "facts" offered slaveholders and their allies. Ceaser argues that Jefferson committed a significant error in reducing politics to such conjectural "facts." Even if proven true, such "facts" should not trump political debate and decision. Scientific "facts" should be judged from the much more architectonic, prudential perspective of politics. The latter is based on a comprehensive view of the rights of citi-zens found in the Declaration and Constitution.

These studies are not exhaustive, nor would double their number be complete. But, they lay a foundation for the student of Jefferson's thought. The essays of Michael Zuckert, Jean Yarbrough, and Garrett Ward Sheldon offer a uniquely balanced and comprehensive introduction to Jefferson's extensive and influential understanding of democracy's foundation in reason and nature. Robert Dawidoff illustrates how Jefferson consciously created the images of an American justice and a perfected individualism capable of inspiring each new generation of his countrymen. This Jeffer-son agreed with Walt Whitman's literary formula: "I will put in my poems that with you is heroism upon land and sea / And I will report all heroism from an American point of view" (*Leaves of Grass*, "Starting from Paumanok"). Booth Fowler, examining the highly critical picture of Jeffer-son offered by recent scholarship, still finds at Monticello a vibrant and thoughtful man capable of speaking to our contemporary sensibility. Joyce Appleby describes how Jefferson wove together a theoretical prefer-ence for agrarianism with his recognition of America's need to develop land and give employment to new immigrants. James Ceaser sees in Jeffer-son's thought on race many of the confusions troubling similar studies in social science today.

It is unnecessary to seek a Jefferson so versatile as to contain the "multitudes" Whitman claimed for himself. For Jefferson does one thing above all—above anyone else. Jefferson gives us a compelling analysis of the two great theoretical polestars of American political thought: equality and liberty. As Alexis de Tocqueville and Abraham Lincoln argued repeatedly, these philosophical principles are our first principles. As Lincoln said, ours is a government, "conceived in liberty and dedicated to the proposition that all men are created equal." Therefore, our understanding of the meaning of liberty and equality will always dictate constitutional interpretation and public policy as long as our republic endures. As statesman, Jefferson sought political and economic solutions and social habits capable of sustaining political equality and liberty. But above all, Jefferson sought to teach the principles of liberty and equality required for a new nation by enshrining the Declaration of Independence as the foundation of the American regime, the theoretical ark of our political covenant. Or, as Lincoln said, the Declaration was the apple of gold, the Constitution the silver frame of the new nation. A nation founded on these democratic principles could create a new order of the ages.

NOTES

1. Roy P. Basler, ed., *The Collected Works of Abraham Lincoln*, 8 vols. (New Brunswick, N.J.: Rutgers University Press, 1952), 3:124, 220, 375–76.

2. Basler, 2:249; 4:112, 240.

3. George Fitzhugh, *Cannibals All! Or Slaves Without Masters*, ed. C. Vann Woodward (Cambridge: Harvard University Press, 1960) 135.

4. Basler, 1:487, 310, 502–3; 2:130, 249, 517, 552, 5:48, 3:410.

5. Basler, 4:112.

6. Alexander Hamilton, James Madison, and John Jay, *The Federalist* (Middletown, Conn.: Wesleyan University Press, 1961), Papers 48–50.

7. Alexis De Tocqueville, *Democracy in America*, ed. J. P. Mayer (Garden City, N.J.: Doubleday and Co., 1969), 177.

8. Joyce Appleby, *Liberalism and Republicanism in the Historical Imagination* (Cambridge: Harvard University Press, 1992), 258.

9. Raoul Berger, "Jefferson and the Law," in *Reason and Republicanism*, ed. Gary L. McDowell and Sharon L. Noble (Lanham, Md.: Rowman and Littlefield, 1997), 128.

10. Franklin D. Roosevelt, "The Commonwealth Club Address" (1932), in *The Public Papers and Addresses of Franklin Roosevelt*, ed. Samuel Rosenman (New York: Russell and Russell, 1969).

11. Jeffrey Leigh Sedgwick, "Jeffersonianism in the Progressive Era," in *Reason and Republicanism*, 202.

Founder of the
Natural Rights Republic

꙳

MICHAEL P. ZUCKERT

Surely the most familiar, as well as the most euphoric, assessment of
the American political tradition yet propounded lies in the opening of
Abraham Lincoln's Gettysburg Address. "Four-score and seven years ago,
our fathers brought forth upon this continent a new nation, conceived in
liberty and dedicated to the proposition that all men are created equal."
Within his biblical cadences, Lincoln proffered at least four important
claims about the American political order. First, it was a "new nation,"
new not only to this time and place, but altogether new to mankind.
America was a great experiment, an addition to the array of human political possibilities. In this judgment, Lincoln echoed the founding generation itself when it adopted the motto *novus ordo seclorum*—a new order
for the ages.

The new order dates from 1776, the year of independence, the year of
the Declaration of Independence. The new order does not date from 1788,
the year of the adoption of the Constitution, or from 1688, the year of the
Glorious Revolution in England, or from 1620, the year the Pilgrims came
to America and made their Mayflower Compact. All these other moments
no doubt tell importantly in the tale of the "new nation," but as prehistory
or history, not as birth date of this particular nation.

The new order was "conceived in liberty." The Americans freely chose
their new order; it was neither imposed on them by force, nor merely inherited by them from history, nor simply slid into without reflection. Free
reflective choice guarantees that the new order was consciously adopted
as good and desirable in itself. Perhaps Lincoln means to call attention

to a yet deeper sense in which the new order is "conceived in liberty"—conceived in the vision of human beings as naturally and essentially free beings, not subjected to others by God or nature, and not destined to live in a way unsuited to free beings. Thus understood, the "new nation" would be one not only founded in but oriented toward liberty; it must be, in a broad sense, a liberal order.

The new nation is "dedicated to the proposition that all men are created equal." In the context of Lincoln's address one meaning of this phrase stands ready at hand: slavery, a denial of both equality and liberty, stands outside the bounds of legitimacy (however it may stand with regard to legality) within the "new nation." But Lincoln explicates his phrase in another way too, for at the very end of this address, Lincoln redescribes the nation dedicated to equality; it is the nation possessing "government of the people, by the people, for the people." That kind of government is democracy, or in the somewhat older-fashioned language of the eighteenth century, a democratic republic. To be dedicated to the proposition that all men are created equal is to be dedicated to a form of governance where the equal people rule.

According to Lincoln, then, America is the new nation constituted in its newness by its liberalism and its republicanism. Lincoln sees America as the (first?) liberal republic, or what amounts to the same thing, the natural rights republic. America is not either the first liberal society or the first republic. If we can trust the testimony of Montesquieu, the French political philosopher so influential on the American founders, there were many republics before America (e.g., Rome and other ancient regimes), and there was at least one liberal regime (Britain). But Montesquieu also insists that these older republics were not liberal (i.e., dedicated to liberty), and he suggests that Britain, as an aristocratic monarchy, has, at most, a republican dimension. America's uniqueness lies in combining what had hitherto existed separately.

Oddly enough, Lincoln's propositions about the American political experience bear directly on debates in the late twentieth-century political and scholarly world over whether America is and has been liberal or republican (among other alternatives) at its core. Lincoln does not accept the either/or implied by the debate as valid for America.

Lincoln's view may reflect the formative power of Thomas Jefferson; as Lincoln once confessed, "I have never had a thought, politically speaking, which did not derive from Thomas Jefferson." Jefferson, according to Lincoln, "was, is, and perhaps will be, the most distinguished politician in our history." It was no accident that Lincoln followed Jefferson so closely, for no American thought longer and harder about natural rights and the natural rights republic than Jefferson. He penned the Declaration of Independence, the document generally taken as the authoritative version of the natural rights philosophy for America. He was one of the first to understand clearly and decisively that the nation's natural rights commitment at the time of the revolution implied a firm commitment to a republic as the only form of government legitimate under the new principles. Since he was by no means alone, nor was he the first to so conclude, my point is not to say Jefferson invented the idea. Rather, in the Declaration he provided an unrivaled statement of the natural rights position, and in his projections of legal and constitutional reform after the revolution he drew out in a most principled manner the implications of natural rights for governmental form and structure. More than any other member of his generation, Jefferson continued to ponder the practical implications of the natural rights theory, until, in his post-presidential years, he propounded a very new and radically republican, radically liberal, radically natural rights–oriented proposal for what a properly constituted American government would be.

My point in focusing on Jefferson, then, is to say neither that he was the cause or chief influence on American natural rights republicanism as it developed, nor that he was even the best American theorist of the natural rights republic—in many ways Madison deserves that honor—but rather that he devoted the most sustained intellectual effort to the topic and helps bring later developments into focus for us. He seems to have grasped clearly the internal dynamic of the new order and the inner meaning and significance of this new politics that Americans of his generation brought forth upon this continent.

Natural Rights

In the epitaph he prepared for himself shortly before his death, Jefferson identified those "testimonials" by which he "most wished to be remembered": "Here was buried Thomas Jefferson, Author of the Declaration for American Independence, of the Statute of Virginia for religious freedom, and the Father of the University of Virginia."[1] Disparate as the three are, a common thread runs throughout—all express or derive from the natural rights philosophy. The Declaration succinctly states that philosophy and justifies the colonists' move toward independence in its terms. The long-run meaning of the Declaration, Jefferson believed, is to be "the signal of arousing men to burst the chains under which monkish ignorance and superstition had persuaded them to bind themselves." In place of this legacy of chains is the new order heralded by the Declaration: "All eyes are opened, or opening, to the rights of man."[2] The Virginia Statute for

Religious Freedom bears on the transition from the old "monkish" order in a particularly close way: religious freedom, the very freedom "monkish ignorance" was most apt to reject, the right established in Jefferson's bill, is itself a "natural right," perhaps the chief right to which the "eyes of mankind were opening."[3]

The last of his "testimonials" proves to be most revelatory of the relationship between his concern for natural rights and his dedication to republicanism. The project of founding the University of Virginia was but a part of a much broader scheme of educational reform that Jefferson put forward soon after the revolution. Jefferson's plan for "the more general diffusion of knowledge" sets the need for a system of public education, including a public university, in the context of the following thought: "certain forms of government are better calculated than others to protect individuals in the free exercise of their natural rights."[4] Protection of natural rights is the standard in terms of which forms of government are judged. According to this standard, if republicanism is good, it is good because it secures rights better than other forms do. The understanding of government contained in the Declaration's natural rights philosophy points toward republicanism, and indeed, toward one particular version of republicanism above all.

The natural rights philosophy holds together Jefferson's list of accomplishments. The first item on his list—the Declaration of Independence—was itself the great statement of that philosophy.

On the Declaration of Independence

An early editor of Jefferson's writings attests to our familiarity or even overfamiliarity with the Declaration when he calls it "the paper which is probably the best known that ever came from the pen of an individual."[5] We have memorized it as school children, we have read it and listened to it on public holidays, we have looked to it when seeking to understand ourselves, taken refuge in it when seeking to justify ourselves, and argued about its meaning and application when facing divisive political questions. The traditional place of the Declaration in our national life has perhaps never been stated better than by Ralph Barton Perry:

> The Declaration of Independence contains the essential ideas of American democracy, and has remained its creed and standard. . . . These principles . . . have invariably been invoked in times of crisis or of patriotic fervor as constituting the mutual bond of American nationality. . . .[6]

Yet this familiarity has had its negative effects as well. Already long ago, Moses Coit Tyler claimed the Declaration suffered "the misfortune of being read too much," with the result, he thought, that it had become "hackneyed."[7] The Declaration's overfamiliarity has not made it any easier to understand, either, if we are to judge by a sampling of the recent literature on the document. That literature, taken as a body, disagrees almost entirely as to its meaning. Some argue the Declaration is a democratic, even a "radically democratic" document;[8] others that it is aristocratic at core;[9] yet others that it is monarchic;[10] and finally, some maintain it is politically neutral.[11] Some find the Declaration to be essentially radical and transforming;[12] others, essentially conservative.[13]

The present state of confusion derives from a variety of causes, some of which are intrinsic to the Declaration itself. The Declaration proceeds with the utmost concision; it seems, moreover, to pronounce its chief propositions to be self-evident truths, a claim which appears to have discharged Jefferson from any felt obligation to explicate at greater length and with fuller defense the key points of the Declaration's theory. Moreover, concepts as notably equivocal as equality, natural law, inalienable right, and consent figure prominently in the Declaration without the kind of discussion which could serve to fix their meanings more precisely. Since the Declaration is so brief, since its key terms are so controversial, it is no wonder that different readers should find different things in it.

Notwithstanding this confusion, I believe a persuasive and coherent account of it can be generated if we avail ourselves properly of appropriate aids to understanding. The Declaration may be concise in the extreme and its terms uncommonly equivocal, but they appear in a set context and structure that goes far toward fixing a meaning for the document. Through structure each element provides a context for every other, and context supplies meaning. Structureless reading presents an open invitation—accepted far too frequently—to read out of context, or to read in.

Two other aids are also helpful. One is John Locke's political philosophy, especially his *Second Treatise of Government*, generally, if not universally, agreed to have been an important source for the Declaration. A second aid derives from the character of the Declaration as Jefferson himself described its "object": "Not to find out new principles, or new arguments, never before thought of," but rather to express "the American Mind." It rests, he said, on the "harmonizing sentiments of the day."[14] If that is true, then other expressions of the same theory ought to be visible in the public discourse of the day. Among other places, those "harmonizing sentiments" can be found in public documents which, like the Declaration itself, clearly seek to express "the American mind" at the time of the

Revolution. Particularly valuable are the Virginia Bill of Rights, drafted by Jefferson's friend George Mason in the same year that Jefferson wrote the Declaration, and the Massachusetts Bill of Rights, written in 1780 by John Adams, himself a member of the drafting committee for the Declaration. These documents, like Locke's writings, can be helpful in corroborating and filling in the understanding we may achieve through a structural reading of the Declaration.

The Declaration's first paragraph announces the intention of the document as a whole: to "declare the causes which impel [the Americans] to the separation" from Britain. The presentation of these causes occurs as a syllogism with the conclusion that "these United Colonies are, and of Right ought to be, Free and Independent States." The major premise of that syllogism consists of a series of propositions which, if true, would yield under certain conditions the conclusion that separation is legitimate or even necessary.

The minor premises are supplied by the list of acts of the king, often called the grievances. These are "facts" to be "submitted to a candid world," which are to establish that "the present King of Great Britain" has "in direct object the establishment of an absolute Tyranny over these States," a shorthand description for the situation held in the major premise to justify "altering or abolishing" an established political order.

Thus the parts of the Declaration are not disparate or disjointed as often asserted, but are tightly constructed, like a geometric proof. The first paragraph announces what is to be proved, the second presents the major premises of the syllogism, or the "axioms" of the proof, the series of paragraphs detailing the grievances presents the minor premises, and the final paragraph draws the conclusion from the two sets of premises. The theoretical part of the Declaration cannot be seen, as it sometimes is, as a series of glittering sentiments mainly present as a showpiece or introduction to the heart of things in the list of grievances.

The theoretical paragraph setting forth the major premise of the Declaration's syllogism is itself tightly structured; it consists of six interrelated "truths" "held" by the Americans to be "self-evident." These truths on examination also prove to have a deductive structure. Nothing in the Declaration is more familiar or more vital than the first truth—"all men are created equal." And nothing in the Declaration is more controversial. So it has been asserted that equality means equality in rights, which the text pointedly does not say; that equality means equal in possession of the moral sense, which the Declaration nowhere mentions; equal in subjection to the moral law, equal in moral dignity, equal in claims on the public fisc, equal in claims to "life chances," equal in claims to political power (and thus that it mandates political democracy), or equal in wealth (and thus that it mandates socialism or a heavily redistributive state).

Such a carnival of speculation is unnecessary, however, if one attends to the other "truths" with which the truth about equality is juxtaposed, for these set a precise context and meaning for it. The series of six truths presents a temporal sequence, a kind of mini-historical narrative of the political experience of the human race. It begins with a prepolitical condition, that is to say, the condition before governments are "instituted among men," tells of the institution—how and why governments come to be made—and then tells of the post-institution phase—the corruption or falling away of government from its ends, followed by an altering or abolishing culminating in a new institution. We have three distinct phases, then, civil society, pre-civil society, and for want of a better term, post-civil society. We might present the three phases and the corresponding truths schematically as follows:

Prepolitical	All men are equal	and endowed with certain inalienable rights
Political	Governments are instituted to secure these rights	deriving their just powers from the consent of the governed
Postpolitical	If government becomes destructive of those ends, there is a right to alter or abolish it	and institute new government

Properly set in its context, "created equal" becomes distinctly less mysterious. By nature, or in nature, human beings are equal, in the sense of not being subject to the authority of any other. Neither God nor nature has established rule among human beings; they do this for themselves. By stating that men are created equal in this sense, the Declaration is saying what some political philosophers said when they posited the original condition as a "state of nature," a state in which no rightful authority exists by nature.

The Declaration thus means something more precise than the claim that the "equality of human beings . . . must lie in the simple fact of their humanity, of their belonging to the same species."[15] This fact does not in any evident way imply equality, nor does this interpretation adequately explicate the way equality functions structurally in the Declaration.

In his rough draft of the Declaration, Jefferson is perhaps clearer; "all men are created equal and independent." John Adams very closely echoed this phrasing in the Massachusetts Bill of Rights: "all men are born free and equal." The Virginia Bill of Rights has the very similar "All men are by nature equally free and independent." All four texts in turn follow Locke. In claiming that "all Men by Nature are equal," Locke insists he does not mean to affirm "all sorts of Equality." Age, virtue, merit, high birth, or benefits given or received may distinguish one person from another.

> Yet all this consists with the equality, which all Men are in, in respect of Jurisdiction or Dominion one over another, which was the Equality I there spoke of.

Being equal means, then, that by nature no man is "subjected to the will or authority of any other man."[16] The point Locke and the Americans are making is a simple yet powerful one: whatever the many inequalities among human beings may be, whether of intelligence, virtue, beauty, or strength, none of them gives a rightful claim of authority over another.

The Declaration is thus not saying that all men are equal in the sense that they should necessarily have an equal share of political power and thus that the only legitimate form of government is a strongly egalitarian democracy. A reading like that (in part) led Charles Beard to deny continuity between the Declaration and the Constitution, for the latter clearly did not institute as egalitarian a democracy as Beard's egalitarian understanding mandated. Yet this is a clear misinterpretation of the Declaration, for the very existence of government, i.e., of rightful authority, abrogates of itself the original equality.

The same democratic misreading pervades the classic study of the Declaration by Carl Becker. He believes that the egalitarian philosophy of the Declaration is democratic and antimonarchical in principle, but then has difficulty understanding the Declaration's failure to denounce monarchy as such: in the list of grievances, it says only that "a prince whose character is thus marked by every act which may define a tyrant is unfit to be the ruler of a free people," implying that a king of another character, a non-tyrannical king, would be fit. Likewise, the Declaration displays a remarkable flexibility regarding legitimate forms of government: it affirms a right in the people to make government "in such form, as to them shall seem most likely to effect their safety and happiness."

It should also be apparent that the Declaration's proclamation of human equality is not a mandate for equality of condition. Inequalities of wealth, for instance, do not of themselves violate the principle of equality contained in the Declaration. Whatever merit this more egalitarian standard may have, it cannot stand on the authority of the Declaration.

The structural reading of the Declaration also raises serious questions about two important and closely related approaches to the American tradition, classical republicanism and communitarianism. The two overlap in their common opposition to liberal political philosophy. The republicans object to the insufficiently political character of liberalism while the communitarians object to the insufficiently social character of liberalism. The republicans harken back to Aristotle and affirm the view they find in him of the dignity and human significance of political life and political participation.[17] Where liberalism speaks of abstract persons and their natural rights, republicanism would speak of citizens, their duties, and their civic virtue. Communitarians also frequently look back to Aristotle and his heirs and their notion that "a human being is a social animal," social in nature, social in duties, attachments, and satisfactions. Like the republicans, the communitarians object to the individualism of liberalism, to "the picture of the freely choosing individual it embodies."[18]

Gordon Wood, one of the outstanding analysts of republican themes in the founding era, supplies a republican reading of the Declaration on equality as follows:

> a rough equality of conditions was in fact essential for republicanism. Since antiquity theorists had assumed that a republican state required a general equality of property-holding among its citizens. . . . Equality was related to independence; indeed, Jefferson's original draft for the Declaration of Independence stated that "all men are created free and independent." Men were equal in that no one of them should be dependent on the will of another.[19]

Wood correctly relates equality to independence, but he incorrectly identifies it as a description of a republican civil condition rather than an assertion of a pre-civil condition. He thus makes hash of the very language of the clause; not that all men *should be* equal, but that "all men *are created* equal." Wood has taken a descriptive statement and transformed it into a "should," and he has completely lost sight of "created," of the reference to the origin or initial situation it contains.

Likewise some communitarians view the Declaration as essentially communitarian. Wilmoore Kendall, for one, concludes that

> the equality clause of the Declaration . . . simply asserts the proposition that all people who identify themselves as one . . . are equal to others

who have likewise identified themselves . . . The Declaration asserts that Americans are equal to, say, the British and the French. If the British and French can claim equality among the sovereign states of the world, so, too, can the Americans.[20]

When the Declaration declares all men to be created equal, it is not referring to individual human beings, but to peoples, to communities. Such an interpretation cannot survive a structural reading of the text, however, for that reading reveals equality to characterize the situation prior to the existence of peoples. Moreover, the same "men" who are said to be "created equal" also are said to be prepolitical possessors of rights. Surely these rights possessors are human individuals. When Jefferson wished to speak of peoples he knew perfectly well how to do so; in the opening paragraph of the Declaration, for example, he spoke of the occasion when "it becomes necessary for one people to dissolve the political bands which have connected them with another." The juxtaposition of the first paragraph's "people" and the second paragraph's "all men" in such close contiguity surely signifies a difference in reference.

For better or worse, then, the Declaration lines up on the liberal rather than the republican or communitarian side of the battles over the character of America. Of course, this does not of itself imply that the theory of the Declaration suffers from the deficiencies imputed to it by the republicans and communitarians. One such deficiency frequently emphasized by critics of liberal individualism is the ahistorical character of the liberal position, well epitomized by the Declaration's notion of "created equal." Human beings never have lived in a state of nature; they are born into society and social life, they are born under subjection to authority. If the Declaration presents, as I said above, a "mini-history" of the race, it is frightfully bad history, say the communitarians.

This is a much misguided criticism, however, for the Declaration does not present literal or empirical history, but moral history. It is speaking of rightful or "just power," not power simpliciter. Nobody is merely born into moral subjection to political power, no matter how civilized and political their origins. The Declaration is not speaking of some primordial prepolitical condition. "All men are created equal"—those born into society right under our noses just as much as those born in prehistory. The sociological or historical facts to which the above-mentioned critics advert are simply irrelevant to the Declaration's claim about equality and rule. Here again Locke is helpful in understanding the point, for he "affirms that all men are naturally in that state [of nature], and remain so, till by their own consents they make themselves members of some political society."[21] He obviously is not referring to some mythical prehistory.

To affirm the state of nature, or this original equality, thus does not entail affirming some historically dubious condition; nor does it necessarily commit one to the view that human beings are naturally asocial. They are without political order by nature, but the Declaration makes no commitment regarding natural society, other than to imply that natural sociality, if there be such, is defective, for it requires supplementation by government, that is to say, by law backed up by force.

The first characteristic of human beings in the state of nature is a lack—the lack of relations of rightful authority, of superiority and subordination, which lack constitutes the original equality or independence. But the second characteristic of persons in the state of nature is a possession—they are endowed with "inalienable rights." These rights precede the institution of government and exist prior to all human law. They are said in the sequel to be that for the sake of which human law and government exist. While human beings have rights in the state of nature, the Declaration makes no mention of their having duties or obligations in the state of nature. The Declaration thus provides no explicit support for the view, sometimes expressed, that the rights in the Declaration derive from prior duties or obligations.

An inalienable right is one that cannot be taken away or given up, and *a fortiori* cannot be presumed to have been given up. Thus human beings should never accept any argument that they ought rightfully submit to any authority which threatens their rights on the grounds that they or their ancestors have somehow given up their rights. Accordingly, the Virginia Bill of Rights speaks of "certain inherent rights, of which, when they enter into a state of society, they cannot by any compact deprive or divest their posterity" (Art. 1). Even if they consciously wish to give up their or their posterity's rights, they cannot do so. It is possible that men, wallowing in "monkish ignorance and superstition," consented and thereby made a government which neither they nor it understood to rest on their consent, or to have as its purpose the securing of their rights. They might even have understood themselves to owe it unconditional obedience. The moment they come to understand their inalienable rights, to understand that there are certain claims they may always rightfully assert, they may rightfully take whatever action is needful, including withdrawing their consent and altering or abolishing the government, precisely because their rights are inalienable. The rightful power to unmake and remake government is the strongest and most persistent token of the inalienability of rights.

The source of the rights is somehow the Creator, but the text is quite inexplicit in saying how. Surely we do not learn of these natural rights to life, liberty, and the pursuit of happiness from the Bible, for in the biblical account, we learn not of rights or claims that human beings have or raise in the original condition, but of free gifts to them from the Creator God and an injunction or duty laid on them.

Harry Jaffa has suggested that "the Declaration has reference to natural, not to revealed theology," which seems a very good suggestion in the light of the text's reference in its first paragraph to the "laws of Nature and of Nature's God."[22] The "Laws of nature's God" are not quite identical to the "Laws of God." The laws of God might, for example, include laws pertaining to nonnatural subjects (e.g., salvation, grace), and be known in nonnatural or nonrational ways (e.g., revelation). The God who legislates in the Declaration is a God who speaks through reason and acts in nature. His laws, then, are none other than the laws of nature themselves, as understood by human reason. If God acts only through the mediation of nature, then the Creator would seem to be nothing other than "Nature's God," and his action the action of nature.

On reflection, natural rights appear more fundamental than natural equality. Each person has rights to life, liberty and the pursuit of happiness, namely, his or her own life, liberty, and pursuit of happiness. With each person possessing these natural rights, it is impossible that any other person could naturally be the ruler of any individual, for a natural or rightful ruler would have authority inconsistent with such wide-ranging natural rights. That someone possessed a natural right to rule would imply that the ruled do not have full rights to determine their own actions and the shape of their own lives. Thus the primordial possession of such wide-ranging natural rights implies natural equality.

The Declaration unequivocally asserts that the purpose of government is the securing of rights, and only the securing of rights. Law, not the duties of others, is the source of security for rights. A political society organized according to the principles of the Declaration is a society dedicated to servicing or allowing the pursuit by individuals of their rights. The existence of legitimate government and laws proves that the various rights cannot be "absolutes." The law can legitimately limit rights, and can intrude into the basic sphere of immunities of the individual not only on behalf of the specific rights of others, but in pursuit of "the public good." Rights-securing requires a community and an effective government, and these in turn have many requisites not translatable directly into rights of specific individuals. Equally important, if less obvious, is what we might call a society's "rights infrastructure"—the social institutions and traits of character that make rights-securing possible. Concern for the rights infrastructure may also require that governments provide services beyond direct protection to rights; for example, Thomas Jefferson was of the view that public education was a requisite to the rights infrastructure. The natural rights theory is quite certain in affirming the ends of political life ("to secure these rights"), but there is nonetheless a great range of possibilities as to what this involves in practice. We need not pursue further here the implications of this orientation to rights in the limited character of the government, in the essentially secular character of the society, in the primacy of the private sphere—in short, in the liberal polity that would result. The Declaration's rights doctrine empowers such features of liberalism as individualism, constitutional government, privatism, and the embrace of the idea that liberty, not virtue as such (the good state of soul of the individual), not salvation, and not glory form the legitimate end of the liberal state.[23] Political life conducted under the auspices of the rights philosophy is in principle open to the potentially varied and variable goals of its citizens; within limits about which neither the founders nor we have arrived at a consensus, human beings are to be left free to "pursue" their own happiness, to follow their own bents. This principled commitment to liberty has produced, among other things, both an impressive economic development—for when left to their own bent, Americans sought material betterment—and, compared to other Western nations, an impressive adherence to religion.

For all the importance of rights, however, the Declaration is noticeably reticent on the source, nature, and specific contours of the rights. For more light on these topics one must consider reasonings not contained in the Declaration. The Declaration's near silence about the source and nature of rights also limits what one can say about the table of rights provided. Why these rights? Since the three rights specified in the text are said to be "among" the inalienable rights, it is clear there must be others, but what they are or how we discover them is not stated. In other places, Jefferson mentions other rights—a right to property, to expatriate, to freedom of conscience. There is nonetheless a kind of coherence to the list supplied, as there is to the more common list of "life, liberty, and property." Although the Declaration substitutes "pursuit of happiness" for "property," other documents of the revolutionary era make clear that this substitution does not necessarily signify a rejection of the latter right, for many of the state constitutions contained both: obviously the one does not in any sense cancel the other.

The rights listed have a systematic coherence. The right to life is a right to what is most one's own, one's life. Given the nature of a human life, it is difficult to see how it could be anything other than one's own, how it could in any sense belong to others. Given the dependence (or base) of life in or on the body, the right to life must contain a right to bodily immunity, the right not to have one's body seized, invaded, or controlled by others.

The right to liberty extends the right to life: not only does one possess a rightful immunity against the depredations of others on one's body, but one has a right to the use of one's body. We can take control of our bodies and invest our body's movements with our intentions and purposes. The natural right to liberty proclaims the prima facie rightfulness of active, intentional use of the body. The right to property involves an extension of rights from the spheres of one's own life, body, and actions to the external world. It proclaims the rightful power of human beings to make the external their own in the same way they can make their bodies their own.

The three basic rights together amount to the affirmation of a kind of personal sovereignty, a rightful control over one's person, actions, and possessions in the service of one's intents and purposes. When seen as an integrated system of immunities and controls, the specific rights sum to a comprehensive right to pursue a shape and way of life self-chosen, that is, a right to pursuit of happiness.

Everything about the institution of government follows deductively from the truths about the prepolitical state. Government is instituted to secure rights: that follows not only from the fact that rights are insecure without government, but also from the fact that there is no supervening claim over rights in the name of which coercion could rightfully be employed. The security of rights can be the only legitimate end of political society. Likewise, since neither God nor nature provides for rule, this must be done by human beings themselves: governments must derive "their just powers from the consent of the governed," a derivation known in the philosophic tradition as a social contract. Since government exists to secure rights and only for that purpose, governments which fail to secure rights can have no legitimacy. The people, therefore, must possess "the right to alter or abolish governments" that have lost legitimacy. This so-called "right to revolution" must be "among" the other rights not earlier specified in the list of primary rights. Given its relation to the primary rights, it too must be an "inalienable right." Thus the right to alter or abolish is a universal right, valid for all political societies, quite independent of their particular histories. A nation with a history of absolutist and tyrannical rule is therefore not morally disbarred by its own history and traditions from reclaiming its inherent rights. It is as legitimate for France or Haiti to assert the right to alter or abolish, as it is for the English colonies in America. Altering, and especially abolishing government leaves rights once again insecure, as they were prior to the existence of government. The new situation of no government implies the same "right to institute new government" as the "original" situation did.

Governments are needed to secure rights because they are otherwise insecure. What makes them insecure is not stated. Within the social contract philosophic tradition a variety of answers was given to that question, and the Declaration pointedly withholds judgment. The character of the government needed as a remedy for the insecurity of rights depends, to some degree, on the nature of the threats. For example, so deep in the nature of man is the source of rights-threatening behavior, according to Thomas Hobbes, that only a very powerfully armed state can hope to secure rights. On the other hand, Locke finds threats to rights to be less severe and more related to natural scarcity. The political solution for Locke is thus a far milder government with greater emphasis on securing the conditions for overcoming natural scarcity. Perhaps the Declaration remains silent on the nature and severity of the threat to rights because that topic escaped the "harmonizing sentiment of the day."

The Declaration's silence on the nature of the threat to rights may have something to do with its openness on kinds or forms of legitimate government. The Declaration is open on form notwithstanding its pronouncement that governments "derive their just powers from the consent of the governed." As Martin Diamond points out, and as the structure of the text confirms, this affirmation of consent applies particularly to the origin or institution of government.[24] However, governments do not "derive" their power once and for all at some originating moment. Governments exercise powers derived or delegated from their constituents, and thus all just power always is derived from the "consent of the governed." That a government derives its powers from the consent of the governed does not mean, however, that governments necessarily operate democratically or through representative assemblies.[25]

That all governments rest in consent is another way of saying that all government is a human artifact, constructed from human agreement or conventions, and, when the human situation is properly understood, serving certain ends only. Non-consent, or the withdrawal of consent, is precisely what happens when the government is perceived no longer to serve the purposes for which it has or should have been constructed, and people act to alter or abolish it. Another implication of the Declaration's doctrine of consent would appear to be an inalienable right to emigrate.

Thus the Declaration can affirm the continuing basis of political power in consent, and yet not commit itself to democratic forms. The Declaration, of course, is not antidemocratic. It endorses whatever form the people settle on as "most likely to effect their safety and happiness." Jefferson and many other founders judged that popular or republican government was the form most likely to satisfy the ends set forth in the Declaration, but they did not render that judgment in the Declaration itself. To say, as one scholar does, that from the point of view of the principles of the Declaration the English monarchy is itself a form of republicanism obscures as much as it elucidates.[26] According to the social contract theory of the Declaration, it is true, the king's authority rests on the consent of the people governed. Thus, Jefferson could refer to the king, in his *Summary View of the Rights of British*

America, as "no more than the chief officer of the people." Nonetheless, neither the Declaration nor common sense itself supports blurring the real difference between a monarchy, or "mixed regime," *jure populo*, and what Madison in *The Federalist* calls "wholly popular forms."

It is striking how far we in the late twentieth century tend to reverse the Declaration's priorities regarding government. The ends of government—the security of rights—are, according to the Declaration, set and certain; the means of government, the form, however, may vary. The criterion of good government has far more to do with securing the end than with some universal test of form. We, on the other hand, are uncertain about the ends that legitimate government should pursue, but are far more certain of the necessity of the democratic form. This shift in emphasis is in large part, however, a result of the further reflections the founders brought to bear on the problems of "the natural rights polity."

The Declaration's affirmations regarding such matters as consent and the right to revolution indicate with special clarity what kind of historical narrative the Declaration is presenting. It is a "history" to be sure, and not a mere "ought." The founders knew that the historical record of mankind did not entirely support the account of the origins they were providing. The Declaration gives a history as that history would be lived by human beings who understood the truth of their situation in nature correctly; the Declaration's history is thus a rational reconstruction rather than literal history; it is not for all that utopian, however, for it can become literal history the moment people understand and act on the fundamental truths of politics and morality.

As rational reconstruction the Declaration implies a theory of justice relevant to the civil societies established according to its precepts. Human beings who knew what they were doing would consent only to a government that promised to secure their rights; they would not consent to a government that threatened to subordinate their rights to the rights of others or the welfare of others per se. Each would require that he or she get out of government what he or she is in it for—security of his or her own rights. This implies that everyone has an equal claim on the government for protection; it means government has an obligation not to sacrifice some to the others. Both majority and minority tyranny are abhorrent. The Declaration stands against class or race politics.

The Natural Rights Republic

Abraham Lincoln directs us to 1776 and the Declaration of Independence as the origin of the American political tradition, but some of our most influential students of the tradition disagree. They not only deny that the Declaration is the origin; they do not find it to be any significant part of the tradition at all. Instead of natural rights liberalism, they see classical republicanism or civic humanism as the defining feature of America, at least during the founding era.

The Declaration of Independence and the natural rights philosophy more generally are almost literally absent from the accounts of American political origins in the so-called republican synthesis. Bernard Bailyn, usually considered to be the originator of the synthesis, began the trend when, in a survey entitled *The Ideological Origins of the American Revolution,* he barely mentioned the Declaration. Yet he admitted the role of natural rights philosophy in the mix of ideas animating the Americans at the time of the revolution. He differed from earlier students of the era like Carl Becker or Clinton Rossiter in downplaying these elements somewhat and elevating instead another stream of thought, identified by him as a "tradition of opposition thought." This tradition had its origin in the commonwealth period following the English Civil War and was carried forward into the eighteenth century mostly by the Whig Opposition, that is, by Whigs who remained in opposition to the Whigs who held power after the Glorious Revolution. According to Bailyn, they "dominated the colonists' miscellaneous learning and shaped it into a coherent whole."[27] Bailyn concedes that these opposition writers "overlapped" in their commitments with Enlightenment thinkers like Locke, and that the natural rights/social contract philosophy did indeed play a part in their thinking about politics.[28] Nonetheless, the dominant opposition tradition had a content and temper quite different from Enlightenment thought. The one produced "glittering generalities" and proceeded at a sophisticated intellectual and emotional level; the other contained a quite specific political analysis and prescription for action, and was crude, simplistic, vulgar, and emotionally charged. Those elements of opposition writings that were most unphilosophical contributed the power that made the whole attractive to a mass public and thereby suitable to serve as an ideology for a mass movement.[29] The substantive core of the opposition tradition, according to Bailyn, was an interrelated set of concepts revolving around the dangers of power. Bailyn would see Lord Acton's famous dictum—"power tends to corrupt, absolute power corrupts absolutely"—as typical of his group of writers. The emphasis on power gave the whole theory a rather negative cast. It was easier to say what they were against and what they feared than what they favored. Like Cecilia Kenyon's Anti-federalists, Bailyn's opposition tradition was composed of "men of little faith."[30]

Bailyn's version of the republicanism thesis left Locke, natural rights and so forth, on stage, but in the wings. Not until subsequent elements of the "republican synthesis" were put in place was the natural rights position completely ushered out of the theater. The most decisive event, probably, was the redescription of the opposition tradition by J. G. A. Pocock. Far more than Bailyn, he was interested in this tradition itself, and only secondarily in its impact on the Americans; accordingly, he inquired far more strenuously into its character and pedigree. His reconstruction of the tradition is extraordinarily complex, but for present purposes may be summarized simply as follows: the opposition tradition Bailyn identified was an Anglicized version of a much older republican tradition, originating with the Greeks, especially Aristotle, and revived by the Italian Renaissance humanists, especially Machiavelli. Thus, Pocock locates the American founding within a very old tradition: it was no *novus ordo seclorum*. On the contrary, "The American Revolution, [was] less the first act of revolutionary enlightenment than . . . the last great act of the Renaissance." America was founded in a "dread of modernity."[31]

Pocock, like Bailyn, also notes the negative cast to the political thought of his civic humanists; they feared change, looked to the past, and produced an orientation that Pocock pronounced "barren."[32] He also discerns a more positive content, however, a content tracing back ultimately to the original Aristotelian impulse of the tradition. Aristotle expressed the core of civic humanism thus understood when he pronounced human beings to be, by nature, political animals. The mature theory of civic humanism as Pocock sketches it thus concerns the meaningfulness of and conditions for political participation. Its preference for republican regimes derives from the latter's embodiment of "participatory ideals"; the constitutional and other developments eighteenth-century forms of civic humanism opposed were those elements of modernity seen to be threatening to the active sort of citizenship favored by the humanists. The humanists as described by Pocock, then, are not at bottom as sympathetic to Lord Acton's dictum as Bailyn's opposition Whigs: they do not oppose politics and political power per se—quite the contrary—but they do oppose concentration and uses of power that threaten the independence of citizens whose liberty for participation stands as their highest human potentiality.

Gordon Wood, the third member of the triumvirate of writers who constructed the edifice of the "republican synthesis," applied the republicanism idea more specifically to the Americans. He modified Bailyn's view of the tradition to which the American founders belonged more along the lines of Pocock's analysis. He finds the source of the tradition where Pocock had, in antiquity; and thus Wood calls the theory he sketched "classical republicanism." Also like Pocock, he emphasizes the positive republican aspect of this tradition: "republicanism was the basic premise of American thinking—the central presupposition behind all other ideas."[33] The emphasis in Wood's presentation differs from that in Pocock's, however. Wood understands the classical dimension of his republicanism as an expression of the naturalness or organic character of the political community. As Aristotle said, the *polis* is by nature and is prior to the individual, as the whole human individual is prior to a part like a hand. Wood's republicanism demanded not Pocock's participative ideal of citizenship or Bailyn's suspicion of all power, but rather the recognition of a supervening common or public good, the good of the whole, superior to and in principle demanding the submergence of individual private goods. Virtue is the habitual pursuit of the public over the private good, liberty the corporate involvement of the people in ruling, and not (as it was for Bailyn) the individual security of natural rights.[34] For Wood, the republican ideal is one more of duty than of self-fulfillment. Wood's republicans seem to share some important commitments with Christians, as well as with classical republican heroes like Brutus or Cato.

Where Bailyn made a place for Lockean liberalism in his version of the "synthesis," Pocock and Wood develop the republican ideal as a full-scale alternative to the natural rights/social contract liberalism of Locke. Pocock is quite explicit about his displacement of Lockean liberalism. "Pocock has seen the history of political thought [says Isaac Kramnick] 'dominated by a fiction of Locke,' whose importance 'has been wildly distorted.' . . . To understand the debates of eighteenth century politics does 'not necessitate reference to Locke at all.' . . . The proper interpretation 'stresses Machiavelli at the expense of Locke.'"[35]

The distance of the republican conception from the theory of the Declaration should be apparent from even this brief sketch. According to the republicanism thesis, human beings are intensely political (Pocock) and/or communal (Wood); according to the Declaration, human beings are not originally or naturally political—the origin is a state of nature understood as an apolitical condition. Although polity is essential, it is not natural; it is made by human beings. Politics, according to the Declaration, is for the sake of natural rights, and natural rights are emphatically prepolitical. The Declaration nowhere intimates that in political participation lies human fulfillment—in place of human fulfillment is the right to pursuit of happiness. Nor does the Declaration endorse the notion that political life requires as duty or virtue the submersion of one's private and particular interests in the common good. The common good, on the contrary, is precisely the coordinated satisfaction of those fundamental individual interests called rights, and the conditions necessary for the broad security of these rights. Within the Declaration's conception of politics, tension between the interests of the individual and the common good are certainly possible, but they are not necessary, inevitable, and defining, as in the "republican synthesis."

Within the natural rights philosophy politics and political participation are instrumental; accordingly the Declaration shows a remarkable openness on form of government—whatever form seems most conducive to rights-securing is fine. The Declaration reveals no inherent antipathy to monarchy. The republicanism thesis is defined by a commitment to a particular form, however, which is either for the sake of expressing the moral demand to seek the common good over one's particular good (Wood) or for the sake of humanly fulfilling participation in republican rule (Pocock).

The understanding of property likewise differs almost entirely between the two political theories. For Pocock's republicans, property is for the sake of gentlemanly or citizenly independence, a precondition for the citizen's participation and public-spiritedness. Property is above all a political, not an economic, phenomenon. Within natural rights liberalism, property is a natural right and, therefore, not particularly tied to its political function. The emphasis is not on static "estate," which can equip one for citizenship, but on dynamic wealth production. Various limitations on the terms and nature of ownership are perfectly compatible with property understood in Pocock's republican way; entail and primogeniture, for example, two practices that keep property concentrated and in the same family line, are suitable to a system aiming to support an independent political class. Such practices are much less compatible with liberal republicanism, however, for, among other things, they deny the inherent character of the property right—the near sovereignty one has over one's property—and they interfere with the dynamics of wealth production.

Few scholarly theories have been subjected to so many sustained bombardments as the "republican synthesis." Nearly every petal in its bouquet has been picked or at least picked over. The picture of Greek and Roman republicanism used by the synthesizers has been challenged;[36] the interpretation of Machiavelli, who supposedly carries forward while partially transforming the Aristotelian political philosophy, has been rejected;[37] the accuracy of the portrayal of James Harrington, who allegedly "anglicized" the Aristotelian-Machiavellian tradition, has been impugned;[38] the vision of "neo-Harringtonianism," which supposedly transformed Harrington in ways that put the tradition into its newfound form as the Whig Opposition, has been said to be blurred, at best;[39] the validity of the application to the Americans has been denied.[40]

Moreover, some of the most important early participants in the creation of the "republican synthesis" have reformulated their own positions in a way that is friendlier to the natural rights liberalism that the synthesis in its classical form turned against. For example, Lance Banning, the author of the importantly republican *The Jeffersonian Persuasion* in the early 1970s, describes his more current writing as an effort "to incorporate some schooling [he has] gotten from the critics of the republican interpretation." The criticism has led Banning to conclude that Pocock and Wood "suggest . . . that early Revolutionary thought was more completely classical or more decidedly pre-modern than was actually the case." Indeed, he now believes, "early revolutionary thinking was by no means truly classical . . . in its image of the good republic."[41]

The counterrevolution against the republican revisionists has thus gone very far, and has been almost altogether successful in trimming the exclusivist claims of the synthesizers. Having passed out of the "either/or" phase of the discussion, scholars now seem to have entered into a "both/and" mode—somehow both liberalism and republicanism are present at the founding and subsequently. Thus Garrett Ward Sheldon speaks of Jefferson beginning with a Lockean period, moving on to a republican period, and then late in life, returning to a Lockean period—the statesman as Picasso. Banning now wishes to speak of something he calls "liberal republicanism"; Michael Lienesch of a "hybrid" of the two traditions. Wood wants to deny he ever saw republicanism and liberalism as contraries.[42]

In some respects this movement toward a more inclusive approach is appropriate: the founding generation and the entire subsequent American political tradition have shown commitments to *both* natural rights liberalism and to republicanism (or its descendant, democracy). The most astute of the founders understood there to be some tension between these various commitments, but the founding generation never conceived that these were contrary, or in principle, incompatible elements. Thus the current scholarly movement beyond "either/or" is indispensable for recapturing the frame of mind prevailing at the origins of the American political tradition.

Nonetheless, the current efforts have not been entirely successful. The combination of elements as contrary to each other as liberalism and republicanism as conceived in the current literature is simply impossible. One needs to see how these two elements fit together for the founding generation, but one can never do that so long as one takes as a point of departure the conceptualization of these matters prevalent in the literature.

The artificiality of the received manner of conceiving the natural rights liberalism/republicanism nexus stands forth with great clarity if we think of Thomas Jefferson. He gave America's most authoritative version of the natural rights philosophy in the Declaration of Independence, he showed how it governed the American constitutional position prior to the Revolution in his *Summary View of the Rights of British America*, and he engaged in the most deep-going reflections of any American of the founding era on the nature and ground of rights. Yet, at the same time, Jefferson was a thoroughgoing and deeply committed republican; he founded a political party devoted to republicanism and he turned his thoughts to the requirements and possibilities of republicanism from his earliest to his last days. He not only developed the most clearly democratic variant of republicanism among the founders, but he also formulated a principle that has became nearly orthodox throughout most of the world: this very democratic form of polity is the only legitimate form of polity, the only one consistent with natural or human rights, the one to which human beings have a right. Jefferson not merely can help us overcome the stale and unfruitful ways in which the origins of the traditions are now discussed; he can also help us understand the remarkable emergence in America of a new and quite unique political orientation, a natural rights orientation both liberal and republican.

Jefferson came to his unique theory of republicanism in the context of three alternative or competing views: the classical or ancient form of republicanism, represented most eminently by Rome and defended most eloquently by Machiavelli and a series of successors including men like Algernon Sidney; a modern form of republicanism, which Jefferson saw as an oligarchic republicanism, defended by many of his fellow Virginia planters and embodied in the revolutionary-era Virginia Constitution; and finally, a modern American form of republicanism, modeled on the British constitution, developed by his friend James Madison, among others, and embodied more or less in the Constitution of the federal union. Jefferson rejected all three as insufficient embodiments of authentic republican principles, which were in turn mandated, Jefferson saw, by the natural rights philosophy.

The version of republicanism to which natural rights philosophy pointed was emphatically not classical republicanism. Neither the theory nor the practice, neither the ideal nor the exemplifications of the ancient republic, held much allure for Jefferson. He spoke fairly often, for example, of Plato, who stands in the background of most later classical republican theory, including that of Aristotle, Polybius, and Cicero. Without exception, Jefferson was hostile to Plato, more violent in his opinions on the Greek philosopher than even his cranky friend John Adams. To the latter, he wrote in 1814:

> Having [some] leisure . . . I amused myself with reading seriously Plato's *Republic*. I am wrong, however, in calling it amusement, for it was the heaviest task-work I ever went through. . . . While wading through the whimsies, the puerilities, and unintelligible jargon of this work, I laid it down often to ask myself how it could have been that the world should have so long consented to give reputation to such nonsense as this?[43]

Classical politics fell short because the ancients did not understand the true foundational principles of politics, natural rights, the social contract, or their implications.

Jefferson paid more explicit attention to ancient republican practice than to ancient republican theory. He was almost as little impressed with the one as the other, although he did recognize that the example of ancient Rome had a certain attractiveness to many of his fellow Virginians. He himself found the Romans a valuable model, up to a point. The Roman republic provides the first and last instance before America itself of an "experiment in government . . . founded on principles of honesty, not of mere force."[44] Nonetheless, Jefferson on the whole had a negative view of Rome.

It was a "seductive example," one which lured otherwise well-meaning men into false, even dangerous political experiments.[45] On the authority of Rome, twice during the difficult years of the revolution, distinguished Virginians had proposed in the legislature that a dictator be created, "a *dictator*, invested with every power legislative, executive and judiciary, civil and military, of life and death, over our persons and over our properties!"[46]

Jefferson used his discussion of this proposal not merely as an occasion to denounce the dictatorship, but more interestingly, to reject the entire model of classical republicanism from which it was adapted. It is just not possible to understand Jefferson as Professor Pocock would have us do, as a partisan of classical politics. Jefferson sees that the vaunted Roman constitution was self-defeating, for it "allowed a temporary tyrant to be erected, under the name of a Dictator; and that temporary tyrant, after a few examples, became perpetual." The dictatorship "proved fatal" to the republic, yet it was also indispensable to it. Rome was marked by "tumults which could not be allayed under the most trying circumstances, but by the omnipotent hand of a single despot."[47] If the Roman republic required an institution inevitably fatal to republican government, then Rome can be no sort of model for a republic. In drawing that conclusion, Jefferson breaks not only with those fellow Virginians who admired Rome, but with much seventeenth- and eighteenth-century thinking about republics, going back to Machiavelli, who had set Rome as the very model of what a republic should be.[48]

The tumults in Rome that required the intermittent but fatal experiments with the dictatorship in turn flowed from the most characteristic features of its constitution. The rulers of Rome were "a heavy-handed unfeeling aristocracy." They governed "a people ferocious, and rendered desperate by poverty and wretchedness."[49] Jefferson sees basically the same Rome that Machiavelli saw—the Rome of a conflict between classes, which, Machiavelli believed, produced salutary results.[50] For Jefferson, however, that class structure produced a system "rent by the most bitter factions and tumults," the ultimate result of which was an even more heavy-handed and unfeeling tyranny.

So far as Rome was willing to countenance a dictator it did not qualify as a real republic, for a dictator is entirely antithetical to republicanism's "fundamental principle . . . that the state shall be governed as a commonwealth," that there be majority rule, and no prerogative, no "exercise of [any] powers undefined by the laws."[51] "Powers of governing . . . in a plurality of hands" and rule of law—these are the minimum requirements of a legitimate republic as Jefferson understands republicanism in the period between the revolution and the framing of the constitution.

Moreover, as an aristocracy, Rome fails to satisfy the principles of legitimacy expressed in the Declaration of Independence and inspiring all the new American constitutions. "The foundation on which all these [constitutions] are built is the natural equality of man, the denial of every preeminence but that annexed to legal office, and particularly the denial of a preeminence by birth."[52] The principles embodied in the Declaration establish the highest principles of legitimacy for American politics, and exclude perhaps every historical republic of note, for all the well-thought-of classical ones had hereditary elements.

Jefferson's hostility to aristocratic republics reveals quite clearly the way in which natural rights liberalism had primacy for the Americans, and how it conduced to an American transformation of the old republicanism. Hereditary elements were not only prevalent in earlier practice, but had been emphasized in earlier theory as well: prior to the American founding it was not understood that the republican principle, or, more broadly, the criteria of good or legitimate government, excluded in principle the possession of some share of political power by a hereditary class.

Hereditary power not only contradicts the true foundation of political power in the natural equality of human beings, but, Jefferson thought, it also prevents the accomplishment of the true end or purpose of political power, the security of natural rights: "Experience has shown that the hereditary branches of modern governments are the patrons of privilege and prerogative, and not of the natural rights of the people whose oppressors they generally are."[53] Jefferson's interpretation of the natural rights principles excludes not merely the chief classical examples—Sparta, Rome, Carthage—but the chief "approved" regimes of modern times as well—Venice and especially Britain. In this latter, Jefferson shows himself to be far less tolerant in his politics than most of the important natural rights thinkers who laid the groundwork for the political tradition in which he was operating. Locke, Montesquieu, and the English Cato, to name but a few of these earlier thinkers, had endorsed the English mixed constitution, with its two hereditary branches, as the very model of government compatible with the underlying natural rights philosophy. Jefferson thus goes substantially beyond the opposition tradition the republican revisionists invoke.[54]

Rome, the paradigmatic classical republic, not only failed to satisfy the most elementary requirements of liberal republican legitimacy, but it was also a society so different from Virginia as to supply no shadow of a precedent for the latter. The people in Virginia are "mild in their dispositions, patient under their trial, [and] united for the public liberty." The rulers in Virginia are not an aristocracy, but are all elected. The result is that Virginians are "affectionate to their leaders."[55] Virginia stands as a very different kind of polity from Rome—not faction and tumult but real affection between leaders and people.

Jefferson took as his chief task in the wake of the revolution the maintenance and reinforcement of Virginia's differences from Rome. Those efforts reveal the main outlines of his early alternative to classical republicanism, whether as portrayed by classical philosophers and historians, or by Machiavelli. They also reveal how deeply Jefferson saw the requirements of proper republicanism to cut into the substance of the polity.

Rome, the classical form of the classical republic, was ruled by a "heavy-handed aristocracy." But since hereditary power counters the first principles of legitimate government, Jefferson's natural rights republic, as sketched in his 1776 Draft of a Constitution for Virginia, would contain no hint of hereditary power, or of any source of political power other than the people. The "authority of the people," says the Jefferson draft, deposes George from his hitherto royal power, and the same "authority aforesaid" establishes "the following fundamental law and principles of government."[56] His draft constitution makes all offices elective, or appointive by officers either themselves elected or accountable to elected officials.

In 1776, when Jefferson drew up his constitution, he was especially moved by the anti-hereditary principle; he was not, for example, opposed to long terms of office per se. Senators in his scheme would serve for nine years, but he was willing to accept much more. "I could submit, tho' not so willingly to an appointment for life."[57] Neither electoral accountability nor ultimate return by the rulers into the population at large was as much a matter of principle for Jefferson as was the avoidance of any hereditary power.

In Rome, the heavy-handed because hereditary aristocrats ruled over "a people rendered desperate by poverty and wretchedness."[58] Heavy-handedness, on the one side, and wretchedness, on the other, conspired to produce the tumult and disorder that necessitated the institution of the dictatorship. Just as Jefferson rejects the aristocratic rulers, so he aims at a very different kind of populace, so that real affection rather than distrust and hatred can prevail between leaders and people. Jefferson proposes a variety of measures to keep the people of Virginia different from the people of Rome. He seeks, for instance, to prevent the future emergence of a desperately poor populace. In his Draft of a Constitution for Virginia, therefore, he establishes as a fundamental right of all persons an entitlement to "an appropriation of [50] acres or to so much as shall make up what he owns or has owned [50] acres in full and absolute dominion."[59] The land is to come from unappropriated public lands only; Jefferson was not advocating expropriating land from those already possessing more than fifty acres, nor was he suggesting a limit of fifty acres on land ownership. He was seeking not equality of possession, but rather to avoid the "desperate poverty" which had characterized the Roman people.

Jefferson would moderate the property holdings of the wealthy not through any violation of their rights to property, but through a reformation of the laws of inheritance. "Legislators cannot invent too many devices for subdividing property, only taking care to let their subdivisions go hand in hand with the natural affections of the human mind." Jefferson himself had, of course, acted the part of such a legislator, for he sponsored legislation abolishing entail and primogeniture. Just as laws of entail were the prerequisite for the accumulation over time of great concentrations of land in the hands of certain families, so the abolition of those laws would permit the breakup of land into smaller and therefore more widely distributed parcels. Jefferson saw his reforms as especially valuable, for they would produce their good effect voluntarily and with no violation of the natural right to property, for most parents would prefer to distribute their property equally among their children.[60] Jefferson also saw his reforms as valuable because they would free land to circulate, allow it its dynamism. Jefferson was not a friend to the static pattern of land ownership characteristic, according to Pocock, of the Harringtonian republicans. So essential did Jefferson consider the law of descents that he included a provision on this subject in his draft constitution of 1776. When that was not adopted, he put these reforms at the top of his agenda for the "revisal" of laws on which the Virginia legislature, under his leadership, embarked after the revolution.

Jefferson's policies on land ownership were meant to prevent the emergence of a "desperately poor" populace, but the Roman people were "ferocious" as well as poor. Their ferocity, both a cause and a consequence of Rome's martial existence, contributed to Rome's factious, tumultuous political life. By contrast, the people of Virginia are "mild." The "ferocious" Romans lived by and for war; the "mild" Americans live by and for agriculture, and to a lesser degree, commerce. Agriculture does not make human beings ferocious; it rather disposes them to all manner of virtues. The "husbandmen . . . look to their own soil and industry."[61] They are not predators on the labor of others, as were the bellicose ancient republicans who sought wealth through conquest, nor are they dependent on others, as are those who devote themselves to manufacturing. The farmer stands at the right mean—neither seeking dominion over others, nor subservient to others as are those who need customers.[62] Their temper is thus mild but not pusillanimous. Jefferson's nonfactious republic requires a people of such temper, and his land policy is to make available to all a way of life productive of industriousness and rationality, and, therefore, of virtue.

The classical republic, not founded on the principle of the natural equality of human beings, produced republics of the factious and tumultuous sort that inevitably failed to maintain their republican character. Jefferson's view of ancient republicanism seems not so far distant, in fact, from that of his later arch-rival Alexander Hamilton:

> It is impossible to read the history of the petty republics of Greece and Italy without feeling sensations of horror and disgust at the distractions with which they were continually agitated, and at the rapid succession of revolutions by which they were kept in a state of perpetual vibration between the extremes of tyranny and anarchy.[63]

No less than Hamilton, Jefferson relies on "advances" in the science of politics to salvage republicanism from its sorry history; no more than for Hamilton can Rome or any ancient republic serve as a model for America.

Jefferson appeals to the letter and spirit of the Virginia constitution against both the Roman dictatorship and the Roman republic. Yet Jefferson finds the Virginia constitution to be very defective also.[64]

Rome was unacceptable because it was an aristocratic republic; Virginia falls short because it is an oligarchic republic. Although Virginia's constitution does not commit the error-in-chief of ancient republicanism, the acceptance of hereditary rule in any part of the constitution, nonetheless it contains echoes of the aristocratic leanings of the classical republics. The Virginians did not create a separate and overbearing hereditary ruling class, but they do keep rule in the hands of a very small group, quite separate from the people. The constitutive principle of the Virginia constitution is a simple one: "confine the right of suffrage to a few of the wealthier of the people."[65]

Virginia aims at being a true commonwealth, through commitment to "republican forms" and rule of law, but, Jefferson demonstrates, its oligarchic foundations prevent it from achieving either goal. One result of the arrangement of the suffrage in Virginia is very like the result in Rome: "the majority of the men in the state . . . are unrepresented in the legislature."[66] The malapportionment of the legislature, favoring the wealthier and better established eastern strip of the state, increases the oligarchic, nonmajoritarian character of the regime.[67] As in Rome, the governors therefore are a quite distinct body from the people they govern. Jefferson, by contrast, is seeking a form of republicanism which minimizes the distance between rulers and ruled, so that "real affection" prevails between them. Harmony cannot persist between the people and their rulers if government is "trusted to the rulers of the people alone," for every such government "degenerates."

> In every government on earth is some trace of human weakness, some germ of corruption and degeneracy, which cunning will discover, and wickedness insensibly open, cultivate and improve.[68]

This tendency to degeneracy, a tendency for rulers to govern in their own interests and not in that of the ruled, is, Jefferson insists, a universal tendency. But "certain forms of government are better calculated than others to protect individuals in the free exercise of their natural rights." To protect the people in their rights, "the people themselves . . . are [government's] only safe depositories."[69] Oligarchic rule secures rights no better than does aristocratic rule.

The republican form, properly understood, or as consistent with the principles of government articulated in the Declaration of Independence, requires not only nonhereditary and multiple offices, but a far more democratic representation of the majority. Therefore Jefferson's draft constitution takes an altogether different approach to representation than the Virginia Constitution does: "All male persons of full age and sane minds" who pay local taxes are decreed electors, and also eligible to stand for office.[70] Likewise his draft provides for the apportionment of legislative seats proportionate to qualified voters, in order to prevent the kind of drastic malapportionment the adopted constitution embodies.

Even though Jefferson suggests in *Notes on Virginia* that the defects of the Virginia constitution stemmed from "inexperience in the science of government," the differences between him and the drafters of the constitution go much deeper than that. Jefferson explains his desire for nearly universal male suffrage in a letter to the more oligarchic-minded Edmund Pendleton: "Whoever intends to live in a country must wish that country well, and has a natural right of assisting in the preservation of it."[71] The principles of legitimacy in the Declaration not only deny the validity of hereditary power but demand a democratic republic. Universal manhood suffrage is required not only as a means to bring about a nonfactious, harmonious politics of "real affection," but as an implication of the primary natural rights: government exists to secure the rights of all, and all therefore possess a right to secure the instrument of their security.

Jefferson's principled differences with the drafters of the Virginia constitution emerge also in his discussion of the failure of that document to secure the rule of law, a failure deriving from a failure to establish a proper system of separation of powers. That failure in turn derived from Virginia's commitment to, not accidental fall into, oligarchical republicanism. "All the powers of government, legislative, executive, and judiciary, result to the legislative body," Jefferson charges, and that is unacceptable, because "concentrating these in the same hands is precisely the definition of despotic power."[72] Jefferson, like Madison later in The Federalist,[73] follows Montesquieu on the function of separation of powers in guaranteeing nondespotic or lawful government.[74]

Jefferson insists there be a genuine separation of powers where the Virginia constitution does not. The drafters of the constitution, Jefferson implies, thought it was enough "that these powers will be exercised by a plurality of hands": what is not monarchic is not despotic. But Jefferson disagrees: "173 despots would surely be as oppressive as one."[75] However, the Virginians had another principle in mind in addition to "plurality of hands": The legislators "are chosen by ourselves." The drafters apparently believe that the "electoral connection" makes the legislature a safe depository for these concentrated powers. But, retorts Jefferson, "an elective despotism was not the government we fought for."[76] Government "founded on free principles," i.e., electorally responsible government, is a necessary but not a sufficient condition for a nondespotic regime. A proper government is one "in which the powers . . . should be so divided and balanced among several bodies of magistracy, as that no one could transcend their legal limits, without being effectually checked and restrained by others."[77]

Admittedly, the Virginians do partially recognize the necessity of a separation of powers, but they leave it at a mere declaration and, in fact, proceed to establish practices according to which "the judiciary and executive members were left dependent on the legislature." The Virginians do not take the problem of concentrated powers seriously because they are "deluded by the integrity of their own purposes, and conclude that these unlimited powers will never be abused, because themselves are not disposed to abuse them."[78] Behind the inadequacy of the provisions for separation of powers lies the Virginians' confidence in their own integrity or virtue. That appears to be connected with the provisions for representation and suffrage in their constitution. These qualifications guarantee that only the "better sort," the "respectable" members of the community, can hold office and take part in the selection of officeholders; one can rely, the Virginia drafters seem to believe, on the virtue of such men. Those features of the constitution to which Jefferson objects, in other words, are commonly inspired by a commitment to placing political power in the hands of "a few of the wealthier people," from whose good qualities—virtue, integrity, incorruptibility, wisdom—good government is to spring.

The Virginians are committed by design and conviction, not by mere inadvertence, to their oligarchic system. Jefferson rejects almost every element of their analysis, including especially their reliance on the virtues of the wealthy. "My observations," Jefferson observes in 1776, "do not enable me to say I think integrity the characteristic of wealth. In general I believe the decisions of the people, in a body, will be more honest and more disinterested than those of wealthy men."[79] If the virtue of any class is to be relied on, it is the virtue of the people. But, as Jefferson says in a slightly different context, "the fantastical idea of virtue and [commitment to] the public good being a sufficient security . . . I assure you was never mine."[80]

Jefferson surely does not mean to substitute a simple reliance on the people for the Virginians' oligarchy. In the very same place where he praises the people as "more honest and disinterested," he indicates he is under few illusions regarding popular political capacities. "I have ever observed that a choice by the people themselves is not generally distinguished for it's [sic] wisdom. This first secretion from them is usually crude and heterogeneous."[81] A proper constitution must rest on the people, but must supplement them in a number of ways. Bicameralism is required not merely for the added checking and balancing a second legislative chamber provides, but perhaps more importantly for the sake of adding wisdom to popular honesty. Thus Jefferson at this period in his career favors an upper house selected not by the people, but by the lower house. "Give to those so chosen by the people a second choice themselves, and they generally will choose wise men."[82] Jefferson seeks to supplement the people not with the wealthy as such, but with the wise, or with "the aristocracy of virtue and talent," or "the natural aristocracy."[83]

Jefferson seeks to secure something like the old mixed constitution as in Britain:

The purpose of establishing different houses of legislation is to introduce the influence of different interests or different principles. Thus in Great Britain it is said their constitution relies on the house of commons for honesty, and the lords for wisdom; which would be a rational reliance if honesty were to be bought with money and wisdom were hereditary.[84]

Jefferson seeks a more effective means to achieve the ends he attributes to the British constitution. Jefferson aims to accomplish much the same thing Madison identified as the goal of the new political science animating the federal constitution: to find a democratic, i.e., nonmixed, remedy for the evils of democracy.[85] Jefferson, no less than Madison, recognizes the need to supplement democracy, in his case with wisdom, or with talent, but to do so without recourse to nondemocratic practices.

Jefferson's democratic republic requires an ambitious scheme of education. The people may be "the only safe depository" of political power, but "even they must be rendered safe," and to that end "their minds must be improved to a certain degree."[86] Thus Jefferson proposes a daring plan of universal education, every child, male or female, to be provided three years of free education. As opposed to most earlier proposals for widespread education, Jefferson's inspiration was political and not religious.[87]

The people are to receive an education "directed" not to their salvation, but "to their freedom and happiness" in this world. History will serve as the center of this education, for "by apprising them of the past [it] will enable them to judge of the future; it will avail them of the experience of other times and other nations; it will qualify them as judges of the actions and designs of men; it will enable them to know ambition under any disguise it may assume; and knowing it, to defeat its views."[88] Education is to fit the people for a certain kind of citizenship—to act the sentinels over their "freedom and happiness." Education will make the people's honesty more effective by arming it with a modicum of defensive wisdom.[89]

Jefferson's educational system would also reinforce or help form the people's honesty itself. "The first elements of morality too may be instilled into their minds; such as, when further developed as their judgments advance in strength, may teach them how to work out their own greatest happiness, by showing them that it does not depend on the condition of life in which chance has placed them, but is always the result of a good conscience, good health, occupation, and freedom in all just pursuits."[90] Jefferson's commitment to natural equality and to democratic republicanism does not extend to a commitment to social or economic equality. The people's education will help make them fit citizens of a free republic dedicated to the security of rights, including the right to property, by leading them to see that plundering the wealthy is no necessary part of their own happiness. With such schemes, Jefferson hopes to reassure his fellow wealthy Virginians that their oligarchic system is not necessary in order to protect their own rights. Of course such a system of moral education can only succeed if the people do not live in desperate poverty. Education "indeed is not all that is necessary, though it be essentially necessary."[91] Nonetheless, Jefferson could go very far in his hopes for education: "Enlighten the people generally, and tyranny and oppressions of body and mind will vanish like evil spirits at the dawn of day."[92]

The educational scheme helps provide not only a fit people for the natural rights republic, but the wise and naturally talented rulers who must supplement the people.

> It [is] expedient for promoting the publick happiness that those persons, whom nature both endowed with genius and virtue, should be rendered by liberal education worthy to receive, and able to guard the sacred deposit of the rights and liberties of their fellow citizens.[93]

Education helps both to identify and to form the "natural aristocracy" who will take the lead in Jefferson's democratic republic. The educational system will be the expected entree to the public sphere for the young men of Virginia. There they will prove themselves in company with their peers; there they will be exposed to what Jefferson considered the undeniably salutary effects—moral and intellectual—of "liberal education." Since "nature has sown talents as liberally among the poor as the rich," the educational system will also be the avenue for finding and raising up the natural aristocrats among the poorer elements of society.[94] Through a complicated system of screening and evaluation, the very best of the poorer youths will be advanced to higher levels of free education. Jefferson's system of education is to be, then, a limited vehicle for social mobility, but that is neither its purpose nor its justification. Its purpose is political—to find and form the talented among the poor and put them into a position from which they may "be called to the charge" of "guarding the sacred deposit of the rights and liberties of their fellow citizens."[95] "Worth and genius" are thus to be "sought out from every condition of life and completely prepared by education for defeating the competition of wealth and birth for public trusts."[96]

Education is a necessary but not sufficient supplement to resting politics securely on the great body of the people; Jefferson insists that the constitution of his democratic republic contain a proper system of separated powers and checks and balances. He would not make the mistake of the oligarchic republicans who thought virtue in the holders of power a sufficient safeguard. (He does not share the theories of our republican synthesizers, either.) However virtuous the Virginia rulers may feel themselves to be—Jefferson diplomatically does not challenge their self-assessment—nonetheless the future holds for America what the past has revealed elsewhere. "Human nature is the same on every side of the Atlantic, and will be alike influenced by the same causes. The time to guard against corruption and tyranny, is before they shall have gotten hold on us."[97]

The Virginia constitution, with its failure to establish a proper separation of powers, illustrates the danger Jefferson fears. All powers, legislative, executive, and judicial, rest in the hands of the legislature. Concentration of power is in itself very bad, for the legislature is thus free to substitute its will for the rule of law that the separation of powers fosters. Not only can the legislature make the general rules which govern society, but it can control the application of them to individuals; it can override all efforts by other officials to resist its self-interested acts of will.

The corruption and degeneracy Jefferson particularly fears is that the rulers, numerous as they may be, electorally responsible as they may be, liberally educated as they may be, will forget their trust—the rights and liberties of their fellow citizens—and pursue their own interests to the extent of destroying the republic and setting up themselves or some of their number as absolute and irresponsible rulers. This is a fate to which Virginia's extraordinarily defective oligarchic republic is especially prone, but it is one that Jefferson fears lies in the future of any republic that is not exceedingly well constructed.

Jefferson never stopped pondering republicanism—within a few years of leaving the presidency, he reconceived the entire topic. He comes now to judge his own earlier draft constitution to have been nearly as inadequate as the Virginia constitution itself, and for much the same reason. Jefferson confesses that his draft contained "gross departures . . . from genuine republican canons." He attributes his errors and those of his fellows to the same erroneous opinion. "The abuses of monarchy had so much filled all the space of political contemplation, that we imagined everything republican which was not monarchy."[98]

By 1816, Jefferson sees all the early American experiments in republicanism, including his own projections, as overly-mild adaptations of European, especially British, models. "It must be agreed," he writes in 1816, "that our governments have much less of republicanism than ought to have been expected."[99] The Revolution, after all, "commenced on [very] favorable ground. It presented us an album on which we were free to write what we pleased." Even though the Americans were not engaged in the Whig enterprise of a restoration of an antecedent order, even though they made their "appeal to the laws of nature" and not to the ancient law or constitution, "yet we did not avail ourselves of all the advantages of our position."[100] The Americans' failure to exploit to the full the opportunity presented by their *tabula rasa* was not due to "any want of republican disposition in those who framed these constitutions, but to a submission of true principle to European authorities, to speculators on government."[101]

European practice and European theory deterred the Americans from following their own better instincts. Some of the Federalist Party, Jefferson thought, aimed at an actual restoration of the British constitution—

complete with hereditary monarch and house of lords—but even the sounder heads who forbore from that remained too much within the orbit of European models. They dismantled the obviously unacceptable elements—monarchy and trailing nobles—but put in their place substitutes too much like the originals, and failed to appreciate the immense difference natural rights republicanism made for a proper constitutional order.

Jefferson's critique of the oligarchic republicanism of the Virginia constitution can easily be recast in terms of these later complaints. The Virginians essentially did away with monarchy and the hereditary principle, but placed power in the hands of an oligarchic class, considering this sufficiently republican because nonmonarchic and nonhereditary. This was deficient because insufficiently popular, and also because in practice the hereditary principle maintains more hold than it ought to have, since the "leading families," largely hereditary elements, tend to acquire a natural call on political power in such a system.

Another example, a particularly striking one, of the hypnotic hold of English models, is the provisions made in most American constitutions for judicial independence.

> In England, where judges were named and removable at the will of an hereditary executive, from which branch most misrule was feared, and has flowed, it was a great point gained by fixing them for life, to make them independent of the executive.[102]

But a suitable arrangement in the context of a monarchy is not necessarily suitable in the context of a popular republic. "In a government founded on the public will," judicial independence is no longer a virtue, for it "operates in an opposite direction, and against that will."[103] Thus, by 1816 Jefferson favored popular election and accountability of judges—all the way up to the highest courts. This represents a truly major shift from his own earlier position. The draft constitution for Virginia of 1776 provided for "good behavior" tenure for judges.

Jefferson's own 1776 constitutional provisions for the Senate in Virginia betray how much the Americans were inclined to substitute for the old British institutions new American versions much like what they were replacing. Jefferson incorporated long terms of office and was even willing to contemplate life tenure. Moreover, he sought an indirect election for the upper house—not the popular electorate directly, but the lower house was to select the upper. By 1816, Jefferson shifted ground substantially. He now favored a shorter term of office, four years, and he now favored direct election of the Senate by a much expanded electorate.[104]

Jefferson in 1776–1787 had favored a different mode of selection for the Senate because he sought to bring different qualities into the two houses of the legislature, honesty reflecting the people as such, in the lower house, and wisdom in the upper house. At the time he was quite explicit about the model for his plan—the theory of the British constitution.

His draft constitution was indeed deeply indebted to the British model as to its aims, the combination of the many and the few, and as to its means, popular dependence in some places, and exclusion of the people (more or less) elsewhere. In this light, Jefferson's draft constitution did remain close (perhaps not as close as he said, however) to its European precedents, sans the hereditary monarchy and nobles, of course.

Even in his later thought, Jefferson does not entirely renounce ways of thought associated with the British constitution. Early and late he considers "the few" to be an indispensable element of a healthy republic. The "natural aristoi" are those distinguished by "virtue and talents," but certainly not those marked by "wealth and birth." The late Jefferson goes so far as to conclude that "that form of government is the best which provides the most effectively for a pure selection of these natural *aristoi* into the offices of government."[105]

These later musings on the natural aristocracy certainly continue themes from Jefferson's earlier writings on constitutions and education, but they contain two emphases which distinguish them from his earlier positions. First, Jefferson no longer thinks of one particular place in the government as the specific home of wisdom, talent, and virtue. So far as possible, these men of ability ought to fill the whole government. Although Jefferson continues to see politics as involving some sort of interplay between the few and the many, he no longer sees it on the pattern of the British constitution's division of two houses with affirmative "set asides" for members of each class. Moreover, no special techniques of selection are necessary or desirable to bring these men of talent and virtue into leadership positions. "I think the best [method] is . . . to leave to the citizen the free election and separation of the aristoi from the pseudo-aristoi, of the wheat from the chaff." The people, Jefferson believes, will "in general . . . elect the real good and wise,"[106] a substantial change of view from his earlier days. The cooperation of the few and the many is to take place on an entirely different basis from any version or adaptation of the English constitution; it is to be truly popular, thoroughly dependent on the people.

Jefferson clearly has come to see British models as seductions that need to be resisted by his countrymen, as he had earlier seen classical models as dangers to American political health. His period of party leadership was devoted, therefore, to rallying the country against what he saw to be the Federalists' concealed but real reversion to the British constitution, either in the corrupted form patronized by Hamilton, or in the purified form patronized by John Adams.[107] The postpresidency phase of his career was devoted to the development and promulgation of his more radical new republicanism. The enemy now is not the more or less unvarnished Anglicism of Hamilton and Adams and their like, but the subtle Amer-Anglo republicanism of the likes of the early Thomas Jefferson and the James Madison who drafted the U.S. constitution.

The Americans fell short of real republicanism in their earlier efforts at political construction because, dazzled by European authorities, they failed to "penetrate to the mother principle, that 'governments are republican only in proportion as they embody the will of their people and execute it.'"[108] In other statements, Jefferson went even further:

> Were I to assign to this term [republicanism] a precise and definite idea, I would say, purely and simply, it means a government by its citizens in mass, acting directly and personally.[109]

The standard of republicanism is what we would now call direct democracy. All forms which retreat from that (and Jefferson knows most will require some retreat) are only republican to a degree; "the further the departure from direct and constant control by the citizens, the less has the government of the ingredient of republicanism."[110]

The contrast to Madison's Anglified republicanism (as Jefferson would describe it) could not be clearer. According to Madison, a republic is "a government which derives all its powers directly or indirectly from the great body of the people, and is administered by persons holding their offices during pleasure for a limited period, or during good behavior."[111] The tone of this is surely different from Jefferson's late republicanism. Nothing here of that activist popular role, that insistence on rule by the will of the people. Thus, Madison considers his life-tenure judiciary, his indirectly elected Senate and President, his distant and rather independent representatives, to be perfectly adequate embodiments of the republican principle.

In his postpresidency years, in other words, Jefferson's conception of republicanism has shifted substantially. It would be a mistake, however, to conclude, as some do, that this shift signifies an equally significant metamorphosis in Jefferson's understanding of the grounds and purposes of government, that it implies, for example, a shift away from the natural rights philosophy and toward a conception of politics according to which

no one could be called happy without his share in public happiness, . . .
no one could be called free without his experience in public freedom,
and . . . no one could be called either happy or free without participat-
ing, and having a share, in public power.[112]

Contrary to such speculation, Jefferson in 1816 continues to express
the criteria of political legitimacy in terms of rights. "Believing, as I do,
that the mass of the citizens is the safest depository of their own rights . . .
I am a friend to that composition of government which has in it the
most . . . popular election and control."[113]

"The true foundation of republican government," then, lies not in
novel ideas of public (as opposed to private) happiness, nor in a sudden appreciation for the classical idea that "man is a political animal," but rather
"in the equal rights of every citizen, in his person and property, and in
their management."[114] The ground of republicanism, in other words, is in
the private and individual rights each has to his or her own. Jefferson's
later republicanism represents an attempt to take these rights extremely
seriously. They are, as he had affirmed in the Declaration of Independence, "inalienable." The European models and their Americanized imitations do not take the ground in natural rights seriously enough. They
proceed as though the rights to the management of one's self and one's
own are alienable, as though they are merely theoretical postulates which
have little abiding significance for the construction of political society.

Jefferson thinks quite otherwise:

Society [is] one of the natural wants with which man has been created; . . . when . . . he has procured a state of society, it is one of his acquisitions which he has a right to regulate and control, jointly indeed
with all those who have concurred in the procurement.[115]

The democratic republic is not merely conducive to rights-protecting, not
merely expressive of the status of all citizens as rights-bearers, but is itself
a right. The flexible and prudential standards Jefferson, following Locke
and Montesquieu, had articulated in the Declaration of Independence are
gone; democracy is now understood to be a right, a matter of principle,
and simply the only legitimate form of government.

Jefferson derives this right by drawing the implications from the conclusions of natural rights philosophy about the nature of government: It is
not merely an instrumental thing, but is itself "an acquisition," that is to
say, it is itself property as well as an instrument for the securing of property
(in the broad Lockean sense). The whole system rests on the underlying

principle that human beings are rights-possessors with the inalienable right to "manage" themselves, "their person and property." Public institutions, the joint-making of the citizenry, must be "managed" consistently with their purpose as rights-securers and their nature as "acquisitions." As property in this sense, government must be made and operated so that it really belongs to, that is to say, proceeds via the actual and active consent, or better, will of the governed. Jefferson's most republican or political moment thus arises in a line of thought more or less the reverse of the picture of republican politics in the republican synthesis. Jefferson formulates this extraordinary right to democracy when he assimilates the public sphere entirely to the theory of private property, when he comes to see the state more completely through the lens of the Lockean theory of property and property rights.

From these axioms, Jefferson in his postpresidential years derives a quite novel principle for constituting and organizing public authority. "We think experience has proved it safer, for the mass of individuals composing the society, to reserve to themselves personally the exercise of all rightful powers to which they are competent, and to delegate those to which they are not competent to deputies named, and removable for unfaithful conduct, by themselves immediately."[116] Applying that principle, Jefferson develops a new kind of complex system of government to replace, more or less, the complex models based on the British constitution. He replaces one kind of complexity, the largely horizontal complexity of Amer-Anglo republicanism (e.g., the U.S. constitution) with another kind of complexity, a more vertical complexity suggested to a large degree by federalism, but going well beyond it. The "secret" of liberty "will be found," Jefferson argues, "in the making [of each man] himself the depository of the powers respecting himself, so far as he is competent to them, and delegating only what is beyond his competence . . . to higher and higher orders of functionaries, so as to trust fewer and fewer powers in proportion as the trustees became more and more oligarchical."[117] What powers can be kept in the hands of each, as a private and individual matter, ought to be so kept. All public power ought to be entrusted to the lowest, most local level capable of exercising it, and each level of government ought to be constructed so as to maximize popular involvement and control. What one does not manage for oneself, one manages with others; where one does not have full control over affairs, one has a share in the management of affairs, so far as is compatible with the affairs being managed at all.

Thus Jefferson spends much space in his later writings detailing the allocation of functions and powers among different vertical levels of government, all of which together form one "gradation of authorities."[118] The "national government," Jefferson thinks, should "be entrusted with the defence of the nation, and its foreign and federal relations."[119] Here Jefferson clearly indicates another area of great difference between himself and his friend Madison. In the latter's Amer-Anglo republican constitution, the national government's responsibilities go substantially further. For example, in the plan he drew up for the Constitution, Madison included a provision (to which Jefferson objected) for the Congress of the national government to exercise a veto power over all legislation in the states, a proposal aimed at securing justice and the protection of rights within the states. The Constitution as adopted certainly failed to go as far as Madison hoped, but it did include provisions which went beyond what Jefferson considered appropriate.[120]

Jefferson would leave exclusively to "lower" levels of his system of authorities many of the matters Madison would wish to see the national government involved in. The state governments ought to "be entrusted . . . with the civil rights, laws, police, administration of what concerns the state generally; the counties with the local concerns of the counties, and each ward [should] direct the interests within itself."[121] Power remains at the lowest level possible, beginning with each person, his or her self and property, and moves upward only as necessary, only as the lower level proves incompetent, trusting, as he said, "fewer and fewer powers" to each level, as fewer and more distant persons hold the power.[122] Jefferson's later republicanism is not so driven by abstract principle that it does not make place for political needs which require some compromise with the principle that power must be kept entirely in the hands of each.[123]

The most remarkable and probably the most important feature of Jefferson's system is the provision for a system of "ward republics." Each county should be divided into much smaller units, wards, approximately six square miles in size, that is, about one-fourth the size of the average Virginia county.[124] The wards, modeled on the New England township, are the places where Jefferson departs most notably from all adaptations of the English constitution; they are the places where the active will of the people can most make itself felt and effective. They are the places, in other words, where Jefferson's "true republicanism" is to be realized.

Whatever tasks they undertake,[125] Jefferson foresees them fulfilling a number of functions central to the health and survival of republicanism. They are, first, to be loci for the exercise of the right that each possesses to share in political power. "Each ward would be a small republic within itself, and every man in the state would thus become an acting member of the common government, transacting in person a great portion of its rights and duties."[126] Secondly, the wards are to be the vehicle by which (most) public tasks get done better and more effectively.[127] To transfer public business from higher and more distant levels to the wards "will have it better done."[128] People care best for what is of most direct concern to them.

The ward system, thirdly, will importantly contribute to the goal Jefferson had set from his earliest days of a harmonious republic, with the populace attached and well affected toward their government. "By making every citizen an acting member of the government, and in the offices nearest and most interesting to him, [the ward system] will attach him by his strongest feeling, to the independence of his country, and its republican constitution."[129] The wards will conduce to political unity; "the whole is cemented by giving to every citizen, personally, a part in the administration of the public affairs."[130]

Enlisting the sentiments and attachments of the people, the wards would be the source of vitality to republican government in America. "These little republics would be the main strength of the great one." The townships of New England have already proved how much energy these "little republics" can generate. "We owe to them the vigor given to our revolution in its commencement in the Eastern States, and by them the Eastern States were enabled to repeal the embargo in opposition to the Middle, Southern and Western States, and their large and lubberly division into counties which can never be assembled."[131]

The energy unleashed in the wards to some extent also serves negative or checking functions as part of a proper system of divided, and therefore safer, powers. "The way to have good and safe government, is not to trust it all to one, but to divide it among the many." The system of authorities, and especially the wards, "constitutes truly a system of fundamental balances and checks for the government," a system better than the old constitution of horizontal checks and balances modeled on England.[132] The decentralization of government made possible by the ward organization provides the best guard against "what has destroyed liberty and the rights of man in every government which has ever existed under the sun," i.e., "the generalizing and concentrating all cares and powers into one body, no matter whether of the aristocrats of Russia or France, or of the autocrats of a Venetian Senate."[133] Since all governments have ultimately "destroyed liberty and the rights of man," and since the wards promise to fend off this sorry fate, no wonder Jefferson concludes, "could I once see [the establishment of the ward system] I should consider it as the dawn of the salvation of the republic."[134] "The wit of man," he says almost at the very end of his life, "cannot devise a more solid basis for a free, durable and well-administered republic."[135]

What is perhaps most striking about Jefferson's new natural rights republicanism is the creative way in which he has assimilated the important contributions James Madison had made to American political science. At the time of the drafting of the Constitution, Madison had compellingly shown (in *The Federalist* 37, among other places) that the dominant approach to politics taken by his countrymen after the revolution was fundamentally mistaken. Americans had defined the political problem too narrowly, as a problem of *safety* only, that is to say, as the problem of keeping government from being oppressive of the rights of citizens. Madison had persuasively argued that safety was but one of several qualities that governments must embody—energy and stability were two others which he identified. Madison wondered aloud in *The Federalist* whether the republican form was compatible with these various and partially conflicting requirements, and concluded that it was, but only if republicanism was understood in the relatively lax way he defined it, and only if his ersatz British constitution qualified as that kind of republic. Jefferson's later republicanism represents an effort to combine the various qualities Madison had identified—safety, competence, energy—with his own more principled, more rigorous definition of republicanism. In doing so, Jefferson sets forth the most thorough-going conception of what an America, characterized through and through by republican commitments and republican forms, would be.

Jefferson's robust version of democratic-republicanism does not bespeak the sway over him of classical republican strains of thought as Arendt, Pocock, Wood, Banning, Sheldon, and others would have us believe. Rather it is a specific thinking through of the natural rights philosophy he had given authoritative expression to for America in the Declaration of Independence. Only its connection to the natural rights doctrine allows us to understand the principled or, as some would have it, rigid and inflexible character of Jefferson's republicanism. He declares war on all hereditary power, which had been held to be perfectly acceptable within classical republicanism, and he declares war on all efforts to imitate the effects of hereditary power, as in Madison's much less populist model of republicanism. Republicanism, or, it would now be fair to say, democracy, becomes both the only rightful government and even a personal or individual right. It was this strain of Jeffersonian theory that the Warren Court picked up on, for example, in its reapportionment decisions.

Jefferson's theory is complex because he derives the right to democracy both from an argument of principle and an argument of practice. Principle establishes a right to a democratic republic because government, as a thing made by the contractors—all the persons subject to its authority—belongs to those who made it, and thus, like any piece of jointly owned property, is rightly controlled and managed by the owners, jointly. So far is Jefferson from rejecting a natural right to property in favor of some "higher" form of democracy that he derives his "higher" democracy from the right to property.

At the same time, he holds the democratic republic to be instrumentally best also. It does better what all governments are to do—secure the rights of its citizens. In modern jargon, Jefferson's case for a right to a democratic republic combines deontological and consequentialist elements. That right is both expressive in itself of a fundamental right and instrumental to other rights. Jefferson thought his theory of the ward republics so important precisely because it combined the competence, safety, stability, wisdom, energy, and allegiance-producing quality required by government in its instrumental role with the principled requirement set by governments as expressions of the rights-bearing quality of human beings.

Jefferson's robust republicanism does not bespeak the sway over him of a counter-liberal republicanism, but it does provide a vehicle wherein the American tradition has assimilated to its basic natural rights liberalism elements more intensely political and reminiscent of premodern republicanism. Going beyond the original natural rights liberalism, politics is no longer simply instrumental, but is, indeed, a good in itself, an expression of the fundamental character of human beings as rights bearers. Thus, politics in America cannot be captured in any utilitarian calculus—the legitimate form is not simply the form that performs best instrumentally. Political participation, too, takes on a meaning somewhat more akin to what it held in earlier forms of republicanism. It is both a good in itself and even a civic duty, not merely an interest or private benefit.

Of course, America as a nation is now only partly defined by republicanism as understood by Jefferson. It is surely not a system in which we find "government by its citizens in mass, acting directly and personally." It would be difficult to say that Americans see themselves, in any significant way, primarily as citizens, or as owners of their governments. Jefferson hoped to see a nation in which "every man is a sharer in the direction of his ward-republic, or of some of the higher ones, and feels that he is a participator in the government of affairs, not merely an election one day in the year"—or one day every four years—"but every day." The kind of self-identification Jefferson's citizens would form is not the kind formed by citizens of America's large, distant, and relatively nonparticipant republic.

Nonetheless, Jeffersonian republicanism has been deeply transformative of American political life and American political opinion. Over time, we have experienced a synthesis of sorts of the Jeffersonian and Madisonian versions of natural rights republicanism. The large and less strenuously republican Madisonian constitutional system has set the fundamental frame for American politics, but it has been infused with a more Jeffersonian spirit: no longer are the Madisonian institutions as removed from the people as they were under the Madisonian constitution. First, the political parties, then the formal modification of the constitution, and finally, the development of the mass media have worked to bridge some of the distance Madison had hoped to establish between governmental institutions and the people.

At the same time, the Jeffersonian popular spirit operates within the Madisonian context of an "elitist" republic, without the vital devolution of authority and without the vibrant wards, which were to elicit and educate the republican spirit of the people. One is tempted to conclude that contemporary American republicanism is on the whole the loser for the synthesis—that either the Jeffersonian or the Madisonian version could be superior to the hybrid version we have. The present system does not foster those qualities of deliberation, sobriety, stability, and wisdom that Madison sought, nor does it supply Jefferson's energizing popular spirit, trained in the responsibilities of citizenship and alert to the depredations of government.

Jefferson believed that his theory of ward republicanism represented the one true and authentic working out of the natural rights position, because it alone gave full and adequate weight to both the expressive and instrumental dimension of republicanism. Madison's more practically sophisticated analysis reveals abiding tensions in Jefferson's system: the exercise of the right to control government can, without large stretches of the imagination, produce outcomes that conflict with the rights to be protected. Madison persisted in his belief that institutional devices supplementary to majority rule remained essential for securing the rights of minorities. Jefferson conceded the principle of minority rights, but refused to countenance institutions geared to their protection.

Likewise, Madison also would question whether Jefferson's ward republics and graded authorities would be sufficient to supply all the energy, competence, and prudence required to run a nation successfully. The subsequent course of American history, while it may not definitively settle the matter, certainly suggests that Madison has a point here.

Yet the persistent concern about the quality of democratic life in America more than suggests that Jefferson, too, had a point of continuing value, and that the amalgam for which he stands continues to have power in the political culture. Today, as since the early days of the republic, we live in a tension between Jeffersonian and Madisonian versions of natural rights republicanism, or, put differently, between the expressive and the instrumental dimensions of republicanism. The debate between liberals and communitarians is the contemporary form in which this tension persists. I know of no simple way to resolve this tension—perhaps it should not be resolved. The American amalgam, perhaps, is just such a tension as the

Greek philosopher Heraclitus described: it is such a thing as "agrees at variance with itself; it is an attunement turning back on itself, like that of the bow and the lyre."[136]

NOTES

This essay is on the whole an edited version of chapters 1 and 7 of *The Natural Rights Republic: Studies in the Foundation of the American Political Tradition* (Notre Dame, Ind.: University of Notre Dame Press, 1996). I have for the most part forborne from any temptation I might have felt to recast the argument, but in a few places I have made changes somewhat more substantial than merely stylistic.

1. Thomas Jefferson, "Epitaph" (1826), in *Thomas Jefferson Writings*, ed. Merrill D. Peterson (New York, 1984), 706–7. Hereafter cited as Peterson, ed.

2. Jefferson to Roger Weightman, June 24, 1826, in Peterson, ed., 1517. Cf. Jefferson to John Adams, October 28, 1813, in ibid., 1309.

3. Jefferson, "A Bill for Establishing Religious Freedom," in ibid., 347.

4. Jefferson, "A Bill for the More General Diffusion of Knowledge," in ibid., 365.

5. Moses Coit Tyler, "The Declaration of Independence in the Light of Modern Criticism," in *A Casebook on the Declaration of Independence*, ed. Robert Ginsburg (New York, 1966), 99.

6. Perry, "The Philosophy of the Declaration," in Ginsberg, *A Casebook*, 173.

7. Tyler, "The Declaration," 100.

8. E.g., ibid., 126; Arthur A. Ekirch, *The Challenge of American Democracy* (Belmont, Calif., 1973), 29; Staughton Lynd, *Intellectual Origins of American Radicalism* (New York, 1969).

9. Paul Eidelberg, *On the Silence of the Declaration of Independence* (Amherst, Mass., 1976), xv, 2, 75, 102.

10. George Mace, *Hobbes, Locke and the Federalist* (Carbondale, Ill., 1979), 12.

11. Martin Diamond, "The Revolution of Sober Expectations," in *The American Revolution: Three Views* (New York, 1975), 67–68; Harry V. Jaffa, *The Conditions of Freedom* (Baltimore, 1975), 58–59; Daniel Boorstin, *The Lost World of Thomas Jefferson* (Boston, 1948), 181.

12. See Lynd, *Intellectual Origins*.

13. Daniel Boorstin, *The Genius of American Politics* (Chicago, 1952), 70; Frank M. Coleman, *Hobbes and America* (Toronto, 1977), 71; Barry A. Shain, *The Myth of American Individualism* (Princeton, 1994), 246–59.

14. Jefferson to Henry Lee, May 8, 1825, in Peterson, ed., 1501.

15. Robert Webking, *The American Revolution* (Baton Rouge, 1989), 100.

16. John Locke, *Two Treatises of Government*, ed. Peter Laslett (Cambridge, 1960), 54.

17. Cf., e.g., Thomas Engeman, "Liberalism, Republicanism and Ideology," *Review of Politics* (Spring 1993): 332–33.

18. Michael J. Sandel, ed., *Liberalism and Its Critics* (New York, 1984), 5.

19. Gordon Wood, *The Radicalism of the American Revolution* (New York, 1992), 234.

20. Willmoore Kendall and George Carey, *The Basic Symbols of the American Political Tradition* (Baton Rouge, 1970), 155.

21. Richard Hooker, *Of the Laws of Ecclesiastical Polity* (London, 1907), I, x, 4; Locke, *Two Treatises* II, 15.

22. Harry Jaffa, *How to Think about the American Revolution* (Durham, N.C., 1978), 35, 41, 59–60; cf. Sanford Levinson, *Constitutional Faith* (Princeton, 1988), 59–65, 88.

23. Cf. Scott D. Gerber, "Whatever Happened to the Declaration of Independence . . . ," *Polity* 26 (1993): 230: "the essential premise of the American Founding is that government exists to secure natural rights, not to cultivate virtue."

24. Martin Diamond, *As Far as Republican Principles Will Admit*, ed. William A. Schambra (Lanham, Md., 1991), 213–15.

25. Ibid., 214.

26. Jaffa, *How to Think*, 119.

27. Bernard Bailyn, *The Ideological Origins of the American Revolution* (Cambridge, 1967), 34.

28. Ibid., 34–35.

29. Bernard Bailyn, "The Central Themes of the American Revolution: An Interpretation," in *Essays on the American Revolution*, ed. Stephen G. Kurtz and James Hudson (Chapel Hill, N.C., 1973), 7–8.

30. Bailyn, *Ideological Origins*, 34, 45.

31. J. G. A. Pocock, "Virtue and Commerce in the Eighteenth Century," *Journal of Interdisciplinary History* 3 (1972): 122. For a fuller account, complete with relevant citations, see Michael P. Zuckert, *Natural Rights and the New Republicanism* (Princeton, 1994), 159–64; 166–70.

32. J. G. A. Pocock, "Between Gog and Magog," *Journal of the History of Ideas* 68 (1987): 340; *Virtue, Commerce, and History* (Cambridge, 1985), 68.

33. Gordon Wood, *The Creation of the American Republic* (Chapel Hill, N.C., 1969), 47.

34. For a fuller account, complete with fuller citations, see Zuckert, *Natural Rights and the New Republicanism*, 155–59.

35. Isaac Kramnick, *Republicanism and Bourgeois Radicalism* (Ithaca, N.Y., 1990), 167.

36. See, e.g., Catherine Zuckert, "Aristotle on the Limits and Satisfactions of Political Life," *Interpretation* 11 (1983): 185–206; Thomas Pangle, *The Spirit of Modern Republicanism* (Chicago, 1988); Paul Rahe, *Republics Ancient and Modern* (Chapel Hill, N.C., 1992), pt. 1.

37. See, e.g., Vickie Sullivan, "Machiavelli's Momentary 'Machiavellian Moment,'" *Political Theory* 20 (May 1992): 309–18.

38. See, e.g., J. C. Davis, "Pocock's Harrington: Grace, Nature, and Art in the Classical Republicanism of James Harrington," *Historical Journal* 24 (1981): 683–98; J. F. Goodale, "J. G. A. Pocock's Neo-Harringtonians: A Reconsideration," *History of Political Thought* 1 (June 1980): 237–60; Harvey C. Mansfield,

Taming the Prince (New York, 1989), 183–86; Vickie Sullivan, "The Civic Humanist Portrait of Machiavelli's English Successors," *History of Political Thought* 15 (Spring 1994): 73–96; Rahe, *Republics*, 408–26.

39. See Goodale, "Pocock's Neo-Harringtonians"; Zuckert, *Natural Rights and the New Republicanism*, 166–83; Rahe, *Republics*, 429–40.

40. See, e.g., Pangle, *Spirit*; John P. Diggins, *The Lost Soul of American Politics* (New York, 1984); Joyce Appleby, *Capitalism and a New Social Order* (New York, 1984); Rahe, *Republics*, pt. 3.

41. Lance Banning, "The Republican Hypothesis: Errors, Contributions, and Misunderstandings," in *The Republican Synthesis Revisited*, ed. Milton M. Klein (Worcester, Mass., 1992).

42. Michael Lienesch, *The New Order of the Ages* (Princeton, 1988); Garrett Ward Sheldon, *The Political Philosophy of Thomas Jefferson* (Baltimore, 1991); Banning, "Republican Hypothesis"; Banning, "Some Second Thoughts on Virtue and the Course of Revolutionary Thinking," in *Conceptual Change and the Constitution*, ed. Terence Ball and J. G. A. Pocock (Lawrence, Kans., 1988).

43. Jefferson to Adams, July 15, 1814, in Peterson, ed., 1341; cf. Jefferson to Short, October 31, 1819, in ibid., 1431–32; and especially, Jefferson to Short, August 4, 1820, in ibid., 1438.

44. Jefferson to Adams, February 28, 1796, in ibid., 1034.

45. Jefferson, *Notes on the State of Virginia*, in ibid., 254.

46. Ibid., 252.

47. Ibid., 254.

48. Niccolo Machiavelli, *Discourses on the First Ten Books of Titus Livius*, ed. Bernard Crick (Middlesex, 1970), I.2.

49. Jefferson, *Notes*, 254.

50. Machiavelli, *Discourses*, I.4, 6.

51. Jefferson, *Notes*, 252.

52. Jefferson to George Washington, April 16, 1784, in Peterson, ed., 791.

53. Ibid. On opposition to hereditary rule as the core of early American republicanism, and on how far that stands from the tradition, see Thomas Pangle, *The Ennobling of Democracy* (Chicago, 1992), 99–100.

54. Cf. Peterson, ed., 148–49.

55. *Notes*, 254.

56. Jefferson, "Draft Constitution for Virginia," in Peterson, ed., 337, 338.

57. Jefferson to Edmund Pendleton, August 26, 1776, in ibid., 755–56.

58. *Notes*, 254.

59. "Draft Constitution," 343.

60. "Autobiography," in Peterson, ed., 32, 45. Cf. Alexis de Tocqueville, *Democracy in America*, ed. J. P. Mayer (Garden City, N.Y., 1969), I.3.

61. *Notes*, 290. Cf. Jefferson to Adams, 1034.

62. Ibid.

63. Alexander Hamilton, James Madison, and John Jay, *The Federalist*, ed. Clinton Rossiter (New York, 1961), no. 9.

64. Jefferson, *Notes*, 243.

65. Ibid., 275.

66. Ibid., 243.

67. Ibid., 244.

68. Ibid.

69. Ibid., 274.

70. "Draft Constitution," 338.

71. Jefferson to Pendleton, 756.

72. *Notes*, 245.

73. *Federalist*, no. 47

74. Charles Secondat, baron de Montesquieu, *The Spirit of the Laws*, ed. Anne Cohler (Cambridge, 1989), Bk. XI.

75. Jefferson, *Notes*, 245.

76. Ibid.

77. Ibid.

78. Ibid., 246.

79. Jefferson to Pendleton, 756. Cf. Machiavelli, *The Prince*, chap. 9; Melancton Smith, Speech in New York Ratifying Convention, in *The Complete Anti-Federalist*, ed. Herbert Storing (Chicago, 1981), 6:148–76.

80. Jefferson to Pendleton, 756.

81. Ibid., 755.

82. Ibid.

83. "Autobiography," 32; *Notes*, 274; Jefferson to Adams, 1306; on natural aristocracy as the true principle of classical republicanism, see Pangle, *Ennobling*, 107.

84. *Notes*, 245.

85. *Federalist*, no. 10.

86. *Notes*, 274. Cf. Jefferson to Littleton Waller Tazewell, January 5, 1805, in Peterson, ed., 1149; Jefferson to John Wyche, May 14, 1809, 1207; Jefferson to John Tyler, May 26, 1810, 1226.

87. *Notes*, 273.

88. Ibid., 274.

89. Lorraine Pangle and Thomas Pangle, *The Learning of Liberty* (Lawrence, Kans., 1993), 110–11.

90. *Notes*, 273. Cf. Pangle and Pangle, *Learning of Liberty*, 287.

91. *Notes*, 274.

92. Jefferson to P. S. Dupont de Nemours, April 24, 1816, 1337.

93. "Bill for Diffusion of Knowledge," 365.

94. *Notes*, 274.

95. "Bill for Diffusion of Knowledge," 365. Cf. Pangle and Pangle, *Learning of Liberty*, 117.

96. Jefferson to Adams, 1308.

97. *Notes*, 246.

98. Ibid.; cf. Jefferson to Kercheval, July 12, 1816, 1396.

99. Jefferson to John Taylor, May 28, 1816, 1394.

100. Jefferson to Major John Cartwright, June 5, 1824, 1491.

101. Jefferson to Taylor, 1394.

102. Jefferson to Kercheval, 1397.

103. Ibid.

104. Ibid., 1400.

105. Ibid., 1305–6.

106. Ibid., 1306.

107. Jefferson to Elbridge Gerry, January 26, 1799, 1056; Jefferson to Dr. Benjamin Rush, January 16, 1811, 1235.

108. Jefferson to Kercheval, 1396.

109. Jefferson to Taylor, 1392.

110. Ibid., 1393.

111. *Federalist*, no. 39.

112. Hannah Arendt, *On Revolution* (New York, 1963), 255.

113. Jefferson to Taylor, 1395.

114. Jefferson to Kercheval, 1398.

115. Jefferson to Dupont de Nemours, 1385.

116. Ibid.

117. Jefferson to Joseph Cabell, February 2, 1816, 1380.

118. Ibid.

119. Ibid., cf. Jefferson to Kercheval, 1399.

120. Cf. Charles F. Hobson, "The Negative on State Laws," *William and Mary Quarterly* 36, no. 2 (April 1979): 215–35; Michael P. Zuckert, "Federalism and the Founding," *Review of Politics* (1986): 187–98; Michael P. Zuckert, "A System Without Precedent," in *The Framing and Ratification of the Constitution*, ed. Leonard Levy and Dennis Mahoney (New York, 1988), 145–49; Lance Banning, "The Practicable Sphere of a Republic," in *Beyond Confederation*, ed. Richard Beeman (Chapel Hill, N.C., 1987), 162–87.

121. Jefferson to Cabell, 1380; cf. Jefferson to Cabell, 1399–1400.

122. Ibid., 1380.

123. Cf. Jefferson's frequent animadversions against Montesquieu's small republicanism, and his endorsement of Madison's federalism: Jefferson to Francois D'Ivernois, February 6, 1765, in Peterson, ed., 1024. Cf. Jefferson to Cartwright, 1493.

124. Jefferson to Cartwright, 1492.

125. See Jefferson to Cabell, 1380; Jefferson to Kercheval, 1399.

126. Jefferson to Cartwright, 1492.

127. Jefferson to Cabell, 1379–80.

128. Jefferson to Kercheval, 1399; cf. Jefferson to Adams, 1308.

129. Jefferson to Kercheval, 1399. Consider the critique of Jefferson offered by Pangle and Pangle, *Learning of Liberty*: "We note with unease the absence . . . of any reference to the virtues of obedience to and reverence for law" (113–14). Jefferson sees such reverence emerging from the educative functions of republican institutions.

130. Jefferson to Kercheval, 1400.

131. Jefferson to Tyler, 1227.

132. Ibid., 1380.

133. Ibid.

134. Jefferson to Cabell, 1227.

135. Jefferson to Cartwright, 1493; cf. Jefferson to Kercheval, 1399.

136. Heraclitus, Fragment 78, in *The Art and Thought of Heraclitus*, ed. Charles H. Kahn (Diels, 102).

Thomas Jefferson
and Republicanism

✣

JEAN YARBROUGH

The starting point for any discussion of Thomas Jefferson's political thought properly begins with the Declaration of Independence. For not only does this document lay out the principles of political right, setting forth in its opening paragraphs the origin and end of all legitimate governments, but it includes as its central idea the one principle that Jefferson, in other respects the great apostle of moral and political progress, insisted was permanent and unchanging: the rights of man.

Michael Zuckert's new book, *The Natural Rights Republic*, properly seeks to restore the centrality of this teaching to the American founding in general and to Jefferson's political thought in particular. But Zuckert does not seek merely to reinstate an orthodox Lockean liberalism, while disregarding the insights of civic humanists, Protestant majoritarians, Whig historians, and Scottish moral sense philosophers. Rather, his point is that, however much these competing philosophies found their way into the principles of the founding, forging a new "amalgam," the dominant line of thinking remains Lockean liberalism. To be sure, Zuckert's Locke is, in important respects, a revisionist Locke, at times closer to Kant than to Hobbes, but it is Locke nonetheless, not Hutcheson or Burlamaqui, whose spirit presides over the Declaration.

And not only the Declaration. One proof of how widely accepted these political principles were is that they appear in so many of the public documents drafted during this period, both before and after the Declaration. But while Americans spoke the common language of equality, rights, and consent, these documents are no better at explaining what these principles mean than is the Declaration. All of them are remarkably concise.

How then should we go about trying to understand the principles upon which the American republic rests? One method, according to Zuckert, is to pay close attention to the structure of the document, and this is particularly useful in explicating the meaning of equality. Equality is a prepolitical condition, signifying that all human beings are naturally free and independent; it emphatically does not imply an equality of condition in civil society. But as Zuckert himself acknowledges more than once, the structure of the document sheds no light on the central idea of natural rights. To be more specific, it does not explain what in human nature serves as the ground of our rights; nor does it help us to know what these rights mean, and, perhaps more important in today's rights-obsessed climate, what their limitations are. So, in chapter 3 of *The Natural Rights Republic*, Zuckert too is forced to go outside the Declaration. But whereas he finds the ideas of nature and rights best elaborated in the *Notes on Virginia*, and more particularly in the metaphor of the natural bridge, I rely principally upon Jefferson's commonplace books and private correspondence to flesh out his understanding of these terms. And again in contrast to Zuckert, who draws exclusively upon Locke to fill in the remaining lacunae in the Declaration, and, not surprisingly, concludes that natural rights in the strict sense all derive from the selfish desire for security, I argue that Jefferson's political psychology, while undeniably influenced by Locke, nevertheless departs from him in three important respects. First, Jefferson follows the Scots in asserting the existence of certain innate moral sentiments, such as fidelity to compacts and a sense of justice, which, when properly developed by education and republican institutions, help to reconcile the tension between self-interest and moral duty.[1] But the Scots were not the communitarians Garry Wills has made them out to be; Scottish moral sense philosophy, rightly understood, is not a grand alternative to Lockean liberalism, but liberalism in a different key.[2] Second, Jefferson rejects the Lockean hierarchy of the passions which elevates the desire for comfortable self-preservation as the single source of all natural rights.[3] In addition to the desire for a comfortable and secure life, Jefferson grounds the natural right to liberty on a second selfish passion, pride in the capacity for self-government.[4] In this sense, Jefferson's political psychology departs from that of the *Second Treatise* by taking a more expansive view of self-love, but it follows Locke in retaining the selfish passions as an important source of our rights. And third, Jefferson, again in contrast to Locke, and here, too, following the Scottish school, does not ground all of our rights on the selfish passions. Though we are of course most interested in our own happiness, the right of each individual to pursue happiness does not arise solely from the selfish part of our nature; happiness is also rooted in the generous desire to do good to others, or what the Scottish moral philosophers call benevolence. Thus, the political psychology of the Declaration is not reducible to the Lockean desire for comfortable self-preservation, but seeks to combine two different, and to some extent competing, selfish passions on the one hand and benevolence on the other.

If Jefferson's understanding of human nature departs in these important ways from the orthodox Lockean view, it would follow that his conception of rights also differs to some extent. And it does in three important respects. First, the appeal to pride in the capacity for self-government suggests a view of liberty that is more positive, or "republican," than Lockean liberalism. The right of citizens to participate in public life, which Jefferson later comes to see as the very definition of a republic, is not an extension of the right to private property, a conclusion which, if it were true, would indeed turn the republican tradition on its head.[5] Rather, the natural right of self-government is a manifestation of human spiritedness, which, for Jefferson, finds its expression in political as well as economic activities. Second, while Jefferson agrees that human beings are motivated by the desire for a secure and comfortable life, and, consequently, seeks to encourage and protect the acquisition of private property, he nowhere unequivocally states that property is a natural right.[6] Third, the appeal to the social as well as the selfish passions points to a somewhat different conception of happiness. Whereas Locke in the *Essay on Human Understanding* links happiness with the desire to avoid pain and seek pleasure and emphasizes the various and contrary ways in which men pursue their individual goals,[7] Jefferson, while nowhere denying the connection between happiness and pleasure consistently maintains that true happiness also requires virtue. In Jefferson's moral economy, pleasure, happiness, and virtue are all connected: we are so constituted that the exercise of virtue, and especially the social virtue of benevolence, gives us pleasure, and hence, completes our happiness.

The Jeffersonian View of Human Nature

In developing his view of human nature it is worth pointing out that Jefferson nowhere specifically mentions Locke, but refers instead to the Scottish moral sense philosopher, Henry Home, Lord Kames. At an early age, Jefferson copied into his *Commonplace Book* the following observation from Kames's tract on property: "Man, by his nature is fitted for society, and society by it's [*sic*] conveniences is fitted for man."[8] And like Kames, Jefferson, too, assumes that human beings are naturally social. "We consider society as one of the natural wants with which man has been created."[9] By this, Jefferson does not mean that human beings always act in ways which affirm their social nature; he seems to accept Kames's observation that primitive people are capable of great brutality and cruelty. Rather, he means that as human beings gradually develop the capacity to recognize and act on their innate moral instincts, they may be able to live together without law and government. In contrast to the purely hypothetical war of all against all posited by Hobbes, Jefferson sometimes views the American Indians as existing in a "real" state of nature, where every man is "perfectly free to follow his inclinations,"[10] without degenerating into violence and force. But at other moments Jefferson takes a more realistic view of "natural" man. Athough a Benevolent Creator has endowed human beings with a moral sense which makes it possible for them to live together in society, this sense by itself is not sufficient to ensure that individuals fulfill their moral obligations to others. Here again, the Indians' treatment of their women offers empirical evidence. Left to the promptings of the moral sense alone, Indian men exert their superior force to impose an "unjust drudgery" upon their women. Without "civilization" to enforce the equal rights of those who are physically weaker, natural societies, operating on the moral sense alone, tend to slide into "barbarism."[11]

But if human beings need government to compel the triumph of sociality, how does Jefferson's view of human nature differ from Locke's suggestion that we are naturally selfish, by which he means that even if men have always lived together with others,[12] they are naturally inclined to put their own interests first? The differences between Jefferson's view of human nature and Locke's are subtle but important. First, although Jefferson acknowledges that the moral sense by itself is weak, the fact that it exists at all means that the task of government can be limited to reinforcing the moral instincts that are already present in some inchoate form within human nature. And for Jefferson, this will require, even by the standards of Lockean liberalism, a very modest role for government in securing rights. In other words, sociability provides the moral grounding for Jefferson's greater confidence in the capacity of the people for self-government.[13] Second, and closely related, sociability means that our rights and duties are neither reducible to the selfish passions, even the selfish passions broadly construed, nor merely conventional, the result of utilitarian calculation. "Morality, compassion, [and] generosity" are also "innate elements of the human constitution."[14] Thus, while Jefferson, like Locke, starts from self-love, he moves beyond it to the social affections in order to bridge the gap between rights and right.

Although Jefferson occasionally admits that self-interest and moral obligation pull in opposite directions, most famously in the case of slavery, in general he believes that republican institutions, universal education, and an agrarian economy will improve, if not actually transform, human nature and so minimize the tension between the two. "Our interests soundly calculated, will ever be inseparable from our moral duties."[15] By this, he does not mean the Lockean argument that our moral duties to others can be rationally deduced from our selfish interests alone, but, on the contrary, that our deepest interests, if correctly understood and carefully cultivated in a proper republican environment, can spontaneously approach our genuine moral obligations. In short, Jefferson's political psychology seeks to combine the realism of an expanded self-interest with the moral dignity of benevolence, expressing a particularly American conception of rights which is at once more spirited and more philanthropic than Locke's.

The Right to Life

The first of our inalienable rights is the right to life, or more precisely, the right to preserve life. In the Declaration, Jefferson deliberately obscures whether this right comes directly from nature or whether it is the gift of a Benevolent Creator, but elsewhere he makes it clear that the ground of this right is our natural desire for self-preservation. Although Jefferson recognizes that this passion is not always and in every circumstance the most powerful human drive—witness, for example, the love of a mother for her child, or the self-destructive passions of hatred and revenge—Jefferson believes that it is usually so. Accordingly, the right to life takes precedence over our moral obligations to others. As if to underscore the unevenness of the conflict, Jefferson develops this point in the very document where he publicly invokes the phrase "the moral law of our nature." In the Opinion on the French Treaties, Jefferson acknowledges that "when performance of an obligation becomes self-destructive to the party, the law of self-preservation overrules the laws of obligation to others." The best he can do is interpret this exception to the moral law narrowly. Although we are not obliged to perform a duty that will result in our own destruction, we "will never read there permission to annul [our] obligations for a time or forever, whenever they become dangerous, useless, or disagreeable; certainly not when merely useless or disagreeable. . . . Yet the danger must be imminent, and the degree great." Nevertheless, even this rule of interpretation proves more porous than it at first appears. For all individuals and nations must judge for themselves when these obligations become self-destructive. As a last resort, Jefferson reminds us that we must all answer to "the tribunal of our consciences," but he leaves unresolved whether conscience or what he elsewhere calls the moral sense is sufficiently powerful by itself to override our more selfish and subjective determinations of when a danger is "great, inevitable, and imminent."[16]

The question, therefore, is whether there is anything in Jefferson's understanding of human nature that might offset the power of self-interest to eclipse all other moral considerations. We are not talking now about the grave and immediate danger to life, for Jefferson frankly acknowledges that in such circumstances the right to life almost always takes primacy. What we mean here is the tendency of reason to ally itself with the selfish passions and to construe every limitation upon liberty as a dire threat to self-preservation. As Herbert J. Storing has pointed out, the tendency of the modern natural rights doctrine, insofar as it is rooted exclusively in the selfish passions, is "for justice to be reduced to self-preservation, and for self-preservation to be defined as self-interest, and for self-interest to be defined as what is convenient and achievable."[17] Indeed, Jefferson himself in his letter to John Holmes provides unwitting testimony to this tendency to view indirect and distant threats to one's own rights as imminent and life-threatening. When Jefferson, commenting upon how the Missouri Compromise might affect emancipation efforts in Virginia, made his famous observation, "we have the wolf by the ears, and we can neither hold him nor safely let him go. Justice is in the one scale and self-preservation in the other,"[18] he does not mean only that emancipation in some cases posed an immediate and grave danger to the lives of Virginia slaveholders. As the rest of the letter makes clear, he also means that Virginians would not support emancipation unless they could first significantly reduce the number of slaves in Virginia by allowing their owners to take them *as slaves* into the newly developing territories. Virginians would be persuaded to end the "moral abomination" of slavery only when they were convinced it was in their interest to do so.

If, however, Jefferson's understanding of rights so far seems vulnerable to the kind of criticism that Herbert Storing and Harry Jaffa have leveled against the Lockean conception of natural rights,[19] his understanding of both liberty and the pursuit of happiness may each, if properly understood, help to mitigate the egoism these critics rightly deplore.

The Right to Liberty

For Jefferson liberty is the natural condition of human life; men in the state of nature are free and independent. They are subject to no master and may do whatever is necessary to preserve their rights to life and liberty. But when men act as judges in their own cause, as they do in the state of nature, the moral sense by itself is too weak to restrain the selfish passions. Thus, men must establish government to ensure that each individual respects the same rights in others that he claims for himself. The purpose of civil society is to preserve the broadest possible sphere of "rightful liberty" to each individual.[20] Thus, the natural right to liberty extends to the full range of activities that individuals may innocently pursue in cultivating their natural faculties and sensibilities. It includes those rights connected with self-development, such as the "rights of thinking and publishing our thoughts by speaking and writing," as well as "the right of personal freedom,"[21] and freedom of conscience. In addition, it encourages personal enrichment by recognizing the right to immigrate, to trade freely, to choose a vocation, and to labor for a livelihood.[22]

At first sight, Jefferson's expansive notion of liberty, especially when taken in conjunction with his deliberate exclusion of property from the Declaration, would appear to lay the ground for the gradual enlargement of rights, in both economic matters and also moral issues, and the steady expansion of governmental powers to secure them. While this interpretation first gained force during the Progressive Era, there are two problems with it. First, the natural right to liberty, as Jefferson understands it, applies only to the exercise of one's own faculties to satisfy one's own needs; it does not (except in unusual circumstances, as, for instance, when laborers are denied their fundamental right to labor for a living) extend to a claim on the faculties and property of others. To argue that government ought to redistribute wealth in order to promote greater socioeconomic equality is to misunderstand the most powerful impulses that lead individuals to form civil societies in the first place. What men seek above all else is "the *guarantee* to every one of his industry and the fruits acquired by it."[23] Thus, although Jefferson excludes property from the Declaration's list of inalienable rights, his understanding of the relation between liberty and property is not all that different from Locke's, and appears to be rooted in the same desire for a secure and comfortable life. Consequently, it is only those rights that conform to this passion that can be justified.

Turning to the more recent debate over what might be called "lifestyle" issues, Jefferson, in contrast to contemporary liberals, believes that all our rights are founded on an unchanging and universal conception of human nature. And nature establishes certain limits to individual liberty. Thus, natural rights do not extend to what today are called "privacy" issues; for example, Jefferson's revised legal code for Virginia would still punish homosexual acts.[24] More generally, his conception of liberty does not extend to what Walter Berns has called "the right to think, speak, and print unguided by moral principle."[25] Indeed, as Jefferson understands it, the natural right to liberty does not even require equal civil rights for women. (Women, of course, are endowed with the same natural rights, but since their nature is different, the content of these rights, especially the right to pursue happiness, differs somewhat from those of men.) This does not mean that political societies may not extend certain legal and political rights to their citizens beyond the natural rights Jefferson deduces from the Declaration. Civil rights for women are indeed consistent with the Declaration's principles.[26] A case can also be made on liberal grounds for tolerating homosexuality, especially in the limited sense of not criminalizing such behavior.[27] But in general, all such rights should accord with "the laws of nature and nature's God." Natural rights, by definition, are more limited than the contemporary concern with "human" or "fundamental" rights, both of which reject appeals to either nature or historical tradition in favor of some abstract or logical idea of liberty which governments are then obliged to enforce regardless of cost or consequences.[28]

If, in these important respects, Jefferson's understanding of liberty so far tracks Locke's argument, there is one important way in which it departs from him. To secure the rights of the people, Jefferson seeks, far more than Locke, to restrict the powers of government and, as a further safeguard, to organize citizens in local associations to keep a jealous eye on their elected representatives. This expansion of liberty to include "the natural right of self-government" after civil society is established is one of the distinctive features of Jefferson's conception of rights, and raises the question of how we are to interpret it. Is the natural right of self-government grounded exclusively in the desire for a comfortable life, which is the source of so many of our private liberties, or is it at least partly grounded in some other passion?

At first sight, the right to self-government does seem to be an extension of the desire for comfortable self-preservation: one reason the people insist on retaining the right of self-government is because they cannot always trust their elected representatives to protect their rights. But there is a second and more "republican" passion at work here: men seek to govern themselves not only because it promotes their interests, but because it gratifies their pride.[29] Jefferson's expanded conception of liberty seems at least partly grounded in pride and its associated passions, the love of honor and laudable ambition, which attend the spirited, as opposed to the appetitive, dimension of human nature. Moreover, to a far greater extent than Locke, Jefferson seeks to channel these more spirited passions not only into economic, but into political activity. Indeed, one of the striking aspects of Jefferson's political thought is the extent to which he views spiritedness in distinctively political terms.[30] While spiritedness may be directed toward the cultivation of the land or the taming of the wilderness, it manifests itself most fully in the proud determination of citizens to live freely under laws which they have established for themselves. So important does this become for Jefferson that he will later define a republic solely by whether it reserves to the people some opportunity to exercise their natural right of self-government on those matters which are "nearest and most interesting" to them.[31]

That the natural right to liberty is not simply reducible to the acquisitive desires is also suggested by Jefferson's repeated (and very un-Lockean) warnings that the rising tide of prosperity would sap the springs of republican virtue. Long before Alexis de Tocqueville warned of the danger of excessive materialism and its corrosive effects on civic life, Jefferson worried that the American preoccupation with making money would drain the public realm of its vital energy and spirit. Thus, although he would vigorously defend the right to acquire and possess private property, unrestrained acquisitiveness, especially when it is joined with modern commercial institutions, remains far more problematic for him than for Locke.

But what does it mean that for Jefferson there are two passions, each linked to a distinct and competing element in human nature, which ground the natural right to liberty? Does pride act as a counterweight to the desire for self-preservation, inspiring citizens to cherish their freedom and capacity for self-government, or does it encourage people to assert themselves even more vigorously on behalf of their selfish and narrow interests? Pride is a dangerous passion. Indeed, the entire liberal enterprise arises out of the very real need to tame the children of pride. And where pride is not restrained, as in the case of many of the Southern slaveholders, it can play a destructive role, emboldening masters to "trample" on the rights of their slaves. But it is also possible to go too far in trying to extirpate this passion; liberal republicanism must seek a balance between self-assertion and security-seeking. Jefferson's conception of liberty achieves this balance: the proud determination of citizens to govern themselves tempers the otherwise private and acquisitive aspects of liberty, and generally dignifies the life of free men. To use the words of Harvey C. Mansfield in a different context, by grounding liberty on these two irreducible passions, Jefferson "tempers our pride with our interests, yet ennobles our interests by combining them with our pride."[32]

And the Pursuit of Happiness

The pursuit of happiness remains the most elusive of the rights announced in the Declaration. Again, Zuckert sees this as an essentially Lockean idea, drawn from the *Essay on Human Understanding*, in which each individual is free to pursue whatever he believes will lead to his own happiness, with the predictable result that most will direct their energies toward material betterment.[33] Here, too, I believe he overstates the Lockean connection. For while Jefferson does indeed acknowledge the variety of human talents, inclinations, and situations, which inevitably lead individuals to pursue different objects, he repeatedly insists that the core of happiness is permanent and universal: there can be no genuine happiness without virtue. "The order of nature is that individual happiness shall be inseparable from the practice of virtue."[34]

Still, I do not mean to exaggerate this point. Jefferson's conception of happiness is not simply moralistic. No one who lived and entertained as well as he did could fail to appreciate the material prerequisites of the good life. But he never made the mistake of believing that wealth, power, good birth, or even bodily well-being could, by themselves, without the cultivation of virtue, bring true happiness. For Jefferson, the "greatest happiness" requires what Aristotle calls virtue and equipment; it depends on "good conscience, good health, occupation, and freedom in all just pursuits."[35]

Nevertheless, the attempt to move beyond this general formulation raises several difficulties. First, Jefferson never systematically explores what he means by happiness in general or the pursuit of happiness in particular. Nor does he ever directly take up the source of this right. Nearly all of his comments about happiness occur in private correspondence addressed to a wide variety of family, friends, acquaintances, and even strangers, in which the meaning of happiness is often casually treated and, as Zuckert notes, almost always tailored to the views of the recipient.[36] Before 1785 even these sources, of particular significance in trying to understand the meaning of the pursuit of happiness in the Declaration, are limited.[37] Second, and closely related to this last point, although Jefferson consistently maintains that virtue is the essential component of happiness, his conception of virtue undergoes a major change, from an early classical emphasis upon individual excellence to be achieved through stoical resignation and control of the passions, to a later modern and Christian stress upon the social virtues, especially benevolence. Thus, even if Jefferson means to link the pursuit of happiness with the practice of virtue when he substitutes this right for property in the Declaration, it is difficult to know precisely which virtues he has in mind in 1776.[38]

Third, even if these matters can be explained, if not systematically, at least plausibly, by reference to Jefferson's writings, there remains the question of how the *right* to pursue happiness can be read as implying a moral *duty* to others beyond the duty not to interfere with their equal right to pursue their own happiness. In a document justly celebrated as a declaration of *rights*, and which never mentions virtue, this reading of the pursuit of happiness is far from obvious.

Fourth, and finally, Jefferson insists that the purpose of the Declaration was not "to find out new principles or new arguments, never before thought of, not merely to say things which had never been said before." Is there any proof that Americans in Jefferson's time understood the pursuit of happiness in this way? Does the equation of happiness with virtue express what Jefferson believes to be the "common sense of the subject"?[39]

Beginning with the last objection, it should be noted that although the connection between virtue and happiness may at first strike the modern reader as farfetched, it was very much a part of the eighteenth-century English heritage shared by the Americans. Indeed, according to Howard Mumford Jones, in his classic study of the term, it was not only eighteenth-century Englishmen and Americans who equated happiness with "a knowledge of moral duties," but the entire Western tradition beginning with the ancient Greek and Roman moralists.[40]

If, however, in maintaining that "without virtue, happiness cannot be,"[41] Jefferson is merely echoing the prevailing sentiments of his day, we still need to know which virtues Jefferson associates with happiness. While space does not permit a detailed exploration of this issue, let me suggest that at the time Jefferson wrote the Declaration, he had come to no clear conclusion about the rank ordering of the virtues. Throughout this early formative period, classical and modern conceptions of virtue continue to overlap and to present themselves as models of human excellence. It is not even clear that Jefferson was aware of the tension between the two.

Because this period is so unsettled, it makes sense to look to those later writings that expand on earlier arguments, the implications of which he no more than dimly perceived when he included the right to the pursuit of happiness in the Declaration. While I emphasize that any interpretation elevating the social virtues over the intellectual virtues remains tentative and provisional, Jefferson's numerous remarks suggest that it is not arbitrary. Moreover, this preference for the social virtues seems most to accord with the "common sense" of the subject.[42] At the same time, this very practical and Protestant view would not rule out the exercise of the intellectual virtues for those who, like Jefferson, are naturally inclined to pursue them. The point here is not to get bogged down in an argument about the hierarchy of the virtues, but to consider how our conception of rights would be different if we understood happiness as being in some broad way connected with the cultivation of virtue.

The Ascendancy of the Social Virtues

One of the most explicit acknowledgments of the battle waging in Jefferson's mind between the classical virtues of wisdom, tranquillity, and self-sufficiency and the Scottish emphasis on philanthropy, benevolence, and sentimental friendship is his letter to Maria Cosway in 1786.[43] In this celebrated dialogue between the head and the heart, Jefferson, for the first time, reverses the classical hierarchy, which equates happiness with intellectual virtue, substituting for it the moral or social virtues that are known by the heart. Unlike the head, whose solitary search for wisdom leads to merely "visionary happiness," the heart is the seat of true happiness and pleasure.

What began as a playful contest between the head and the heart, the intellectual and the moral virtues as the ultimate source of human happiness, eventually ends in a rout. Returning to the morality of the ancients more than a decade after the famous dialogue, Jefferson now finds that Cicero and Seneca place far too much emphasis on individual perfection and not enough on the moral duties we owe to others. Although Jefferson continues to admire the ancients for their precepts relating "chiefly to ourselves and the government of those passions which, unrestrained, would disturb our tranquillity of mind," he now concludes that they are "short and defective" in elaborating the duties we owe to others. It is not that the ancients ignored the social virtues altogether, for, as Jefferson immediately adds, "they embraced, indeed, the circle of kindred and friends, and inculcated patriotism, or the love of our country in the aggregate, as a primary obligation: towards our neighbors and countrymen they taught justice, but scarcely viewed them within the circle of benevolence. Still less have they inculcated peace, charity and love to our fellow men, or embraced with benevolence the whole family of mankind."[44]

If, then, Jefferson comes to believe that the essence of virtue is benevolence or "doing good to others," it would follow that benevolence lies at the heart of his understanding of happiness. But where in human nature is there a foundation for this conception of virtue and happiness, and how is it connected to our rights? Perhaps the fullest discussion of this first question occurs in a letter to Thomas Law, written in 1814.[45] Although this is nearly forty years after the Declaration was written, it enlarges upon themes Jefferson had already been exploring when he wrote the Declaration, and so may provide some clue to the ground of this third and most elusive right.

The letter to Law seeks to locate the "foundation of morality" in human nature. Following the Scottish school, Jefferson rejects the argument of Hobbes and his followers that the moral duties we owe to others are ultimately reducible to the promptings of self-love. At the same time, he rejects the alternative claims of the rationalists (Reid, Clarke, and Wollaston) that virtue is grounded in reason, truth, or some notion of fitness. Neither truth, nor the love of God, nor the love of the beautiful, nor self-love provides a true "foundation of morality." Jefferson devotes special attention to the enlightened form of self-interest put forth by the French philosopher Helvetius, who had argued that we do good for others because we receive pleasure from such acts. Jefferson agrees with Helvetius, "one of the best men on earth," that these good acts do indeed give us pleasure. But he here denies that this is the reason we approve of them or perform them. Instead, Jefferson insists that moral action cannot be grounded on the pleasure we receive from doing good to others because this would return virtue to a selfish foundation. Thus, the pleasure we receive is the byproduct of something more fundamental: the natural and immediate inclination, registered by the moral sense, to consider as a motive for our actions the good of others. In other words, the ground of moral virtue is the unselfish "love of others, a sense of duty to them, a moral instinct, in short, which prompts us irresistibly to feel and succor their distresses, and protests against the language of Helvetius 'what other motive than self-interest could determine a man to generous actions?'" It is this view of man as a social animal, naturally endowed by a Benevolent Creator with an innate moral sense, that directs us to pursue our own happiness by promoting "the happiness of those with whom he has placed us in society, by acting honestly towards all, benevolently to those who fall within our way, respecting sacredly their rights, bodily and mental, and cherishing their freedom of conscience."[46]

So far we have shown that Jefferson believes we have a natural duty to promote the good of others, but how is this duty connected with the right to the pursuit of happiness? And how can the Declaration be interpreted to imply a duty to promote the good of others when the document speaks only of rights? If anything, the language of the Declaration would seem to reinforce the tendency to view all moral questions exclusively from the perspective of rights,[47] since it says almost nothing about duties, save for the duty to throw off oppressive governments, and never mentions virtue.

Yet this is precisely why we need to recover the true meaning and ground of our rights as Jefferson understands them. And neither a structural nor a purely Lockean analysis of the Declaration is sufficient. For one of the great differences between Locke and the Scottish school is that the latter insists that both our rights and our duties are grounded on the social as well as the selfish passions. As the letter to Law makes clear, Jefferson follows the Scots, rather than Locke, on the question of moral duties; regrettably, he nowhere directly addresses the question with respect to rights. But given his agreement with the Scots that human beings are naturally social, that the generous impulses are as much a part of our constitution as the selfish passions, and that our moral obligations to others are rooted exclusively in the social affections, it makes sense that he would ground the right to the pursuit of happiness on more than the selfish desire for comfort, security, and material satisfaction. Moreover, if the right to pursue happiness derives partly from the social passion of benevolence, this would explain how a right can also imply certain duties. For as naturally social creatures, endowed with generous impulses, the right to pursue our own happiness and the moral duty to promote the good of others tend to be reciprocal. As Abraham Lincoln observed, the Declaration embodies a "right principle of action" other than self-interest.[48]

Although the moral implications of understanding happiness in this way are profound, the impact on politics is minimal: the rights and duties connected with happiness are not the objects of governmental concern. As the Declaration makes clear, government is obliged to protect only the *pursuit* of happiness; it cannot compel us to act benevolently toward others, even if this is part of what makes us truly happy. For Jefferson, the tasks of the liberal republic are few: government ought to restrain individuals from committing aggression against each other, compel them to contribute to the necessities of society, and require them to submit to an impartial arbiter. "When the laws have declared and enforced all this, they have fulfilled their functions."[49] It was not then, and is not now, the purpose of government to enforce the full range of our natural rights and duties. As James Wilson, who also followed the Scots in these matters, put it in his lecture on natural rights: "The rights and duties of benevolence are but rarely, though they are sometimes, the objects of municipal law."[50] Thus, although the right to the pursuit of happiness entails certain moral obligations to others, which places it on a different moral footing from those rights that are grounded exclusively in the selfish passions, it does not fundamentally alter the limited role that Jefferson, speaking on behalf of all Americans, envisions government playing in our lives. The Declaration presupposes a vision of human happiness, linked to the exercise of the most exalted liberal virtues, but it leaves individuals free to pursue happiness as they see fit.

The Jeffersonian Hierarchy of the Passions

If, however, each of the three great rights in the Declaration rests on a different, and to some extent, competing passion, how do these rights fit together? Is there, in Jefferson's political psychology, a hierarchy of the passions which would bind our rights into a coherent whole, without reducing human beings to mere self-seekers or requiring of them an unrealistic capacity for virtue? Or is human nature merely a bundle of contradictory desires to be acted upon by each individual as he or she sees fit? If there is no hierarchy among the passions, how can we rationally choose among our rights when they, as they sometimes do, conflict?

Jefferson does not address these questions directly, but his scattered comments suggest that the pursuit of happiness is the most comprehensive of our rights.[51] Happiness is the end to which human beings devote their lives and liberties. And although their different circumstances, talents, and inclinations will lead them to pursue different paths, there is at bottom one good that remains constant: true happiness depends upon virtue and virtue means, above all, the social virtues that bind us to one another. Doing good to others can take a variety of forms: it can mean respecting the rights of others, exercising benevolence, or at least civility, to one's fellow men, or it can mean pursuing the useful knowledge which will improve the lot of humankind.[52] But ultimately all the virtues, both moral and intellectual, are directed toward the good of others.

Does this mean that we are obliged to pursue the good of others over our own good? Not for Jefferson. In those few cases where our own good is at stake, Jefferson does not require benevolence to overrule self-love. But for the most part, he assumes that we are so constituted that virtue and self-interest can, with the appropriate republican institutions, be made to coincide. A Benevolent Creator has endowed us with a moral sense and has so arranged our nature that we receive pleasure from doing good to others; the exercise of the social virtues *is* our interest. Whether human beings recognize it or not, their happiness depends in part on the happiness of others.

For this equation to work, however, each of the passions must play its part. Just as pride ennobles self-interest, and self-interest tempers pride, so too does concern for others enlarge our conception of self-interest. At the same time, pride and self-love must be enlisted to restrain the impulse to do good within reasonable limits. It is not that the tension between these passions ever completely disappears, as the inability of so many, though not all, slaveholders to put aside their self-interest poignantly attests, but it is significantly reduced by the operation of the moral sense and the constructive interplay of the passions.

Yet precisely because there are tensions among these rights, Jefferson should have taken greater pains to help Americans understand their true meaning. For while it may be self-evident that all human beings possess certain inalienable rights, it is by no means self-evident what these rights mean, where they come from, or how they can be fitted together. As Jefferson himself observed, the ideas expressed in the Declaration were culled from a number of sources, some popular, but others, especially "the elementary books of public right, as Aristotle, Cicero, Locke, Sidney, etc.,"[53] emphatically not. Jefferson's failure to instruct Americans in the deeper meaning of the principles they shared and to which he eloquently gave voice has encouraged future generations even less sure of their political and moral heritage to believe that they are free to interpret their rights in whatever manner they wish, including ways which sap their independence and pride, and subject them increasingly to the dictates of a government less interested in protecting liberty and the natural right to self-government than in ensuring equality of condition and increased political power for itself.

Thus, at a time when the explosion of the "rights industry"[54] threatens paradoxically to dissolve society into a mass of isolated and ever more powerless individuals and warring tribes, where parents are divided against children, women against men, the elderly against the rest of society, one race against another, and so on, it makes sense to try to recover the original ground and meaning of our rights, and to set forth their requirements and limitations more explicitly than Jefferson does. Properly understood, the conception of natural rights set forth by Jefferson offers four important lessons for us.

First, it reminds us that rights are not simply wishes or aspirations, but are grounded in the most permanent and powerful human passions. These are not the desires of a particular race, class, or gender at a given historical moment but the irresistible and universal longings of men and women everywhere. They are neither wholly nor narrowly selfish; still less are they simply altruistic. Together they form a coherent whole, originating in the desire for security, and culminating in the proud pursuit of those objects that give moral meaning and purpose to life.

Second, and closely related, nature serves not only as the ground of our rights but also as a brake on their steady expansion beyond, and even in contradiction to, anything Jefferson envisioned. Thus, in contrast to contemporary liberals, who are often uneasy with the very idea of nature because it serves as a limit on individual freedom, Jefferson's conception of rights is bounded by the idea of man as a rational and moral being, subject to "the laws of nature and nature's God." This does not, as I mentioned earlier, mean there are no rights beyond those that Jefferson recognized (his list of inalienable rights is admittedly incomplete), but it does mean that there should be no "rights" that conflict with or erode the capacity for "rational liberty."

Third, rights, as Jefferson understands them, are claims that individuals as free moral agents assert for themselves, employing their own faculties and powers. They are not entitlements that others can assert for us on our behalf; a people too dispirited and de-moralized to defend their own rights cannot look to other, more powerful groups to exercise their rights for them.[55] Of course, citizens may join together with others to exercise their rights and, in a democratic republic, where individuals by themselves are often weak, it is inevitable that they will do so. But republican self-government can flourish only where citizens are sufficiently engaged, either individually or collectively, to act for themselves.

Fourth, the exercise of equal rights leads inevitably to inequality of outcomes, most obviously in matters of property and wealth, but also in matters of intellect and virtue. Yet in contrast to many of today's rights' advocates, Jefferson is more inclined to accept the social and economic inequalities that result from the formal possession of equal rights. To be sure, Jefferson is suspicious of great wealth and family position. But as long as these inequalities do not become so great or so menacing as to threaten the very survival of republican government, they must be permitted because this is the reason why people come together in the first place: to be able to rise as far as their different talents and efforts enable them. Jefferson's conception of rights favors equality of opportunity over equality of condition, and liberty over equality.

The natural rights republic does not, of course, put an end to all political debate. Rational men and women have differed, and will continue to differ, over the practical and theoretical implications of our fundamental principles. But for Jefferson, perhaps more than any other founder, this is as it should be, since the preservation of our republican way of life depends, above all, on keeping alive in each generation the liberty-loving spirit of its citizens.

NOTES

1. Zuckert assimilates his more "Kantian" reading of Locke to Jefferson and argues that it is reason, rather than the moral sense, which leads individuals beyond their purely selfish claims toward a mutual recognition of the rights of others. He argues further that this mutual recognition is "more than a mere matter of calculation: it becomes a rational principle and can become a matter of conscientious conviction." However plausible this may be for Locke, Zuckert offers no textual evidence that this is how Jefferson understood the matter, and indeed, overlooks the considerable textual evidence in support of the Scottish school. See esp. Michael P. Zuckert, *The Natural Rights Republic* (Notre Dame, Ind.: University of Notre Dame Press, 1996), 71–78.

2. On this point, see esp. Frank D. Balog, "The Scottish Enlightenment and the Liberal Political Tradition," in *Confronting the Constitution*, ed. Allan Bloom (Washington, D.C.: AEI Press, 1990), 191–208.

3. Here again Jefferson seems to follow the Scots, rather than Locke. See also the similar argument made on behalf of Alexander Hamilton by Gerald Stourzh, *Alexander Hamilton and the Idea of Republican Government* (Stanford, Calif.: Stanford University Press, 1970) esp. 90–95; and for a discussion of this theme in *The Federalist*, see David Epstein, *The Political Theory of "The Federalist"* (Chicago: University of Chicago Press, 1984).

4. See esp. Harvey C. Mansfield, *America's Constitutional Soul* (Baltimore, Md.: Johns Hopkins University Press, 1991), esp. chaps. 6–7.

5. Zuckert, *Natural Rights Republic*, 234–35.

6. Although Jefferson deliberately omits property from the Declaration's admittedly incomplete list of inalienable rights, Zuckert treats Jefferson's position as identical to Locke's (ibid., 79–81). In making his argument, Zuckert relies upon Jefferson's letter to DuPont de Nemours, in which he asserts that the "right to property is founded in our natural wants, in the means by which we are endowed to satisfy these wants, and the right to what we acquire by these means." But, elsewhere he observes that "it is a moot question whether the origin of any kind of property is derived from nature at all," since property in the sense of stable ownership, rather than first possession, "is the gift of social law, and is given late in the progress of society." Cf. Jefferson to DuPont de Nemours, April 24, 1816, with Jefferson to Isaac McPherson, August 13, 1813, in *The Writings of Thomas Jefferson* (hereafter *WTJ*), ed. Albert Ellery Bergh (Washington, D.C.: Thomas Jefferson Memorial Association, 1907), 14: 487–93 and 13:326–38, respectively. Zuckert is rightly concerned to refute the misguided idea of Richard Matthews and others that in omitting property from the Declaration, Jefferson was signalling his rejection of the Lockean or liberal view in favor of something "much grander." But Zuckert overstates the case when he conflates Jefferson and Locke.

7. See Zuckert, *Natural Rights Republic*, 84–85.

8. Jefferson, *The Commonplace Book of Thomas Jefferson: A Repertory of His Ideas on Government*, ed. Gilbert Chinard (Baltimore, Md.: Johns Hopkins University Press, 1926), 107.

9. Jefferson to P. S. DuPont de Nemours, April 24, 1816, *WTJ*, 14:487–93.

10. Jefferson to Francis W. Gilmer, June 7, 1816, *WTJ*, 15:23–27.

11. Jefferson, *Notes on the State of Virginia*, ed. William Peden (Chapel Hill: University of North Carolina Press, 1955), Query VI, p. 60. Hence Zuckert's conclusion that the system of rights replaces the moral sense as a more effective source of just social relations. But it would be more accurate to say that it is government which effectually secures both rights and the moral sense, neither of which is sufficiently powerful by itself to overcome the selfish passions. Zuckert, *Natural Rights Republic*, 70–71.

12. Ruth W. Grant, "Locke's Political Anthropology and Lockean Individualism," *Journal of Politics* 50 (February 1988): 42–63.

13. Cf. Zuckert, *Natural Rights Republic*, 68–72.

14. Jefferson to P. S. DuPont de Nemours, April 24, 1816, *WTJ*, 14:487–93.

15. Second Inaugural Address, March 4, 1805, in *The Works of Thomas Jefferson* (hereafter *Works*), ed. Paul Leicester Ford (New York: Putnam, 1904), 10:127–36.

16. Opinion on the French Treaties, April 28, 1793, *WTJ*, 3:226–43.

17. Herbert Storing, "Slavery and the Moral Foundations of the American Republic," in *The Moral Foundations of the American Republic*, ed. Robert H. Horwitz (Charlottesville: University of Virginia Press, 1977), 226; Harry V. Jaffa, *Crisis of the House Divided* (Garden City, N.Y.: Doubleday, 1959), 308–29.

18. Jefferson to John Holmes, April 22, 1820, *WTJ*, 15:248–50.

19. Storing, "Slavery and the Moral Foundations"; Jaffa, *Crisis of the House Divided*, 308–29. And cf. Zuckert, who agrees that rights, or what he terms "proto-rights," initially arise from the selfish desire for security and are, strictly speaking, amoral. But, once human beings rationally recognize a need for reciprocity, these previously amoral claims acquire "a genuine moral quality." The mutual recognition of rights is more than mere calculation; it becomes a rational principle upon which human beings may conscientiously act. No wonder Zuckert is "tempted to adopt the Kantian formula of 'rational rights' rather than 'natural rights.'" But however true this is for Kant, or even for Zuckert's "Kantian" reading of Locke, there is no evidence, nor does Zuckert offer any, that this is what Jefferson, speaking on behalf of his countrymen, had in mind. See esp. Zuckert, *Natural Rights Republic*, 73–78.

20. This, of course, includes blacks and people of color. As the original draft of the Declaration makes clear, Jefferson considers the slaves to be human beings, and he denounces the king for denying them their rights to life and liberty. Because all men are naturally free, slavery can never be legitimate; no man can rule another without his consent.

At the same time, however, the principles of equality and liberty did not require Americans to extend the rights of full citizenship to emancipated blacks. That all men are created equal and are endowed with certain inalienable rights does not mean that everyone has an equal right to become a member of a particular polity. All the Declaration requires is that blacks be restored to their natural liberty to form themselves into a distinct people. They do not have the right to join an existing polity unless that people chooses to admit them. Thus, expatriation is consistent with the Declaration's principles, but so, too, are the Fourteenth and Fifteenth Amendments.

21. Jefferson to David Humphreys, March 18, 1789, *WTJ*, 7:319–21.

22. Jefferson, Summary View of the Rights of British America, July 1774, *WTJ*, 2:87; Thoughts on Lotteries, *Works*, 12:435–50; Jefferson to David Humphreys, March 18, 1789, *WTJ*, 7:319–21; Jefferson to James Madison, October 28, 1785, in *The Republic of Letters: The Correspondence between Thomas Jefferson and James Madison 1776–1826*, ed. James Morton Smith (New York: Norton, 1995), 1:389–91.

23. Note accompanying Jefferson's revision of Destutt de Tracy's *Treatise on Political Economy* included in the "Prospectus" sent by Jefferson to Joseph Milligan, April 6, 1816, *WTJ*, 14:456–66.

24. See esp. Bill No. 64, and the discussion in Paul Rahe, *Republics: Ancient and Modern* (Chapel Hill: University of North Carolina Press, 1994) 3:17–23.

25. Walter Berns, *Freedom, Virtue, and the First Amendment* (Chicago: Henry Regnery, 1965), 28.

26. Jean Yarbrough, *American Virtues: Thomas Jefferson on the Character of a Free People* (Lawrence: University Press of Kansas, 1998), chap. 4; Thomas G. West, *Vindicating the Founders: Race, Sex, Class, and Justice in the Origins of America* (Lanham, Md.: Rowman and Littlefield Publishers, 1997), esp. chap. 3.

27. Steven Kautz, *Liberalism and Community* (Ithaca, N.Y.: Cornell University Press, 1995), but cf. West, *Vindicating the Founders*, chap. 4. For a general discussion of what Jefferson means by toleration, see my *American Virtues*, chap. 5.

28. Ronald Dworkin, *Taking Rights Seriously* (Cambridge, Mass.: Harvard University Press, 1978), esp. 131–49.

29. See esp. Mansfield, *America's Constitutional Soul*. In the concluding section of his last chapter, Zuckert makes a similar point: "going beyond the original natural rights liberalism, politics is no longer simply instrumental, but is indeed, a good in itself . . . Political participation, too, takes on a meaning somewhat more akin to what it held in earlier forms of republicanism. It is both a good-in-itself and even a civic duty, not merely an interest or a private benefit" (*Natural Rights Republic*, 240). But it is not clear how he squares this conclusion with his statement earlier that Jefferson's "most republican or political moment" arises out of a line of thought that "assimilates the public sphere entirely to the theory of private property, that is, when he comes to see the state more completely through the lens of the Lockean theory of property and property rights" (234–35).

30. Yarbrough, *American Virtues*, esp. chap. 4.

31. Zuckert is critical of this development because he believes it leads away from the "flexible and prudential standards Jefferson, following Locke and Montesquieu, had articulated in the Declaration of Independence." In the late Jefferson, what Zuckert calls democracy becomes the only legitimate form of government. I disagree. Republicanism bottomed on the wards is a necessary ingredient of the best regime, but Jefferson recognizes that most people are not ready for self-government and does not insist upon it for them. Moreover, the opportunity for citizens to participate in local politics is balanced against the need to recruit only the most wise and virtuous for higher public offices. In this respect, Jefferson's "democratic" republic is actually a mixed regime.

32. Mansfield, *America's Constitutional Soul*, 83; also Joseph Cropsey, "The United States as a Regime and the Sources of the American Way of Life," in *Political Philosophy and the Issues of Politics* (Chicago: University of Chicago Press, 1977), 1–15.

33. Zuckert, *Natural Rights Republic*, 83–85; 26–27.

34. Jefferson to Correa de Serra, April 19, 1814, *WTJ*, 19:209–11.

35. *Notes*, Query XIV, p. 147; Jefferson to Peter Carr, August 6, 1788, in *The Papers of Thomas Jefferson*, ed. Julian P. Boyd (Princeton, N.J.: Princeton University Press, 1954), 13:470.

36. Zuckert, *Natural Rights Republic*, 87–89.

37. Adrienne Koch, *The Philosophy of Thomas Jefferson* (Chicago: Quadrangle Books, 1964), 1.

38. For still a different view which argues that at the time of the Declaration Jefferson was still a Lockean, who had not yet discovered the moral sense, see Garrett Ward Sheldon, *The Political Philosophy of Thomas Jefferson* (Baltimore: Johns Hopkins University Press, 1991), 45–52 and 155.

39. Jefferson to Henry Lee, May 8, 1825, *Works*, 12:408–9.

40. Herbert Lawrence Ganter, "Jefferson's 'Pursuit of Happiness' and Some Forgotten Men," *William and Mary Quarterly* 16 (October 1936): 558–85; Howard Mumford Jones, *The Pursuit of Happiness* (Cambridge, Mass.: Harvard University Press, 1953), 63–64; Harold Hellenbrand, *The Unfinished Revolution: Education*

and Politics in the Thought of Thomas Jefferson (Newark: University of Delaware Press, 1990).

41. Jefferson to Amos J. Cook, January 21, 1816, *WTJ*, 14:403–6.

42. See esp. Charles S. Hyneman and Donald S. Lutz, *American Political Writing during the Founding Era, 1760–1805*, 2 vols. (Indianapolis: Liberty Press, 1983).

43. Jefferson to Maria Cosway, October 12, 1786, *WTJ*, 5:430–48.

44. Jefferson to Dr. Benjamin Rush, with a Syllabus, April 21, 1803, *WTJ*, 10:379–85. It is noteworthy that here Jefferson is comparing the ancients with the morality of Jesus, not with the moral sense philosophers. For a fuller discussion of how these two fit together, see my *American Virtues*, chap. 2.

45. Jefferson to Thomas Law, June 13, 1816, *WTJ*, 14:138–44.

46. Jefferson to Miles King, September 26, 1814, *WTJ*, 14:196–98.

47. Thomas L. Pangle, *The Ennobling of Democracy: The Challenge of the Postmodern Age* (Baltimore, Md.: Johns Hopkins University Press, 1992), 91–92. See also James Q. Wilson, *The Moral Sense* (New York: Free Press, 1993).

48. Abraham Lincoln, "Speech on the Repeal of the Missouri Compromise," October 16, 1854, in *Abraham Lincoln: His Speeches and Writings*, ed. Roy P. Basler (New York: Grosset and Dunlap, 1962).

49. Jefferson to Francis W. Gilmer, June 7, 1816, *WTJ*, 15:23–27.

50. James Wilson, *Lectures on Law*, "Natural Rights," in *The Works of James Wilson*, 2 vols., ed. Robert Green McCloskey (Cambridge, Mass.: Belknap Press, 1967), 2:594; also 1:242. And for a discussion of natural rights in the Scottish school, see Balog, "The Scottish Enlightenment and the Liberal Political Tradition."

51. Zuckert stresses the comprehensiveness of happiness, but lays undue emphasis upon the variety of objects individuals desire, while saying nothing about the connection between happiness and virtue. See esp. *Natural Rights Republic*, 83–85.

52. Jefferson to David Rittenhouse, July 19, 1778, *WTJ*, 4:42–43.

53. Jefferson to Henry Lee, May 8, 1825, *Works*, 12:408–9.

54. Mary Ann Glendon, *Rights Talk* (New York: Free Press, 1991); Richard E. Morgan, *Disabling America: The "Rights Industry" in Our Time* (New York: Basic Books, 1984).

55. For a longer discussion, see Mansfield, *America's Constitutional Soul*, 185ff.

3

Eclectic Synthesis:
Jesus, Aristotle, and Locke

⁂

GARRETT WARD SHELDON

Thomas Jefferson was known for his eclectic tastes, and these extended to his tastes in political philosophy. His democratic theory, uniquely American, drew from a broad range of intellectual sources, often regarded as mutually exclusive, in his day and our own. British liberalism, classical republicanism, Christian ethics, Scots moral sense philosophy, Smithian free trade economics: all moved together in Jefferson's mind and philosophy. The history of Jefferson scholarship has tended to attribute the complexity of his thought to theoretical dilettantism, a paradoxical character, vile hypocrisy, or possibly the thin air of Jefferson's mountaintop estate.[1] A closer examination of these interwoven strands of Jefferson's political theory reveals, however, a brilliant synthesis, a superb blending of many traditions by a mind that drew from several seemingly disparate, but actually coherent, philosophical schools. Jefferson's reconciliation of Christian, Lockean, and Classical Greek worldviews captured the American democratic spirit and culture more successfully than the philosophies of any of his contemporaries, as Alexis de Tocqueville properly acknowledged. Jefferson combined the three dominant ideologies (Christianity, British liberalism, and classical republicanism) that scholars have identified as stimulating the American Revolution and founding the American republic.[2] The ethics of Jesus, the limited government and individual rights of Locke, and the political participation and public virtue of Aristotle all found a home in Thomas Jefferson's civic philosophy.

Christianity

Thomas Jefferson was raised in the Established Anglican Church of Virginia. This, the official Church of England in the British Colony, received public tax support for its clergy, legally compelled church attendance, and persecuted dissenting churches and ministers (like Presbyterians and Baptists). This English church, which later would become the American Episcopal church, was already in Jefferson's time a worldly, decadent, and sophisticated denomination. Its governmental status encouraged officious pride and lax morals, or what Jefferson's friend James Madison called "Pride, ignorance and knavery among the Priesthood and Vice and Wickedness among the Laity," exacerbated by the "diabolical Hell" of religious persecution.[3] This depraved state of religious purity led Jefferson to author the Virginia Statute for the Establishment of Religious Freedom in 1776. For Jefferson, Christian ethics were essential for a civilized society and virtuous republic; but the only way for religious morals to avoid the corruption of the state church was freedom of belief and conscience. Freedom of religion for Jefferson meant breaking the corrupt monopoly over faith of the official state church and promoting open discussion of beliefs, which he hoped would distill and inculcate the "ethics of Jesus": love, charity, forbearance, repentance, and forgiveness, all essential to any harmonious society and democratic republic. As Jefferson wrote to Adams:

> If by *religion*, we are to understand *sectarian dogmas*, in which no two of them agree, then your exclamation . . . is just, 'that this would be the best of all possible worlds, if there were no religion in it.' But if the moral precepts, innate in man, and made a part of his physical condition, as necessary of a social being, if the sublime doctrines . . . taught us by Jesus of Nazareth in which all agree, constitute true religion, then, without it, this would be, as you again say, 'something not fit to be named, even indeed a Hell.'[4]

For Jefferson, Jesus gave a moral philosophy suited to man's true, God-given nature: "His moral doctrines, relating to kindred and friends, were more pure and perfect than those of the most correct of philosophers and . . . went far beyond in inculcating universal philanthropy not only to kindred and friends, to neighbors and countrymen, but to all mankind, gathering all into one family, under the bond of love, charity, peace, common wants and common aids. . . . [Herein lies] the peculiar superiority of the system of Jesus over all others."[5]

Christ's ethical teachings of love, repentance, and forgiveness, of universal brotherhood and charity, provided, for Jefferson, "the most sublime and benevolent code of morals which has ever been offered to man" for his life in society.[6] "Epictetus and Epicurus gave laws for governing ourselves, Jesus a supplement of the duties and charities we owe to others."[7] But, the Christian ethics which Jefferson felt suited man's social nature and contributed to America's virtuous republic were often lost, in his opinion, in the elaborate ceremonies, dogmas, and institutions of the various churches.

While extolling the ethical teachings of Jesus Christ, Jefferson distinguished between the "genuine" lessons of Jesus and the "spurious" dogmas of various disciples and sectarian orders. In order to separate the true teachings of Christ from their specious imitations (which Jefferson considered as easily distinguishable as "the gold from the dross," the "grain from the chaff," or "as diamonds in a dunghill,"[8] he composed a *Philosophy of Jesus* and a *Life and Morals of Jesus*, by extracting those portions of the Gospels which he thought presented the ethics in their purest, most simple form.[9] Ironically, it was his abiding and reverent belief in these Christian ethical teachings that led Jefferson to criticize the institutionalized church, but which also led many to question his religious sincerity. His specific attacks on the church and clergy (especially the Established Anglican Church of Virginia in which he was baptized and served as vestryman) reveal his adherence to essential Christian ethical principles. Jefferson repeatedly chastised the church for not living up to its divine mission, for not upholding the purity of the Christian faith in a corrupt world, and for allowing a decadent, immoral clergy to continue in leadership positions. He attacked the church for neglecting its duties, for its venality and hypocrisy in serving worldly political authorities rather than measuring them against the high standards of Christian faith, and for preaching poverty, peace, charity, and humility while practicing extravagance, persecution, and self-righteous pride.[10] Indeed, Jefferson's principal complaint against the church was that its distortions of Christ's ethical teachings, essential to a virtuous republic, drove good people away:

They [clergy] are mere usurpers of the Christian name, teaching a counter-religion made up of the *deliria* of crazy imaginations as foreign from Christianity as is that of Mahomet. Their blasphemies have driven thinking men into infidelity, who have too hastily rejected the supposed author himself, with the horrors so falsely imputed to him. Had the doctrines of Jesus been preached always as pure as they came from his lips, the whole civilized world would now have been Christian.[11]

Jefferson's remedy for this perversion of true Christian teaching was the establishment of absolute religious freedom in America. Religious freedom and toleration, for Jefferson, were to serve the higher purpose of encouraging debate and dialogue among the various denominations, from which the simple ethical teachings of Christ, vital to Jefferson's vision of a virtuous republic, might be distilled and disseminated. As he wrote to Dr. Benjamin Waterhouse, "I rejoice that in this blessed country of free inquiry and belief, which has surrendered its creed and conscience to neither kings nor priests, the genuine doctrine of one God is reviving, and I trust that there is not a *young man* now living in the United States who will not die [a true Christian]."[12] He hoped that through freedom of religious practice and discussion, those basic teachings of Christ common to all denominations would gain ascendancy, bringing all religious people together and promoting peace and justice in the American republic. In his first inaugural address, Jefferson expressed this hoped-for effect of religious freedom, describing the country as "enlightened by a benign religion [Christianity], professed, indeed, and practiced in various forms, yet all of them including honesty, truth, temperance, gratitude, and the love of man; acknowledging and adoring an overruling Providence."[13] For him, a corrupt church was a greater threat to Christian truth than freedom of conscience and religious liberty. The truths of Christianity were so persuasive that if the simple lessons of the Gospels were ever heard, they would be instantly convincing. And those simple Christian truths were more likely to be concealed by a corrupt state church than by free, independent churches.

Thus, rather than emanating from a hostility or indifference toward Christianity, Jefferson's advocacy of religious freedom was designed to preserve true Christian teachings from the corruption of worldly institutions: "Had not the Roman government permitted free inquiry Christianity could never have been introduced. Had not free inquiry been indulged at the ear of the reformation, the corruptions of Christianity could not have been purged away. If it be restrained now, the present corruptions will be protected, and new ones encouraged."[14] Even if religious freedom would permit some heterodoxy, overall, more Christian orthodoxy would be propagated than under a church monopoly.

Jefferson's "Bill for Establishing Religious Freedom" began this process of cleansing the church by denouncing the established Anglican Church for "impiously" obstructing the Christian faith:

> Almighty God hath created the mind free . . . all attempts to influence it by temporal punishments, or burthens, or by civil incapacitations, tend only to beget habits of hypocrisy and meanness, and are a departure

from the plan of the holy author of our religion. . . . [T]he impious pre-
sumption of legislature and ruler, civil as well as ecclesiastical . . . [to]
have assumed dominion over the faith of others . . . tends also to corrupt
the principle of that very religion it is meant to encourage.[15]

Only "Christian" means of evangelism—teaching, preaching, discussion, and prayer—were legitimate and effective for Jefferson. But the dis-
establishment of the Anglican Church did not, for Jefferson, automatically
result in complete religious freedom (by which he understood the expo-
sure to various denominational creeds, from which the true, simple teachings of Jesus might be distilled). So, for example, Jefferson opposed the
establishment of a Chair of Divinity at the University of Virginia, not because he wished to exclude religion from that public institution, but because a *single* Chair of Divinity would imply representation of only one
denomination (just as had the established church): "It was not, however,
to be understood that instruction in religious opinion and duties was
meant to be precluded by the public authorities, as indifferent to the interests of society. On the contrary, the relations which exist between man
and his Maker, and the duties resulting from those relations, are the most
interesting and important to every human being, and the most incumbent
on his study and investigation."[16] Jefferson actually designed the University Rotunda with rooms for student religious gatherings, worship, and
devotions.

Jefferson's solution to the problem of one dominant religious sect in
the public university was not to exclude all religion from the institution,
but to invite the free expression of *all* denominations within the university's walls.

A remedy . . . has been suggested of promising aspect, which, while it
excludes the public authorities from the domain of religious freedom,
will give to the sectarian schools of divinity the full benefit the public
provisions made for instruction in the other branches of science. . . . It
has, therefore, been in contemplation, and suggested by some pious individuals, who perceive the advantages of associating other studies with
those of religion, to establish their religious schools on the confines of
the University, so as to give their students ready and convenient access
and attendance on the scientific lectures of the University. . . . Such establishments would offer the further and greater advantage of enabling
the students of the University to attend religious exercises with the
professor of their particular sect, either in the rooms of the building
still to be erected . . . or in the lecturing room of such professor. . . .
Such an arrangement would complete the circle of useful sciences

embraced by this institution, and would fill the chasm now existing, on principles which would leave inviolate the constitutional freedom of religion.[17]

Thus, to use contemporary Supreme Court language, Jefferson was an accommodationist, so long as all religious groups were included.

The presence of all religious denominations within the walls of the public university and use of public space for religious observances would give students the opportunity to be exposed to all dogmas. From this, Jefferson hoped, they might distill that which was common to them all—the basic ethical teachings of Jesus—to the benefit of the virtuous American republic, without imposition of a single religious creed or violation of their religious freedom. Christian truth had a power of persuasion and did not require explicit state support to survive and flourish. It required only liberty.

The same understanding of freedom of religion is revealed in Jefferson's description of religious life in Charlottesville. The absence of church buildings compelled the separate denominations to worship together, taking turns conducting services in the public courthouse:

> In our village of Charlottesville there is a good deal of religion, with only a small spice of fanaticism. We have four sects, but without either church or meeting house. The courthouse is the common temple, one Sunday in the month to each. Here Episcopalian and Presbyterian, Methodist and Baptist, meet together, join in hymning their Maker, listen with attention and devotion to each other's preachers and all mix in society with perfect harmony.[18]

So, Jefferson's commitment to religious liberty was to advance the common Christian ethics of love, charity, repentance, and forgiveness that any civilized society requires to operate smoothly and effectively. A democratic republic, in which citizens interact with each other more than in older hierarchical societies, requires this underlying Christian culture in particular. The "sublime and benevolent" teachings of Jesus in the Gospels were, for Jefferson, the superior system of values in human relationships. Without such a moral foundation in America, freedom could easily turn into license and violence. With the ethics of Christianity widely known and accepted, economic and political liberty could be enjoyed safely and prosperously. The rights granted by Locke's British liberal philosophy and the close political participation of Aristotle's classical polis could exist, if an underlying Christian ethos upheld them. Freedom of religion was the best guarantor of this.

Lockean Liberalism

Like most educated British colonials in the eighteenth century, Jefferson became acquainted with John Locke's political theory while studying law in college. He refers to Locke's *Second Treatise of Government* in his *Commonplace Book* and mentions possessing the books "Locke on government—8 vol." in a letter of August 1771.[19]

John Locke conceived of man as naturally "free, equal and independent," possessing natural rights to "Life, Liberty and property."[20] Legitimate government, therefore, is formed by a Social contract of free individuals who delegate a portion of their rights to the state in order to better protect their lives, liberty, and property. The authority of government is limited to that which the citizens consent to grant it. Its main purpose is to protect individual rights from violations by others (thieves, murderers, kidnappers, etc.). If the state itself becomes a "criminal," invading the rights of its citizens, it is a right of the citizens to change it and establish a new government that will serve its proper purpose.

Jefferson's adoption of Locke's theory is most evident in the revolutionary document, the Declaration of Independence. Where Locke said in *The Second Treatise*, "Men being . . . by Nature, all free, equal and independent," Jefferson writes, "all men are created equal and independent."[21] Locke refers to "Man . . . with . . . an uncontrolled enjoyment of all the Rights . . . of the Law of Nature . . . that is, his Life, Liberty and Estate"; Jefferson echoes with "from that equal creation they derive rights . . . of life, & liberty, & the pursuit of happiness."[22] Locke summarizes the formation of government as "to join in society with others . . . to unite for the mutual Preservation of their Lives, Liberties and Estates"; Jefferson states, "to secure these ends, governments are instituted . . . to provide new guards for their future security."[23] Locke described the peoples' "Right to Revolution" against an abusive state that violates their rights thus: "When by the Arbitrary Power . . . without the consent and contrary to the common interest of the People, there also the Legislative is altered . . . [and] Government is dissolved, the People are at Liberty to provide for themselves, by erecting a new Legislative"; Jefferson agrees with the statement that "whenever any form of government shall become destructive of these ends, it is the right of the people to alter or abolish it and to institute new government."[24] Jefferson's originality in adopting Lockean theory lies in applying these categories to "free and independent" colonies as well as to individuals, when he argues for political sovereignty of the North American legislatures (Virginia, Massachusetts, etc.). This adaptation of Lockean liberalism in the service of "equal and independent" political communities as well as individual rights allows Jefferson to incorporate a more classical Greek content to those communities after the Revolution.[25] And, these natural rights conform to a basically Judeo-Christian world view in his understanding of individual rights as "the gift of God." Jefferson once wrote that he "trembled" when he contemplated America's violations of slaves' rights and that "God is just."[26]

Classical Republicanism

After the American Revolution, Jefferson's concern with constructing a new American republic brought out a classical bent to his political philosophy. This is most evident in his conception of human nature as social (derived from the ethics of the Bible, Aristotle, and Scots moral sense philosophy), requiring development and realization in small, participatory, democratic communities resembling the ancient Greek polis. This non-Lockean psychology and less limited view of government completed Jefferson's political thought, without totally abandoning its British liberal and Christian strains.

In contrast with Lockean materialism, which conceived of man's nature as separate, isolated, and independent, Jefferson conceived of man as naturally social and political. He copied this quote from Lord Kames into his *Commonplace Book*: "Man, by his nature is fitted for society, and society, by its conveniences is fitted for man."[27] Jefferson attributed man's social nature to an innate "moral sense." The individual's moral sense, which renders society his natural home, consisted, for Jefferson, of three distinct but interrelated qualities: (1) the human capacity for moral choice, or the knowledge of good and evil and the freedom to act on that knowledge in choosing the good;[28] (2) an innate identification with others, a feeling of sympathy for others' concerns and sufferings, and a pleasure in the relief of others' pain and their attaining happiness;[29] and (3) from the combination of these two qualities, a natural sense of justice, making social life possible and beneficial, since this appreciation for justice allows the individual to feel concern for the good of others and for the whole community of which he is a part. This inherent sense of justice remained for Jefferson "the first excellence of a well-ordered" society and a necessary ingredient for individual happiness.[30] Hence, Jefferson encouraged his young ward Peter Carr to be "good, learned and industrious," insisting that such virtues would make him "precious to your country, dear to your friends, happy within yourself."[31]

The Scottish philosophers who developed the Moral Sense school were Presbyterian Christians who drew from the biblical view of a human "conscience"; as St. Paul wrote, "when the Gentiles, which have not the law . . . shew the work of the law written in their hearts, their conscience also bearing witness." (Romans 2:14–15). Even unbelievers have a basic knowledge of good and evil and therefore are accountable for their actions.

The existence of this innate capacity for justice was not invalidated, for Jefferson, by its apparent absence in some individuals: "The want or imperfection of the moral sense in some men, like the want or imperfection of the senses of sight and hearing in others, is no proof that it is a general characteristic of the species."[32] Indeed, Jefferson took man's social nature so for granted that he was more inclined to accuse God of some mistake rather than to admit its absence: "The Creator would have been a bungling artist, had he intended man for a social animal, without planting in him social dispositions."[33]

The moral conduct appropriate to this divinely ordained social nature did not, for Jefferson, consist in a primary concern with individual interests or with the building of a moral philosophy on the basis of human selfishness and greed. Rather, this innate moral quality dictated a concern for the good of others and for the whole community: "the essence of virtue is in doing good to others."[34] Of the liberal ethics of self-interested calculation, Jefferson wrote:

> I consider our relations with others as constituting the boundaries of morality. With ourselves we stand on the ground of identity, not of relation, which last, requiring two subjects, excludes self-love confined to a single one. To ourselves, in strict language, we can owe no duties, obligation requiring also two parties. Self-love, therefore, is no part of morality. Indeed, it is exactly its counterpart. It is the sole antagonist of virtue, leading us constantly by our propensities to self-gratification in violation of our moral duties to others.[35]

Hence, individual desire or selfish will does not equate to ethical good.

Jefferson believed that this innate moral sense made just actions pleasurable,[36] but he acknowledged that this ethical sense, with its "noble pleasure," was distributed unevenly among individuals, as were the other senses.[37] As such, Jefferson found the presence of man's innate moral quality "the brightest gem with which the human character is studded, and the want of it more degrading than the most hideous of bodily deformities."[38] But where a deficiency in the moral sense was present, Jefferson had confidence in man's capacity for development through moral education.[39] Like the senses of sight and hearing, which could be refined and sharpened with training, this ethical capacity was also susceptible to instruction and cultivation. Furthermore, along with these other faculties, the moral sense could be strengthened through exercise and refined through habitual practice.[40] Hence, Jefferson encouraged Peter Carr to "lose no occasion of exercising your dispositions to be grateful, to be generous, to be charitable, to be humane, to be true, firm, orderly, courageous, etc. Consider every act of this kind as an exercise which will strengthen your moral faculties and increase your worth."[41] For Jefferson, a person's "worth" was not Hobbesian worldly power, wealth, or prestige.

Thus, for Jefferson, the moral sense which provided the basis for human society also required society for its education and development. Ethical conduct was neither simply an innate, individual matter, nor purely the responsibility of society; rather, it was both. Man is born with an inherent moral capacity and political society is necessary to cultivate and perfect that potential.[42]

Jefferson placed the duty of educating individuals' moral capacities on philosophers, the clergy, and legislators.[43] As he considered it the business of legislators to educate citizens' ethical sensibilities, politics for Jefferson could not be limited to purely liberal strictures of protecting private rights and individual interests. Rather, the moral sense, which included knowledge and choice of the good, sympathy for others' sufferings, and concern for the well-being of society generally, constituted a public sense of virtue, requiring both education and practice in political life. For Jefferson, the political structure which provided both education and practice in public life, thereby cultivating man's moral sense, was the participatory democracy of ward government.[44]

Thomas Jefferson's political philosophy is most classically republican in his conception of political society. His emphasis on political participation, an economically independent and educated citizenry, a natural aristocracy of wisdom and virtue, and the corruption of this classical republic and its balanced constitution by a centralized commercial regime, all reveal his affinity for ideas found in Aristotle, Cicero, Montesquieu, and Harrington.[45] The center of Jefferson's classical republican theory is his conception of ward democracy, with its educational, political, and economic components, and its theory of leadership and representation fundamental to Jefferson's idea of federalism.[46] The essential nature of ward government to Jefferson's vision of the good political society was expressed in a letter of 1816: "As Cato, then, concluded every speech with the words '*Cartago delenda est,*' so do I every opinion, with the injunction, 'divide the counties into wards.'"[47] Jefferson's ward districts bore a striking resemblance to the ideal Greek polis, which also strove to realize man's social nature through direct citizen participation in local community life.[48] As such, classical republics were necessarily limited in size and population, so Jefferson adapted them to the large American continent through an original theory of representative democracy which grew out of, rather than competed with, ward divisions.[49] Having declared the wards "small republics," created out of the smallest existing jurisdictions (the counties), Jefferson provided a precise definition of these political entities: "Were I to assign to this term a precise and definite idea, I would say, purely and simply, it means a government by its citizens in mass, acting directly and personally, according to rules established by the majority; and that every other government is more or less republican in proportion as it has in its composition more or less of this ingredient of the direct action of the citizens."[50]

Among those things which Jefferson considered immediately relevant to ward residents in addition to the elementary schools, and well within their competence, were "care of their poor, their roads, police, elections, the nomination of jurors, administration of justice in small cases, elementary exercises of militia and all those concerns which, being under their eye, they would better manage than the larger republics of the county or state."[51]

Such minor republics, which Jefferson saw as akin to New England townships, were for him "the wisest invention ever devised by the wit of man for the perfect exercise of self-government, and for its preservation,"[52] because "by making every citizen an acting member of the government, and in the offices nearest and most interesting to him, will attach him by his strongest feelings to the independence of his country, and its republican Constitution."[53] While he saw direct participation in local political life drawing out citizens' affections for their community and its public virtue, Jefferson also regarded the wards' small size as contributing to public deliberation and the development of citizens' minds, as evidenced by his repeated plea: "reduce your legislature to a convenient number for full but orderly discussion."[54] Like Aristotle, Jefferson regarded the exercise of "reasoned speech" as the highest political activity.

In addition to cultivating the citizens' hearts and minds, classical participatory democracy would also prevent the degeneration of the state into a tyranny; for Jefferson warned, "If [the people] become inattentive to the public affairs, you and I, Congress and Assemblies, Judges and Governors, shall all become wolves."[55] In other words, for Jefferson, democratically educated citizens are the best insurance against government violations of individual natural rights: "when there shall not be a man in the State who will not be a member of some one of its councils great or small, he will let the heart be torn out of his body sooner than his power be wrested from him by a Caesar or a Bonaparte."[56]

Still, in spite of Jefferson's devotion to small, classical republics, he was not blind to their geographical limitations. "Such a government," he wrote, "is evidently restrained to very narrow limits of space and population."[57] In a country the size of the United States, therefore, Jefferson conceived of a kind of representative democracy as a natural extension of ward republican government. "This I should consider as the nearest approach to a pure republic, which is practicable on a large scale of country or population."[58] But unlike the immediate structure of ward republics, which might benefit from notions borrowed from ancient Greece, this representative adaptation of local participatory democracy to a large nation required entirely original ideas: "The full experiment of a government democratical, but representative, was and is still reserved for us. . . . this . . . has rendered useless almost everything written before on the structure of government; and in a great measure, relieves our regret, if the political writings of Aristotle, or of any other ancient, have been lost, or are unfaithfully rendered or explained to us."[59]

Jefferson provided an entirely new political theory; but his original theory, designed for the unique conditions of America, still drew heavily from the past. He constructed this larger, representative republic out of the smaller, participatory republics, insisting that "these little republics would be the main strength of the great one."[60] The means of connecting the local ward republics with the increasingly centralized republics will be discussed at length below, but its general principle is that the elementary republics of the wards, the county and state republics, and the republic of the Union, would form a system of fundamental checks and balances for the government,[61] founded on every citizen personally taking part in the administration of the public affairs.[62]

This Jeffersonian standard of American federalism provided the basis for his critique of what became the existing structure of American constitutional government, especially after developed by John Marshall and other Federalists. What remains of republicanism after the Federalists' manipulation of Constitution and Court "is not the fruit of our Constitution, but has prevailed in spite of it."[63]

Jefferson consistently regarded the classical ward republics as "the keystone of the arch of our government."[64] His concept of small participatory democracies constituted his mature political theory, and his conception of human nature as naturally social and requiring the exercise of one's moral and political faculties for individual development and for the public good generally, contrasted with his earlier, revolutionary theory premised on Lockean liberalism. And yet, just as his revolutionary appeal to Lockean categories defended autonomous, republican legislatures, his later appeal to classical republican politics, he believed, would enhance the preservation of fundamental rights and liberties. From his mature perspective, Jefferson did not emphasize the individual's freedom from social ties, but rather, insisted that the absence of an active public realm cultivating man's social and moral capacities would not lead to freedom and happiness but to "sinning and suffering." Apart from a meaningful public life, Jefferson believed, individuals would be reduced to miserable "automatons" devoid of true, intelligent choice.[65]

Thus, Thomas Jefferson's political philosophy blended Christian ethics, Lockean liberalism, and classical republicanism in a coherent synthesis. Acceptance of Christ's moral precepts formed the ethical culture necessary to democratic freedom; Locke's natural rights philosophy defined basic human rights and the parameters of government; and Aristotle's polis provided the public participation and values of civic virtue to maintain and develop the social individual and a healthy republic. While differing in fine points of philosophy, these three schools of thought formed the dominant ideologies of America's founding, and Jefferson combined them more skillfully than most other Early American writers.

NOTES

1. See Peter Onuf, ed. *Jeffersonian Legacies* (Charlottesville: University Press of Virginia, 1993), my *The Political Philosophy of Thomas Jefferson* (Baltimore: Johns Hopkins University Press, 1991), and Michael P. Zuckert, *The Natural Rights Republic* (Notre Dame, Ind.: University of Notre Dame Press, 1996).

2. Donald Lutz, *A Preface to American Political Theory* (Lawrence: University Press of Kansas, 1992).

3. Merrill D. Peterson, ed., *James Madison* (New York: Harper, 1974), 29.

4. Jefferson to John Adams, May 5, 1817, *The Adams-Jefferson Letters* (hereafter *A-JL*), 2 vols., ed. Lester J. Cappon (Chapel Hill: University of North Carolina Press, 1959), 2:512. See also Eugene R. Sheridan's introduction to Dickenson Ward Adams, ed., *Jefferson's Extracts from the Gospels* (Princeton: Princeton University Press, 1883).

5. So, Jefferson's criticism of the ancient moral philosophers runs along these lines: "In developing our duties to others, they were short and defective. They embraced, indeed, the circles of kindred and friends, and inculcated patriotism, or the love of our country in the aggregate, as a primary obligation; towards our neighbors and countrymen they taught justice, but scarcely viewed them as within the circle of benevolence. Still less have they inculcated peace, charity, and love of our fellowmen, or embraced with benevolence the whole family of mankind." Jefferson to Dr. Benjamin Rush, April 21, 1803, *The Complete Jefferson* (hereafter *CJ*), ed. Saul K. Padover (New York: Tudor, 1943), 948.

6. Jefferson to John Adams, October 12, 1813, *A-JL*, 2:384.

7. Jefferson to William Short, October 31, 1819, *Writings of Thomas Jefferson* (hereafter *WTJ*), ed. Albert Ellery Bergh (Washington, D.C.: Thomas Jefferson Memorial Association, 1904–1905), 15:220.

8. Quoted in Adrienne Koch, *The Philosophy of Thomas Jefferson* (New York: Columbia University Press, 1943), 23; and see Adams, *Jefferson's Extracts from the Gospels.*

9. Jefferson wrote: "The essentials of Christianity as found in the gospels are 1. Faith. 2. Repentance. That faith is everywhere explained to be a belief that Jesus was the Messiah who had been promised. Repentance was to be proved sincere by good works." *The Papers of Thomas Jefferson* (hereafter *Papers*), ed. Julian Boyd (Princeton: Princeton University Press, 1950), 1:550.

10. See Jefferson to John Adams, May 5, 1817, *A-JL*, 2:512; to Wendover, March 13, 1815, *CJ*, 953–55; and to Dr. Benjamin Waterhouse, June 26, 1822, *CJ*, 956.

11. Jefferson to Dr. Benjamin Waterhouse, *CJ*, 956. See also Jefferson to John Adams, May 5, 1817, ibid.; and to Peter Carr, August 10, 1787, *WTJ*, 6:258–59.

12. Jefferson to Dr. Benjamin Waterhouse, ibid. Jefferson's letter ends "die a Unitarian," which for him at this time *was* a true Christian (see Daniel Boorstin, *The Lost World of Thomas Jefferson* [New York: Henry Holt, 1948], 156). Mark A. Beliles in *Thomas Jefferson's Abridgment* (Charlottesville, 1993), 1–11, argues that Jefferson was an orthodox Christian early and late in his life but was Unitarian from roughly 1800 to 1820.

13. Jefferson, First Inaugural Address, *CJ*, 385.

14. From Jefferson's *Notes on the State of Virginia, CJ*, 675.

15. Jefferson, Bill for Establishing Religious Freedom, *CJ*, 946. It was in relation to an established state church that Jefferson made his famous reference to the "wall of separation" between church and state to the Connecticut Baptists (though even there he wishes for religious freedom to encourage citizens' "social duties," i.e., knowledge of Christian ethics):

> I contemplate with sovereign reverence that act of the whole American people which declared that their legislature should "make no law respecting an establishment of religion, or prohibit the free exercise thereof," thus building a wall of separation between church and state. Adhering to this expression of the supreme will of the nation in behalf of the rights of conscience, I shall see with sincere satisfaction the progress of those sentiments which tend to restore to man all his natural rights, convinced he has no natural right in opposition to his social duties. (Letter to A Committee of the Danbury Baptist Association, January 1, 1802, *CJ*, 518–19)

16. Jefferson, October 7, 1822, *CJ*, 957.

17. Ibid., 957–58.

18. Jefferson to Dr. Thomas Cooper, November 2, 1822, *WTJ*, 15:404, quoted in Henry Wilder Foote, *The Religion of Thomas Jefferson* (Boston: Beacon Press, 1963), 7–8. Despite this ecumenical sentiment, Jefferson, two years later, contributed to the building of separate houses of worship, showing a decided partiality to his own Episcopal church. His account book of March 8, 1824, reads: "I have subscribed to the building of an Episcopal church, two hundred dollars; a Presbyterian church, sixty dollars and a Baptist, twenty-five dollars" (p. 8).

Jefferson's general appreciation of the relation between ethics and politics is revealed in a letter to Judge Augustus B. Woodward (March 24, 1824, *WTJ*, 16:19), in which he states that he regards "ethics, as well as religion, as supplements to law in the government of men"; and to William Johnson (June 1823, *CJ*, 322) that "the state's moral rule of their citizens" will be enhanced by its "enforcing moral duties and restraining vice."

19. Gilbert Chinard, ed., *The Commonplace Book of Thomas Jefferson* (Baltimore: Johns Hopkins University Press, 1926), 214; *Papers*, 1:77–79.

20. See Garrett Ward Sheldon, *The History of Political Theory* (New York: Peter Lang, 1988), chap. 9.

21. John Locke, *Second Treatise of Government*, ed. Peter Laslett (New York: New American Library, 1965), 95; Jefferson, *Papers*, 1:423–27.

22. Locke, ibid., 87; Jefferson, ibid.

23. Locke, ibid., 123; Jefferson, ibid.

24. Locke, ibid., 216, 220; Jefferson, ibid.

25. See Sheldon, *Political Philosophy of Thomas Jefferson*, 49–51, 88–91.

26. Ibid., 140.

27. *The Commonplace Book of Thomas Jefferson*, ed. Chinard, 107. Cf. Bolingbroke's remark that God made man "by nature fit for society" (quoted in Isaac Kramnick, *Bolingbroke and His Circle* [Cambridge, Mass.: Harvard University Press, 1968], 89). Cf. Aristotle, "man is by nature a political animal," *The Politics*, trans. T. A. Sinclair (Baltimore: Penguin, 1972), bk. 1, chap. 2, p. 28.

28. Jefferson to Peter Carr, August 10, 1787, *WTJ*, 6:257; to John Adams, February 25, 1823, *A-JL*, 2:589. Cf. Aristotle, "the real difference between man and other animals is that humans alone have perception of good and evil, right and wrong, just and unjust" (*Politics*, bk. 1, chap. 2, p. 29); and "for man's moral choice to be completely excellent, he must know what he is doing; secondly, he must choose to act the way he does, and choose it for its own sake; and in the third place, the act must spring from a firm and unchangeable character" (*Nicomachean Ethics*, trans. Martin Ostwald [Indianapolis: Bobbs-Merrill, 1962], bk. 2, 1105a, p. 39; cf. Genesis 2:15; 3:5).

29. Jefferson to Thomas Law, June 13, 1814, *CJ*, 1033; to John Adams, October 14, 1816, *A-JL*, 2:492. Cf. Rousseau's notion of *pitie* in *The Second Discourse*, trans. Roger and Judith Masters (New York: St. Martin's Press, 1964), 102; and Aristotle's conception of "noble pleasure" derived from moral choice and in the service of justice: "There is a difference between pleasures that come from noble sources and pleasures that come from bad sources, and the pleasure of a just man cannot be felt by someone who is not just" (*Nicomachean Ethics*, bk. 1, 1099a, p. 20, and bk. 10, 1174a, p. 278). Also, cf. Aristotle's *Politics*, bk. 3, chap. 9, p. 121 ("it is our love of others that causes us to prefer life in society").

30. Jefferson to John Adams, February 25, 1823, *A-JL*, 2:589.

31. Jefferson to Peter Carr, August 10, 1787, *WTJ*, 6:262.

32. Jefferson to Thomas Law, June 13, 1814, *CJ*, 1033; thus Jefferson took Aristotle's position of not defining individuals on the basis of their apparent incompleteness, but rather on the basis of their essential *telos* or complete development as human beings.

33. Ibid. Cf. Bolingbroke's remarks in Kramnick, *Bokingbroke and His Circle*, 86–89.

34. Jefferson to John Adams, October 14, 1816, *A-JL*, 2:492.

35. Jefferson to Thomas Law, June 13, 1814, *CJ*, 1032–33. Cf. Aristotle, "this kind of justice is complete virtue or excellence.... It is complete virtue and excellence in the fullest sense, because it is the practice of complete virtue. It is complete because he who possesses it can make use of his virtue not only by himself but also in his relations with his fellow men" (*Nicomachean Ethics*, bk. 5, 1129b–30a, p. 114).

36. Jefferson to Thomas Law, June 13, 1814, *CJ*, 1033; to John Adams, October 14, 1816, *A-JL*, 2:492; to Peter Carr, August 10, 1787, *WTJ*, 6:262.

37. Jefferson to Peter Carr, August 10, 1787, *WTJ*, 6:257. This variability in capacity or development of this innate moral sense did not diminish its universality for Jefferson: In spite of other prejudices, he did not deny the moral sense to either Negroes or Indians (see *Notes on the State of Virginia*, in *CJ*, 664), declaring only that it seemed absent in Napoleon (to John Adams, February 25, 1823, *A-JL*, 2:589). Cf. Aristotle, references to the variable capacity for goodness (*Nicomachean Ethics*, bk. 2, 1103b, p. 34, 1109a, p. 50, bk. 8, 1156a–57a, pp. 218–20). One of the best expressions of the pleasure of the moral sense sympathies is in Jefferson's famous "Head and Heart" dialogue in a letter to Maria Cosway, October 12, 1786, *Papers*, 10:449.

38. Jefferson to Thomas Law, June 13, 1814, *CJ*, 1034.

39. Ibid., 1033.

40. Jefferson to Peter Carr, August 10, 1787, *WTJ*, 6:257. Cf. Aristotle, "virtues . . . we acquire first having put them into action. . . . we become just by the practice of just actions" (*Nicomachean Ethics*, bk. 2, 1103a–1103b, pp. 33–34). See also Boorstin, *Lost World of Thomas Jefferson*, 146.

41. Jefferson to Peter Carr, August 10, 1787, *WTJ*, 6:258.

42. Cf. Aristotle, *Nicomachean Ethics*, bk. 2, 1103, p. 33.

43. Jefferson to Thomas Law, June 13, 1814, *CJ*, 1034.

44. Cf. Aristotle's views on the relation between political participation and the development of individual virtue: "Lawgivers make the citizens good by inculcating [good] habits in them. . . . the main concern of politics is to engender a certain character in the citizens and to make them good and disposed to perform noble actions" (*Nicomachean Ethics*, bk. 2, 1103b, p. 34, bk. 1, 1099b, p. 23); also, "a citizen is in general one who has a share both in ruling and in being ruled. . . . in the best constitution it means one who is able and who chooses to rule and be ruled with a view to a life that is in accordance with goodness" (*Politics*, bk. 3, chap. 13, pp. 131–32).

45. J. G. A. Pocock, "Cambridge Paradigms and Scotch Philosophers," in *Wealth and Virtue*, ed. Istuan Hont and Michael Ignatieff (Cambridge: Cambridge University Press, 1983), 236; Pocock, *Virtue, Commerce, and History* (Cambridge: Cambridge University Press, 1985), 41–44; Pocock, *The Machiavellian Moment* (Princeton, N.J.: Princeton University Press, 1980), 393; Pocock, "Machiavelli, Harrington, and English Political Ideologies in the Eighteenth Century," *William and Mary Quarterly* 22 (October 1965): 553–65; Gordon Wood, *The Creation of the*

American Republic (Chapel Hill: University of North Carolina Press, 1969), 53–58; Lance Banning, *The Jefferson Persuasion* (Ithaca, N.Y.: Cornell University Press, 1978), 29–46.

46. Jefferson's conception of small ward republics seems to be influenced by his understanding of the Greek polis, the English hundreds, New England townships, and Indian tribes. See Richard K. Matthews, *The Radical Politics of Thomas Jefferson* (Lawrence: University Press of Kansas, 1984), 83.

47. Jefferson to Joseph Cabell, February 2, 1816, *WTJ*, 14:423. Also, to Major John Cartwright, June 5, 1824, *WTJ*, 16:46.

48. Jefferson's "mixed" response to Montesquieu's theories revolve around his attempt to adapt classical small republics to a large country, which the French philosopher insisted could not be done (see Jefferson, *Commonplace Book*, 32–33, 267). That which Jefferson retained of Montesquieu was his most classical republican qualities: emphasis on civic virtue, public participation, small republics, public education, and an economic dimension to democracy.

49. Cf. Aristotle, *Politics*, bk. 1, chap. 6, 9, pp. 114, 121; that Jefferson was familiar with Aristotle's *Politics* is evidenced by the presence of the book on his bedside table late in his life (see Merrill C. Peterson, *Thomas Jefferson and the New Nation* [New York: Oxford University Press, 1970], 1008).

50. Jefferson to John Taylor, May 28, 1816, *WTJ*, 15:19; to Samuel Kercheval, July 12, 1816, *WTJ*, 15:33 ("let it be agreed that a government is republican in proportion as every member composing it has his equal voice in the direction of its concerns"). Cf. Montesquieu, "The people, in whom the supreme power resides, ought to have the management of everything within their reach; that which exceeds their abilities must be conducted by their ministers" (*Spirit of the Laws*, 1:9).

51. Jefferson to John Adams, October 28, 1813, *A-JL*, 2:390; also to Samuel Kercheval, July 12, 1816, *WTJ*, 15:37.

52. Jefferson to Samuel Kercheval, July 12, 1816, *WTJ*, 15:38.

53. Ibid., 15:37. Cf. Aristotle's definition of citizenship: "there are different kinds of citizens, but . . . a citizen in the fullest sense is one who has a share in the privileges of rule" (*Politics*, bk. 3, chap. 5, p. 112).

54. Jefferson to Samuel Kercheval, July 12, 1816, *WTJ*, 15:36. This also reflects Jefferson's mature appreciation of classical political theory, as does his comment to Monsieur Coray that "Greece was the first of civilized nations which presented examples of what man should be" (see entire letter). Other evidence for Jefferson's attitudes toward modern conflictual and ancient consensual politics appears in his autobiography, where he contrasts the American Congress's "very contentious . . . morbid rage of debate" with the young French aristocrats in Paris during the late 1780s, whose debates are marked by "coolness and candor of argument . . . logical reasoning and chaste eloquence, disfigured by no gaudy tinsel of rhetoric or declamation, and truly worthy of being placed in parallel with the finest dialogues of antiquity, as handed to us by Xenophon, Plato, and Cicero." *Autobiography*, introduction by Dumas Malone (New York: Putnam, n.d.), 70, 114.

55. Jefferson to Col. Edward Carrington, January 16, 1787, *WTJ*, 5:58. Boorstin, for whom Jefferson's political philosophy provides no positive form of

community or moral dimension, but only natural rights protection from state power, emphasizes what he calls this "prophylactic" purpose of democracy (*Lost World of Thomas Jefferson*, 190–95).

56. Jefferson to Joseph C. Cabell, February 2, 1816, *WTJ*, 14:422. The same argument for the strength of republican government occurs in Jefferson's First Inaugural Address: "It is the only one where every man, at the call of the laws, would fly to the standard of the law, and would meet invasion of the public order as his own personal concern" (in *CJ*, 385).

57. Jefferson to John Taylor, May 28, 1816, *WTJ*, 15:19. Cf. Aristotle's observation in *Politics*, bk. 7, chap. 5, p. 266; and Montesquieu's *Spirit of the Laws*, 1:120:

> It is natural for a republic to have only a small territory; otherwise it cannot long subsist. In an extensive republic there are men of large fortunes, and consequently of less moderation.
>
> In an extensive republic the public good is sacrificed to a thousand private views; it is subordinate to exceptions, and depends on accidents. In a small one, the interest of the public is more obvious, better understood, and more within the reach of every citizen; abuses have less extent, and, of course, are less protected.

58. Jefferson to John Taylor, May 28, 1816, *WTJ*, 15:19.

59. Jefferson to Isaac Tiffany, August 26, 1816, *WTJ*, 15:66; though even here, evidence exists showing that Jefferson's idea of the states' "compact" into a federated Union may have been an attempt at replication of the "confederation" of Greek city-states, of which Athens was a part (see his notes on Stanyan's *Grecian History* (1739) in *Commonplace Book*, entries 717, 729).

60. Jefferson to Gov. John Tyler, May 26, 1810, *WTJ*, 12:394.

61. Jefferson to Joseph C. Cabell, February 2, 1816, *WTJ*, 14:422.

62. Jefferson to Samuel Kercheval, July 12, 1816, *WTJ*, 15:35.

63. Ibid.

64. Jefferson to John Adams, October 28, 1813, *A-JL*, 2:390.

65. Jefferson to Samuel Kercheval, July 12, 1816, *WTJ*, 15:40.

4

Rhetoric of Democracy

✿

ROBERT DAWIDOFF

I.

American political theory owes many of its most powerful notions to Thomas Jefferson's expression of them. Jefferson's political thinking differed from the systematic and closely reasoned thinking of John Adams, James Madison, or Alexander Hamilton. Jefferson's theory was always visionary, that is, his writings about political things expressed a vision of actual things in their guise as ideal things. The *Notes on the State of Virginia*, for instance, portrays a Virginia yeoman farmer who serves as an ideal of the kind of citizenry a free democratic republic requires in order to thrive. Jefferson's yeomanry in the *Notes* inhabited a pastoral version of Virginia, but they bore little resemblance to the poor white farmers who actually lived there. Jefferson's ringing proclamation of equality and freedom in the preamble to the Declaration of Independence was the work of a slaveholder in a republic that in fact had a restricted understanding of the "all men" who were "created equal." But it was Jefferson's own compromised position with respect to these ideals that has authenticated his expression of them for succeeding generations. He did not idealize because he failed to see things for what they were. On the contrary, his scientific, enlightened observations of nature—even where his fancy took him far afield—showed his capacity to render accurately what he observed. His plans for the Northwest Territory and his architecture are sufficient reminders of his immense and solid capacity for all manner of practical if avant-garde activities.

99

Jefferson knew the lay of the land and he knew that men were not angels, but his political visions had a different relation to the actualities his scientific, architectural, and practical political methods so shrewdly observed. Jefferson's genius was for principles and political landscapes that blended the real and the ideal in a way that resembles neoclassical painting. He embodied and recognized the stubborn human facts that stymied their realizations. Reversing the usual translation of the real into the mythic, Jefferson invested the mythic with the practical hope of realization. His political writings do not parse the difference between principle and human fact. They rather present the terms and scenes in which American citizens might explore the terrain of free government from the perspectives of Madisonian understanding of self-interest and the eighteenth-century neoclassical ideals of liberty, citizenship, and natural science that Jefferson's own heroes, Bacon, Newton, and Locke, exemplified. Much as we have come to see Jefferson as the apostle of these ideals—or the failure to live up to them—his legacy has raised the stakes of politics into ones that test the nation's founding principles and necessitate the conflict between interest and principle in American political life.

Above all it was Jefferson's language, his way with words, that distinguished him, even in the company of excellent writers he kept. Franklin was his only contemporary peer in finding the words that stuck in the American memory. But Franklin's genius was for encoding the most sophisticated wisdom in stories that Americans read and made their own. Jefferson composed visions that have been the source for the stories Americans would come to tell about themselves. Jefferson's analogous invention to Franklin's "Poor Richard" was his yeoman farmer, and his portrayal of the yeoman remains a pastoral story about the people. Franklin's unequaled feel for the dangers the popular and democratic might pose to the superior intellect informed his invention of an alternative persona to his own, one memorably successful in beguiling and perhaps deceiving the French *philosophes* and Americans of every stripe to this day.[1]

An example of this difference can be seen in two wonderful children's books, ones, as it happens, where I first learned to know and love Franklin and Jefferson. Robert Lawson's *Ben and Me: A New and Astonishing Life of Benjamin Franklin As Written by His Good Mouse Amos*[2] is an enchanting tale for young children of Ben, the genius in homespun whose adventures and inventions we see from the mouse-eyed view, Lawson being Disney-like in his grasp of the way democracy makes critters of us all. Vincent Sheehan's lovely "Landmark Series" Jefferson biography is, by contrast, a book for older children that resembles most Jefferson literature, striking themes such as democracy more comfortably than making Jefferson himself a familiar character.[3] Attempts to make Jefferson a character in the popular culture's stories have seldom succeeded. The 1940 movie *The Howards of Virginia* is a painful example, not least because Cary Grant, who plays the rough-hewn frontiersman of the title, might have made a subtly persuasive Jefferson, and Richard Carlson's Jefferson is more hero's best friend than Thomas Jefferson. But more recent attempts like *Jefferson in Paris* or even the PBS documentary series fail to make a plausible American democratic character out of this brainy, elusive character who was never humble and who is not suitable to inhabit the kinds of tales that democracy spins about itself.[4]

But Americans have always made up stories from Jefferson's words.[5] Lincoln's memorable invocation of Jefferson's words even as he redeployed them in the Gettysburg Address was perhaps the noblest Jeffersonian story, but it was not singular. Jefferson's expression of political theory, what I would call his political visions, is the stuff of American democratic self-understanding. It was not so very long ago that American children regularly responded to adults telling them not to do something with "I can too, it's a free country!" That is a key to Jefferson's continuing importance as a political theorist. He set the terms of American thinking about liberty and democracy and government by writing down the visions that Americans have inhabited ever since. Political theorists prefer weightier themes than this, but Jefferson's medium was his writing, and his writing reveals something of the significance of his abiding importance as a political thinker. As Michael Zuckert says of Jefferson's own view of his contested role in writing the Declaration: "Jefferson as scrivener to the American mind—that and only that."[6]

The American colonies at the time of the Revolution were a little like a bright but unlettered prince, an Alexander, perhaps, who needed tutors to help him realize his prospects. The colonies were lucky in their tutors. Among them Thomas Jefferson, more than anyone, gave us our national words and translated into sentences the sentiments we have chosen to be guided by. It is of interest, therefore, to think about Jefferson in terms of his preferred medium, the written word. Jefferson never claimed to have originated the natural rights philosophy. He read and wrote. To understand his political thinking, we need to think about his chosen medium, his writing; to understand his writing, we would do well to begin at Monticello.[7]

Few men ever get to make their immediate worlds over as much to their liking as Jefferson did in Albemarle. If he had a tremendous effect on the big world of America, the smaller stage of Monticello concentrated his notions in actualities small enough to compass. Two scenes in particular at Monticello concern Jefferson's writing. The spare obelisk rising plainly down the road from the house in the family burying-ground memorializes the "Author of the Declaration of American Independence / of the Statute

of Virginia for religious freedom / & Father of the University of Virginia."
It is as an author first that Jefferson chose to be remembered. The modesty
of his statement that the Declaration was an expression of the American
mind was also his ambitious claim on an audience of the American future.
Jefferson figured that Americans would always be reading some of what he
wrote. The suspicion arises that he wanted them, while they were at it, to
read the *Statute for Religious Freedom*, which specifies more controversially
what the Declaration advances in general terms on the wave of a people's
indiscriminate fervor. He also commended to the care of his audience his
university, which might just institutionalize the impulses, perpetuate the
ideals, and train the sorts of public men Jefferson valued. Knowing how
connected his future glory and his authorship would be, Jefferson enjoined
American posterity to a canon of his writings on his memorial stone.

Certainly few writers have ever achieved what Jefferson enjoyed—a
permanent national audience. If Jefferson fancied himself a sometime
recorder of American sentiments, what writer would not envy him that
post, since, in recording it, Jefferson suffered no alienation from the
American mind. He expressed in the highest terms the eighteenth-century
Enlightenment version of the wisdom of the ages, sentiments sealed in
blood and a constitution, words acted upon as writers only dream of. In a
country where the canonic writers have tended to be alienated, unappreci-
ated, ambivalent, at odds with the national audience, or sentimentalized to
the point of eclipse, there is something lasting and potent in the thought
of an American author who has had Jefferson's originating rapport with the
nation. Nor did Jefferson ever feel the need to dismount the high horse of
his own intellectual journeys. He made no sacrifices to the demands of a
democratic or popular audience. He had one style, one language.

The second setting at Monticello that frames Jefferson's political writing is his study. In a house of elegant and convenient arrangement, where
the social and individual requirements and amenities, the soft and keen
edges of our natures, are so attended to, no room is more attentively out-
fitted with comfort and contrivance than Jefferson's own. His study—
writing area and library—was the open heart of his private world. The in-
struments of his reflection—books, telescope, measuring devices, the
light-giving windows out from which he might look, even his bed of
rest—all center on his chair, candles in the arms, couch under his long
legs, desk drawn up over, with his writing materials and his own copying
machine as the focus of his labors. As his study reminds us, there was something Jefferson wrote for almost everything he did. His writing was so
much an aspect of his doing that the two did not really form separate activities at all. It is extraordinary how much of what we know about Jefferson we
know from his own hand, his records, his books, his letters, and his notes.

He was writing all the time; the scratch and dip of his quill punctuated his life as surely as his breathing or the natural changes he so deliberately noted. He started writing early and stopped only a few days before he died; when he broke his right wrist, he wrote with his left hand.

Jefferson seems to have been one of those people for whom writing is the act of thinking. His topics shifted interchangeably. His reflections were a kind of doing. There was no categorical difference in his attention to natural observations, correspondence, political squibs, philosophic writings, or his ceaseless plans and inventions, which unlike Franklin he did not build but rather invented, much as he borrowed from Locke to invent the preamble to the Declaration. Improvement was Jefferson's hallmark. Jefferson did not share the modern notion of a *writer* as a worthy occupation. He did admit of an alternative to the gentleman's civic obligations to the state, one that might raise the tone of life and advance the cause of humanity. This vocation was philosophic, by which Jefferson meant what we call scientific. He wrote to David Rittenhouse on 19 July 1778 stipulating "an order of geniusses" above the obligation of public service "& therefore exempted from it. No body can conceive that nature ever intended to throw away a Newton upon the occupations of a crown."[8]

Accepting his own responsibility for public service, Jefferson exempted the scientific genius as those in the nineteenth century might the literary genius from some of the rules of ordinary life. However much Jefferson may have valued or possessed what we call literary genius, it never occupied the central position for him. He did not see genius in this sphere as connected to its own higher calling and he fashioned no role for such. The ideal of the engaged intellectual as a willing and venturesome participant in public life might in some ways be said to resemble Jeffersonian views of the public responsibility of the educated. But the self-consciousness of the modern intellectual writer, the sense of alienation, the frank ideological task, and the adversarial relation to the culture, would have distressed him. That human type is closer to the sort of newspaperman Jefferson was known to employ but not to recommend.

The Jeffersonian voice in his writing was reticent and clear, elegant and graceful, easeful but not easy, generous of spirit, clear in expression, and enthusiastic; and it was always governed by the disciplines of his life. Jefferson was not a teacher, but he was didactic to the bone. It is rare to find a Jefferson letter that does not transmit some news, but news meant the news of Enlightenment, not the gossip of the Rialto. It is a commonplace that Jefferson's generation performed, as it were, in the presence of posterity. They also kept worldly audiences in view. Jefferson assimilated many such audiences in his life and letters. It is as if they kept him company, albeit at a respectful or collegial distance.

Jefferson wrote well, sometimes with memorable felicity, but the most powerful impression of reading his correspondence, as well as his formal writings, is how meet to his purposes his sentences were. Jefferson wrote an eighteenth-century prose that was formal, balanced, reserved in expression, polite, and aristocratic. It is not that he did not say what he meant, rather, what he meant seldom boiled down to the plainest speech. The eighteenth-century sentence had a purpose largely lost to the modern reader. It was meant not to cut through, but to include an ethos of enlightened communication. The hallmark of its elegant style was not necessarily to find the shortest route to meaning. Each sentence Jefferson wrote was meant to span a variety of discourses and make it possible to speak of all subjects in the same language. Specialization was meant to occur within the sentence, not in different kinds of sentences. The English sentence Jefferson wrote was an act of comprehension, launched for truth more than pleasure, although the latter was supposed to be founded in the former. For Jefferson, writing was not itself the subject of reflection, it was an instrument. Just as a house could not be beautiful unless it stood and fit certain architectural theories, so a sentence must do its duty. Such beauty or elegance as it had must be founded in its use. *Dulce et utile* was the motto for his writing as for everything else.

Some have observed that Jefferson's use of the passive is a significant and troublesome characteristic of his writing. It is true that Jefferson's writing was not aggressive in the way that Franklin's or Adams' was. His writing was a fluid in which Jefferson floated notions. Grievance and philosophical hope both float in the tides of the Declaration. In expressing the American mind, as he said, one must not be too idiosyncratic. But Jefferson's prose is distinguished for what it permitted him to say. The content is almost impossible to separate from style. The voice was not loud. Jefferson was not the character in his writing that Franklin was in his nor the person that Adams was in his diaries. Jefferson's sentences constructed an arena for rational philosophic action. They were a superb medium for Jefferson to present his ideas and his investigations, and they do not betray him more than occasionally as a subjective presence. Jefferson acted in his sentences, but his action was notoriously undirected.

Jefferson's prose also served humbler and more stringent purposes. He could turn a homely phrase and concentrate complicated situations in vivid metaphors. Slavery prompted some of his most powerful metaphors, "holding a wolf by the ears," for instance. His prose welcomed all the bits and pieces that made up his intellectual breadth: the Greek phrases, the calculations and measurements, the descriptions, quotations, allusions, lists. Like the walls at Monticello, his prose set off with impassive hospitality the elegant and the practical, the fresco and the tusk. The brilliance of his political writing is seen in its capacity to retain its high ideals and even abstract content despite years of democratic use and abuse.

The Jeffersonian voice reflected the conviction that human relations reach their highest expression through rational exchange. His reserve was probably founded in character. But it was also the reserve and caution of a man who had more faith in the exchange of information according to natural philosophic rules than in the commerce of political sympathy. He relied on the tendency toward the same ends, the reading of the same books, more than on the direct encounter of personalities. He shied away from the sort of fight that John Adams relished, and he seldom wrote with the self-conscious comic flare that marked Franklin. It has been said that Jefferson had little sense of humor, but there is a lightness and sometimes an irony and a wit that refreshed Jefferson's writing. He was amiable rather than funny, however, and the airiness and elegance of the lovelier moments in his writing are earnest and serious and have little of the special grace the sense of humor prefers to the graceful. Jefferson lacks the human pungency of an Adams or Lincoln. It is also noteworthy that Jefferson did not rely as Lincoln did on the Bible. He rewrote the Bible, and, however much that challenges current notions of Jefferson as a devout Christian, it is intricately connected to his capacity to receive other than biblical commandments for the new nation.

Thomas Jefferson believed that knowledge was power. Echoing through almost every sentence he wrote is the validating confidence that this notion brings to communication of almost every sort. How hard it is to find a Jeffersonian text that does not get down to this truth. Whether of books, crops, architecture, conversations, weather, discoveries, or explorations, the Jeffersonian yield is knowledge. Nor did Jefferson let things be. He actively reduced life to knowledge, considered according to the Enlightenment rules of reason. The Puritans had believed that the signifying Fall of Adam branded the human brain incomplete. Knowledge required faith and grace. Human reason could not fathom the workings of creation unaided. For those such as Jonathan Edwards, logic and natural philosophy were tools that spanned the awkward, tragic chasm between man's capacity and God's omniscience. Jefferson did not believe this. However much, as a wise and experienced man for whom life did not always go well, Jefferson understood that the human condition required character and endurance, he did not seem to have doubted the capacity of the human mind, using reason, to understand the order of the world. However much he resorted to the ancient creeds of endurance, he never substituted something else for the knowledge a man might gain. Knowledge is power, and *dulce et utile*, twin mottoes of his life, formed the matrix of his political writing. His views on language are analogous to his political views during the Revolution and suggest that his writing was more than the vehicle of his political visions.

In 1786 Jefferson wrote an informal treatise, *Thoughts on Prosody,* which he addressed to Chastellux.[9] It arose out of a dispute with the Frenchman over whether English verse "depended, like Greek and Latin verse, on long and short syllables arranged in regular feet," which Chastellux denied. Jefferson concluded in time that his friend was right. To the student of Jefferson's political thinking, the *Thoughts* sound an echo. Jefferson here takes the authoritative view of true English culture that had become impossible to maintain in the constitutional struggle of the previous decade. The legalism of poetic feet, the units of the poetic line, parallels the proper construction of constitutional legalism. We may discern here the often forgotten price that the colonists paid for their independence. As provincials, they had an exaggerated interest in, an unrelaxed correctness about, English things. Politics forced Jefferson to transcend this, and he, like his colleagues, rose immortally to that challenge. Culturally, for all the founders, the Englishness that had been their standard was harder to forgo. The Americans remained an English literary people. English prosody remained Jefferson's as certainly as the English constitution no longer did. English stayed his language and became the vehicle of his work. The *Thoughts* suggests that he reclaimed the literary heritage for Americans in something of the way *A Summary View of the Rights of British America* tried to reclaim English constitutionalism. The interest of this for the student of his political theory is that it explains that the effectiveness of his writing did not reflect what we call the writer's "talent." Rather, it developed from a consistent understanding of the purpose and character of language that expressed the power and influence of his political visions. The comprehensive purpose of his writings grounded them rather than a free-standing philosophic method or substance.

Jefferson's thoughts on prosody do not rival Samuel Johnson's, because they do not connect to anything in poetry that goes beyond conventional and external aspects of form. But they do reveal something of the method we recognize in his political writings, and they should restrain the understandable impulse to read Jefferson's political theory in the same way we read political writers such as Madison or later Calhoun, for whom expression was not a serious issue.[10] Like all the founders, Jefferson valued the classics, but his reason for preferring blank verse to rhymed points to a difference that resonates in how his political writings differ from theirs:

> If we continue to read rhymed verse at a later period of life it is such only where the poet has had force enough to bring great beauties of thought and diction into this form. . . . But as we advance in life these

things fall off one by one, and I suspect we are left at last with only Homer and Virgil, perhaps with Homer alone.

Jefferson's taste in English poetry had something to do with his political expression as well. From Thomas Gray, William Shenstone, and William Collins he absorbed the beautiful, clean statements of sensibility and the sublime. Sentiment added to sound made sense to Jefferson. So far, his was the conventional English taste of the "Age of Sensibility," a good taste, no doubt. It prized sentiment, tender and plaintive, a susceptibility to the claims and beauties of Nature, and the independence of the gentleman of high purpose from the "clamors fierce and loud" of "the angry crowd." These tastes reveal Jefferson as the conventional, characteristic man of his class and breeding that his philosophical and political daring sometimes distracts us from recognizing. Poetry, for reading people of his sort, was thought to provide an acceptable language of feeling in a container of pleasure. It was formal and intimate, public and private, at the same time. Thus, its morality was central to its purposes. Quoting poetry, Jefferson drew on its expressions either to authenticate philosophical and moral views already held or to help him respond in situations for which no private or other public language of feeling existed. But it also was a language ideally suited to his political theories, which tended toward the articulation of reasoned sentiments rather than philosophic arguments. The English poetry Jefferson liked served the salad days of his fervency. In time, his precocious expectation of confining himself to Homer came essentially true. His espousal of a Greek philosophy of the personal life, his Epicurean conviction, seems to have suited him more than the poetry of his youth. He did not lose his taste for it as much as his sense of the use of it, a fatal loss to Jefferson, *dulce* without *utile*.

2.

Jefferson's only book is a source for, and a test of, any interpretation of his political thinking. *Notes on the State of Virginia* was written in response to the inquiries of Francois de Barbe-Marbois, secretary of the French legation, for information, and presented itself as an act of high diplomatic and enlightened communication.[11] Written to inform, the *Notes* was published in a hesitating, awkward, but deliberate way. Whatever its origin, it bears the Jeffersonian trademark: all his writings were composed situationally. The *Notes* is an intriguing book. It is sometimes argued, sometimes plausibly, that it makes a concerted argument, and perhaps it does. It makes sense on the level on which it is presented, namely, as scientific responses to the queries of "a Foreigner of Distinction, then residing among us." The questions bind the *Notes* and appear to give direction to a story that is really the drama of the author's own investigations of Virginia. Jefferson is the person to whom the queries about Virginia happened to be addressed. His answering them authenticated him as a Virginian, a patriot, a gentleman, a scientist, a traveler, and a man of the world. Jefferson revealed himself by casting his delicate shadow on what he knew.

Query VI shows Jefferson's method in the *Notes*. "A notice of the mines and other subterraneous riches; its trees, plants, fruits, etc." may appear dry, but it recapitulates the history of Virginia in fact and in fancy both as a kind of *el dorado* and a kind of hell. Virginia was an early archetype of the New World, a focus for that vaunted European ambivalence about its own expansion. Virginia was a land of riches, a country of desolation, the scene of human growth, a habitat where the species degenerated, the home of freedom, and the home of slavery. Jefferson in Query VI establishes the natural riches of Virginia with an eye to the lavish tradition of description that had prevailed. The descriptions are moderate in tone, full of the specifics and attached scientific dispute, as if to establish Virginia as a country in fact, a subject at last freed for serious discussion and estimation. He concludes the query with his famous defense of American nature against the aspersions cast by Count Buffon, ending in a spirited brief in behalf of American civilization.

Three essentials sealed Jefferson's argument. His true subject, Virginia, binds information, discovery, advocacy, defense, and celebration all together. Virginia is related to all kinds of information. Second, the republic of science, whose scattered membership constituted one of Jefferson's principal audiences, required that Jefferson take up a certain attitude as well as collect data. What we may consider straying is, in this context, not straying at all. Jefferson regarded all his information with an enlightened scientific eye, and by the canons he accepted, he had no need to distinguish, even where we might. Third and most important, he used himself as the eye through which all is seen and argued. Abundant information, the degree to which Jefferson's interests and information and the very world coincide, and the relative uninsistence of his personal presence may misdirect, but if you look at how he established credibility, you will find Jefferson himself. Query VI, for example, presents an objective answer to a question, but it is also Jeffersonian rumination, an occasion for Jefferson to collect information, sift hearsay, judge theories, visit mines, question authorities, redraw maps, classify species, and examine seashells. Considered as a performance, it is extraordinarily confident and versatile. He commences, "I knew a single instance of gold found in this State," and recounts his own observations. The reader feels reported to, answered, addressed, and informed. Here and there, Jefferson employs the second person to enforce this effect. But Virginia's plentitude is no fairy tale, and the Virginian who tells it to us speaks our language. Franklin played the noble savage, rube *savant*. Jefferson assumed the guise of the *philosophe* representing his native country at the court of the republic of science, as he did in the Declaration's preamble.

At stake in Jefferson's works are visions of real things: a university, a natural aristocracy in the disinterested service of a people, a rational system of weights and measures. The Jeffersonian imagination envisioned the possible, the desirable, and the hopeful, set in a pervasive future that might invade the present and that surely colored the past. Reading Jefferson one is reading stories about the way life in America should be, stories in which the vast learning and wide reading and experience expressed in the advanced scientific language of the day seem to furnish such a future. Jefferson's information grounds and releases a vision of the politically possible, infuriatingly frustrating to his interlocutors in practical measures but everlastingly liberating to his readers. The *Notes* abounds in this special sort of Jeffersonian vision, which is his way of reading the scientific tea leaves and picturing the future. In the book Virginia becomes a scientifically delineated and republican paradise, the right setting for the free government Jefferson has in mind.

Jefferson's account of agrarian virtue in the query on manufactures in the *Notes* remains a quintessential Jeffersonian expression, plausible, fantastic, not exactly arguable, irresistible to Americans in one form or another down the years, the very model of a political vision:

> Those who labour in the earth are the chosen people of God, if ever he had a chosen people, whose breasts he has made his peculiar deposit for substantial and genuine virtue. It is the focus in which he keeps alive that sacred fire, which otherwise might escape from the face of the earth. Corruption of morals in the mass of cultivators is a phenomenon of which no age nor nation has furnished an example. It is the mark set on those, who not looking up to heaven, to their own soil and industry, as does the husbandman, for their subsistance, depend for it on casualties and caprice of customers. Dependance begets subservience and venality, suffocates the germ of virtue, and prepares fit tools for the designs of ambition. (Query XIX)

It was generally the case that when Jefferson summoned God or the Creator, he was about to soar above the plane of natural philosophy as scientifically demonstrated and to venture into a discussion of the self-evident. This attractive setting—the Jeffersonian version of the middle landscape,

English in its celebration of a kind of order and independence, American in setting and in its political hopes—resembles something of what makes people still partial to the idea of the family farm, the still-hallowed connection between the health of the American regime and the grounding of it in the independent cultivators of the soil. Here Jefferson develops a view of the people whom God would have chosen but whom the republic chooses instead.

The vision is a pastoral, an idealized farmer-citizen in an idealized landscape-republic. Everything you can possibly know about Virginia leads you to this man, Jefferson claims. Unlike his cofounders, he sensed the requirement for views that might guide a future hopefully. That husbandman of Jefferson's is not a particularly accurate version of the Virginian farmer of the late eighteenth century, who probably depended on a deferential hierarchical order to stay in check and who was more likely to be the chosen person of the Christian God than the Lockean one. Still, at a crucial moment of his argument, Jefferson imagined such a fellow in an old-new fashion, a traditional sturdy yeoman, English and classical, native to Virginia and to the republic.

Jefferson's attractive pastoralizing of the farmers was not decorative. In his book and as a practical matter it was a didactic fantasy, meant to instill in that necessary class the kinds of virtues and habits and self-image that such citizens must have if the republic is to survive. As almost always in the Jeffersonian fiction, there is a tough-minded core, namely, the realization that the desired goal may require a transformation of present conditions. Jeffersonian writing characteristically attempted that visionary transformation.

The true enemy of the agrarian republic was slavery; the reality of Jefferson's countryside was the slave society with its aristocrats, its perversions of community, and its proliferating dance of dependency. Jefferson's sections on slavery in the *Notes* concentrated on the damage the institution did to those habits of independence and virtue that a republic must cultivate in her citizens (Queries XIV, XVIII). The slavery sections also demonstrate the necessity to Jefferson of a natural aristocracy that would replace the habituated ruling class. We see, as perhaps John Adams could not, how necessary to Jefferson was his hope of a meritocracy. Adams saw in New England, enfranchised around him, a respectable if imperfect oligarchy and citizenry. Jefferson loathed the merely privileged in his own class. They affronted with their exercise of privilege his belief that power must be the reward for the modern, the virtuous, the hardworking, and the best.

Slavery, like so many other situations in Virginia, made Jefferson a visionary. The best country in the world seemed to him in the grip of a backward, superstitious, and detrimental social system that might well prove its undoing. Jefferson was not much in advance of his class or country in racial views. He opposed slavery and tried to give the African-American his due, but he did not envision a multiracial paradise. Instead, he imagined a terrible retributive revolution. The slave rebellion was his nightmare version of the healthy letting of the blood of tyrants. It posed the peculiarly Jeffersonian problem that led to the equally peculiar Jeffersonian fiction. On the one hand, Jefferson opposed slavery and tyranny. He believed firmly in the right of the oppressed to rebel, stating that rebellion was a healthy social process. On the other, seeing the imminence of such a war of black slaves, like his own slaves, against the white masters like him, he recoiled in horror, a horror that had its fair share of straightforward slaveholder feelings. Jefferson could not bring himself beyond the point of pious hope that slavery would be ended and that slaves could be colonized. He wanted slaves and blacks out of Virginia, and he significantly removed them from his picture of the idealized agrarian republic. The current interest in the DNA evidence for Jefferson's fathering of some of Sally Heming's children should remind us of Jefferson's role in the construction of a dubious and color-coded view of "race." This view, necessary to sustain slavery and a "racial" hierarchy, also implicates Jefferson's understanding of Nature in the anything but "natural" creation of a racial classification to explain away the contradictions between American liberty and American chattel slavery. Jefferson's experience as a slaveholder suggests another way in which his political visions can structure the continuing attempt to reconcile American principle with American practice. Ironically, perhaps, thinking about Jefferson—the facts of his life and his "disinterested" pursuit of reason—may help Americans to recognize ourselves as that mixed race population Jefferson himself helped to create but could not bring himself to value.

Having failed to figure out this toughest issue and having failed to transcend his personal stake in the institution and its attitudes (as did almost everyone else, it must be said), Jefferson did two things. He propounded an interesting series of arguments against slavery which tie the future of the republic to its extinction, most famously in the Declaration, but in the *Notes* as well. The equality and freedom of all mankind is a principle worth keeping as a standard even if one does not quite know how to implement it at any given time. Jefferson also glimpsed horror, revolution, and race war, and his memorable images for the slavery situation—holding a wolf by the ears, the fire-bell in the night[12]—caught his true sense of things and his dilemma. Again, it is the writing as much as any systematic thinking through that effected his political thinking.

Jefferson's writings on slavery located the terrain in which Americans must confront the contradiction between their claim to liberty and the institution of chattel slavery that made a mockery of that claim. Jefferson explored the contradictions, even though he did not resolve them into action. In the *Notes*, he "trembles" when he remembers that God is just. Now Jefferson did not often have recourse to this just and wrathful God: he believed that people were capable of being just and that life was susceptible of improvement. Slavery, however, created a political and moral problem for Jefferson that only this grim reaper of a God could address and then only on the familiar Jeffersonian plane of imagination. This is one of the few appearances of this old deity in Jefferson's work, albeit a memorable one. The contradiction Jefferson resolved in a rather extreme and intense imagining of an avenging biblical God, with accompanying images of trouble and bloodshed; and his "prophecy" of a rending civil conflict came true. If Jefferson was unable to think and act his way clearly through the thicket of slavery, he also uniquely provided the metaphors for the ultimate solutions to his conundrums. It is "a hard mystery of Jefferson's," as Robert Frost wrote, but it is also a clue to the importance of his writing that his images predicted what his thinking could not resolve, and bequeathed a visionary place, not a solution. Lincoln inhabited that place and acknowledged that it was Jefferson's deed of gift.

Nature, as Michael Zuckert emphasizes, is the key. If there was a consistent passion in Jefferson's life, it was Nature. Every day Jefferson noted weather, growth, and species, reassuring himself that life on earth was of a connection, if not of a piece. In his observations of nature, Jefferson's different discourses coincided. The natural setting was at once something to be measured, described precisely, and placed and wondered at in the language of sensibility and the sublime. The rational language of the time offered Jefferson a two-pronged possibility of understanding nature, for the sublime was the object of the rational language of feeling, which expressed without specific religious faith what scenes of nature did to the observer. This language was learned from poetry.[13]

And so it is immensely interesting to discover in the *Notes* a passage where this conjunction seems to fall short of resolution. The scene is the Natural Bridge, a natural wonder in Virginia especially dear to Jefferson, not only as an example of the sublime works of Nature but also because it was on his own land. The passage occurs in Query V on Virginian cascades and caverns:

> The Natural bridge, the most sublime of Nature's works, though not comprehended under the present head, must not be pretermitted. It is on the ascent of a hill, which seems to have been cloven through its length by some great convulsion. The fissure, just at the bridge, is, by some admeasurements, 270 feet deep, by others only 205. It is about 45 feet wide at the bottom, and 90 feet at the top; this of course determines the length of the bridge, and its height from the water. Its

breadth in the middle, is about 60 feet, but more at the ends, and the thickness of the mass at the summit of the arch, about 40 feet. A part of this thickness is constituted by a coat of earth, which gives growth to many large trees. The residue, with the hill on both sides, is one solid rock of lime-stone. The arch approaches the Semi-elliptical form; but the larger axis of the ellipsis, which would be the cord of the arch, is many times longer than the transverse. Though the sides of this bridge are provided in some parts with a parapet of fixed rocks, yet few men have resolution to walk to them and look over into the abyss. You involuntarily fall on your hands and feet, creep to the parapet and peep over it. Looking down from this height about a minute, gave me a violent head ach. If the view from the top be painful and intolerable, that from below is delightful in an equal extreme. It is impossible for the emotions arising from the sublime, to be felt beyond what they are here: so beautiful an arch, so elevated, so light, and springing as it were up to heaven, the rapture of the spectator is really indescribable! The fissure continuing narrow, deep, and streight for a considerable distance above and below the bridge, opens a short but very pleasing view of the North mountain on one side, and Blue ridge on the other, at the distance each of them of about five miles. This bridge is in the county of Rock bridge, to which it has given name, and affords a public and commodious passage over a valley, which cannot be crossed elsewhere for a considerable distance. The stream passing under it is called Cedar creek. It is a water of James river, and sufficient in the driest seasons to turn a grist-mill, though its fountain is not more than two miles above.

We accompany Jefferson on his walk at the bridge, his muted presence authenticating our visit and his precise language of surveying the scientific sublime describing it for us. This is how Jefferson meant to learn from Lewis and Clark, indeed, how he collected much of the information for the *Notes*, the very point of his own painstaking recording of his observations. The universal language of measurement, the shared assumptions of natural philosophy, and the collegiality of the cosmopolitan Enlightenment are combined in his method.

As Jefferson approaches the bridge, his language shifts abruptly to describe not the natural wonder, but the human experience of it. With a sudden use of the second person, he lurches into an easily rendered, conventional statement of the sublime, employing the language of poetic emotion to express human feelings in the way that measurement expresses human knowledge. Jefferson handles each well. He resumes the language of measurement as he returns from the bridge to its setting, as it recedes into the countryside, across a commodious public road. The passage is a satisfying example of two linked kinds of descriptive writing merging to create a vivid impression of a distant wonder.

And yet there is something amiss. Between the scientific and poetic slips another tone. Jefferson stands on top of the bridge and looks over into the abyss, and has an episode of dizziness, falling "involuntarily" to his knees and feeling in a "violent" headache the unsettling power of the natural. The "painful and intolerable" view is what for the nineteenth century (and perhaps earlier) engendered the sublime. The terror of the world has more to do with it than the airy grace of a natural arch. The sublime was meant to express with awe and terror a human understanding of the world beyond the resource of ordinary language. It was not just another way of being precise about something. It challenged the descriptive power of language with experiences that seemed to transcend comprehension even as they tyrannize conscious feeling.

The picturesque might be a more domesticated emotion. Jefferson has his indescribable rapture with his feet firmly planted on the ground. Struck down and dizzied by the simple physical force of the natural world, his headache the image of his experience, conventional language would not serve him. He had to hold on too fast for dear life to attitudinize or record. This is the experience of the natural that prompted the nineteenth century, as exemplified by the Romantics and Emerson, to doubt the finality of that scientific-literary grasp of the world that Jefferson stuck by. They made changes in language to express the doubt, expanding the range of the literary first person from Jefferson's careful observer to include and emphasize the rapturous self of his headache. The tension between the rational and the emotional that this passage shows powerfully informed the intellectual and moral agendas for American thinkers in the first half of the nineteenth century. The close supplementary reading of Jefferson that Zuckert executes so impressively elides effectively what the images of distress in Jefferson's writing suggest. Jefferson's prose created terms on which Americans yet struggle to resolve those things he could not. Locating those irresolutions, not as they existed in Jefferson's scattered prose but in a supertext of his political theory, may usefully complete Jefferson's project in ways he never did. It also risks missing the significance of his legacy: it was in his failure to resolve central contradictions that Americans have found him abidingly useful, if not sweet.

3.

In our own day the private has become of engrossing interest to the public. Jefferson's guise as the amorous slaveholder and sophisticate has dominated more and more the public's perception of him. It is of particular interest to engage Jefferson's own view of the private and public in his famous letter to Maria Cosway. On 12 October 1786, Jefferson wrote to Mrs. Cosway, who with her husband had just left Paris and Jefferson's company.[14] Whatever the exact nature of their relationship, it was of a sentimental, passionate, and intense sort, and Jefferson felt her departure very keenly. In his letter, Jefferson presents to Mrs. Cosway a "dialogue" between "my Head & my Heart" as he confronts his feelings about her, "seated by my fireside, solitary and sad." The letter has been prized for its own sake and for its presumed rare insight into Jefferson's private emotions. It is an engaging instance of Jeffersonian authorship, and although it does not catch him *in flagrante*, it suggests the Jeffersonian version of what feminists expressed with their catchphrase "the personal is the political." It is another characteristic Jeffersonian political vision which creates a setting and terms through which the citizen can reconcile apparently contrary impulses. That these impulses are passion and reason make this letter of uncommon interest to the student of his political thinking.

Jefferson cast his letter in the form of a conceit, the dialogue of the head and the heart being a familiar convention founded on contemporary moral psychology, an accepted metaphor for the contrary pull of human passion and human reason. The conceit paid Mrs. Cosway is the compliment of Jefferson's desolation after losing the company of husband and wife following their recent spate of high times; it also conveys a deeper emotion of Jefferson's about Mrs. Cosway and safely explores his own feelings for her delectation. All of this is carried off in the high convention of the conceit, presumably extending the mood of gallantry and deliberate charade that must have masked some of their feelings during their frequent personal encounters.

The first mood of the dialogue is playful and ironic, a light rendering of the stance of sensibility's formulae of wretchedness. Jefferson's Heart is inclined to be sad but initially expresses itself in the conventional language of sensibility, drawn out by Jefferson with some irony. Thus, in answer to the Head's gruff observation that "you seem to be in a pretty trim," the Heart renders his claim: "I am indeed the most wretched of all earthly beings. Overwhelmed with grief, every fibre of my frame distended beyond its natural powers to bear, I would willingly meet whatever catastrophe should leave me no more to feel or to fear."

The Heart rants and in exaggerated grief flatters the absent Maria Cosway, laying these emotions safely at her door. The Head in turn provokes the Heart in a send-up of prudence and philosophical coolness toward passion. Together they tell the history of the affair. Jefferson had been busy with his country's business and his own, busy with friendship and philosophy, chastened by his own life to avoid the forming of new attachments that would be dangerous to his hard-won tranquillity. Jefferson describes himself as happy enough and no stranger to loss; he is properly self-protective. The Head blames the Heart for once again exposing them both to the havoc of feeling, the tribulations of loss. The Head and Heart, in playing philosophical charades, speaking a double language of flirtation, also express Jefferson's feelings about his attachment after it has already upset his peace of mind. The Head tends to look at things from Jefferson's point of view before meeting Mrs. Cosway; the Heart speaks of what life is like since Jefferson came to know her.

Jefferson's feelings run characteristically on American subjects. The Head quickly reminds the Heart that the Cosways belong to Europe; "perhaps you flatter yourself they may come to America?" The dialogue plunges into a discussion of America, its tone changing perceptibly from the elegant to the earnest. The Heart rhapsodizes about the subjects an artist would find to paint in Virginia. The familiar setting of the *Notes* becomes the scene of a romantic friendship. In his book, Jefferson was solitary. Here, Mrs. Cosway joins him amid the picturesque glories of Virginia. Jefferson shows how his feelings have indeed caught the mood of his literary tastes. He creates for himself and Mrs. Cosway a Virginian pastoral to which she repairs after a grief he is peculiarly placed to understand—he who has lost all. Jefferson's chief loss was that of his wife, who died in 1782. He disowns his desire, forbears making a proposal, and utters a pious hope that no grief should come to the Cosways, which means in context that there is no reason for Mrs. Cosway to join him in Virginia. The Head forces the Heart to create a romantic fiction, which in essence obviates a liaison.

Although presented as adversaries, Jefferson's Head and Heart understand and complement one another pretty well. The Head commences a discussion of the false light in which America is seen from Europe as a way of saying that the Cosways will not visit unpersuaded. The Heart responds with a proud patriotic defense of American progress only to bring the Head back to the earlier case at hand, the pain of separation from the Cosways as it reflects on the Heart's conduct of life. The Head advances a view that the "art of life is the art of avoiding pain." It draws the lesson that to retire into self and duty is the prudent course; intellectual pleasures are presented as safe and a kind of sublimity is broached:

> Those, which depend on ourselves, are the only pleasures a wise man will count on: for nothing is ours which another may deprive us of. Hence the inestimable value of intellectual pleasures. Ever in our power, always leading us to something new, never cloying, we

ride, serene & sublime, above the concerns of this mortal world, con-
templating truth & nature, matter & motion, the laws which bind
up their existence, and that eternal being who made & bound them
up by these laws.

At the core of this letter, beneath the charming skein of its conceit—
whatever Jefferson's real relations with Mrs. Cosway—we see that there is
no serious way in which even his excited Heart can compete for Jefferson's
attention with his Head. Nothing in Jefferson is so intimate as his discreet,
idyllic picture of himself and Maria Cosway in the Virginia of the *Notes*.
However much he was under the sway of his feelings—however powerful
a moment he gave to his Heart—Jefferson once again showed the limits of
the personal in his vision of life. It is important to consider whether the
limit he imposed on passion did not implicitly address Madison's view of
self-interest.

4.

Fortified by some acquaintance with Jefferson's life and times, one can read
his writings with an enormous sense of discovery and delight. They offer
pleasures intensely political and intellectual and only mildly personal.
There are also frustrations. His mind seems to change, and the consistency
of his particular views is hard to track. There clings to him a quality of elu-
siveness. It is always chastening to feel how little of his private self Jefferson
felt a person need advance in order to advance the causes of freedom and
enlightenment. There is also that annoying Jeffersonian utilitarianism:
everything turns to account, all of life has lessons, duties, mottoes, and
above all, uses. The moral and the useful and the virtuous and the ener-
getic, the wise, and the studious can spoil the fun. There are times when
the reader longs for a sense of the romantic emotionalism of the nineteenth
century or merely wonders whether the only proper reaction to the Old
World is to resist its corruptions in the name of the New. Jefferson's prose
sometimes seems to flow too freely. His facility enables him to escape too
effortlessly the confines that bedevil others.

Reading Jefferson, one can experience the trouble he gave those masters of the concrete and the consistent, Hamilton and Adams, and appreciate how his subtle tolerance for contingency might drive a literalist like
John Randolph of Roanoke madder; no wonder Randolph called him
"St. Thomas of Cantingbury." Jefferson was so damnably blithe and sure.
It is not difficult to imagine how irritating it might have been for Madison,
so serious and so alert to argument and to the tug of the real and practical in

thought and ideal, to hear even Jefferson's softened critique of his Constitution. One feels it all the time. Jefferson was too versatile, gifted with too optimistic a philosophic temper. Look at all he missed. And yet Madison could not resist him and neither can we. Jefferson flew higher than most of his peers. If he lacked the extraordinary grip on the political past of an Adams, on the political present of a Hamilton, and on the political future of a Madison, who understood better than he what they were doing, from the writing of the Declaration on?

It was Jefferson who gave voice in writing to the terms of American nationality. Jefferson belongs in the tradition of American literature because American literature was concerned with the same ideas as American political theory. His political visions are the bridge (man-made and not "natural") between those falsely separate traditions. Reading Jefferson should be preliminary to reading the American writers who came after him. To go from Edwards to Emerson does not make sense. The literary descent from Mather to Franklin to Jefferson to Emerson makes as much sense as the line from Mather to Edwards to Emerson. Newton inspired Franklin *and* Edwards *and* Jefferson. Americanists should attend to what Americans made of the wisdom of the ages and the wisdom of their times. Jefferson made the most complete republican American synthesis and mastered democracy first as well, amazingly at the same time. The very inconclusiveness of much of his work has made it possible for him to inspire the American generations. Jefferson's sense of the limits of the human imagination suggested to him that human reason be consoled for its limits by the classics, with their spirit of calming resignation and that keen sense of public duty connecting the individual to society. This was not the conclusion to which Emerson was drawn. It is worth restoring to the history of American letters, however. Jefferson has been the subject of much good American writing, but his political visions rather than his character have been the subject of the best. In addition to the Gettysburg Address, the political literature of the United States addresses Jefferson, whether that of Frederick Douglass, Elizabeth Cady Stanton, or W. E. B. DuBois and other figures of liberation, or of Calhoun, Henry Adams, Albert Jay Nock, or other conservative critics of the tendencies of American democracy.

Jefferson's real rival is not Emerson, it is not even Hamilton. It is Madison, whose standing as the favorite founder among the intellectual classes has deservedly grown. Madison and Jefferson understood each other as allies, and their partnership will survive other people's partisanship regarding them.[15] But there is a sense that the Madisonian grasp of what is difficult and unyielding in the world and his tough-minded arrangements for a republican future please us now more than that Jeffersonian vagueness in the middle distance. Selfishness makes a lot more sense than happiness. That peculiarly Jeffersonian fiction, the vision of the American future, the pastoral of the American democratic republic, supplied the imaginative grounds of faith in the republic. The Jeffersonian political imagination generated notions of freedom of expression, notions with which Jefferson himself did not always keep pace. He emphasized the value of the practical (but not the material), the connection between philosophy and the common life, and the responsibilities of the highest human types to the activities and purposes of the republic and its ordinary citizens. The Jeffersonian vision appeals to the person who has the luxury of looking beyond self-interest, and it continues to appeal to those who think of themselves in any era as Jefferson's natural aristocrats. And oddly enough, it has worked as Jefferson hoped and Adams and Madison dared not hope: it has helped bind those people to the democratic republic. The care with which Jefferson invested both the ordinary and the superior person with a role in a free and enlightened future is his companion piece to Madison's harder-headed political thinking. Jefferson's writings envision the connections between the highest human qualities, the ones the analysis in *The Federalist*, no. 10, leaves out, and the republic. The republic will always need more than the metabolic luck of a system of dispersed human self-interest to survive.

Jefferson in mid-twentieth-century America was the patron saint of the literary and educated classes. In April of 1962, John Kennedy welcomed the nation's leading writers and intellectuals to a White House reception honoring American Nobel prize winners by remarking: "I think this is the most extraordinary collection of talent, of human knowledge, that has ever been gathered together at the White House, with the possible exception of when Thomas Jefferson dined alone." Jefferson was important in an era when the revival of "disinterested" expertise and the self-conscious attempt to reverse what Richard Hofstadter called American "anti-intellectualism" was at its height. But it was Jefferson's private array of accomplishments, as much as the fate of his political visions, that was at stake.

Despite Jefferson's emergence as a *bête blanc* of American history during those same years, the view of Jefferson as the talented, cultivated, versatile genius has transformed him once again. Now Jefferson might be said to have become the patron of the high-toned American lifestyle. The classes who are "serious" about their wine, cars, houses, editions, education, possessions—foodies and yuppies and so forth—can and do claim Jefferson. The J. Peterman catalogue's first big item was its Jefferson shirt, and a look at the catalogue from Monticello[16] confirms one's sense that Jefferson is once again being taken up so that Americans can come to grips with a new phenomenon. This appears to be the gaining of a version of the luxury, the leisure from physical labor, and the education that Jefferson so exceptionally enjoyed. It will be interesting to see whether Americans of this sort discover in the tasteful abundance of material privilege anything like Jefferson's own understanding of the true importance of such privilege. It is another one of those Jeffersonian political visions that expresses the terms on which Americans struggle with the contradictions of a regime founded on individual freedom and equality, in which materialism is an ingenious strategy to extend the life of free institutions by begging the question of human meaning. That this is Jefferson country is emphasized by one of the brutal facts of his own life. Others of Jefferson's class emancipated their slaves in their wills, even John Randolph of Roanoke. Jefferson did not, and the determining reason seems to be that he could not afford to do so. His slaves in effect financed his "lifestyle," including his matchless libraries, Monticello, and his wonderful things; they paid with their freedom for his genius.

The words of Jefferson's most important political visions abide, however. Robert Frost's "The Black Cottage" speaks of Jefferson's public legacy of these words. It is a long and wonderful poem, well worth reading for itself. It was published in Frost's celebrated 1915 collection *North of Boston*.[17] The following lines are part of an account given by a minister who is telling the poet about the black cottage they pass in their rambling and especially the old woman who had lived there. She lost her father and brothers in the Civil War, and the minister is explaining what she thought the war was about, not union or slavery, but:

> She wouldn't have believed those ends enough
> To have given outright all she gave.
> Her giving somehow touched the principle
> That all men are created free and equal.
>
> And to hear her quaint phrases—so removed
> From the world's view today of all those things.
> That's a hard mystery of Jefferson's.
> What did he mean? Of course the easy way
> Is to decide it simply isn't true.
> It may not be. I heard a fellow say so.
> But never mind, the Welshman got it planted where it will trouble us
>   a thousand years.
> Each age will have to reconsider it.

The key to Jefferson's political theory resides in these echoing sentences. Important as it remains to parse his thinking and make his views into the kind of systematic account he did not, this must not obscure what Frost recognized, their hard, abiding mystery.

In his last letter, written on 24 June 1826 to Roger C. Weightman, Jefferson apotheosized his authorship.[18] His subject was the approaching celebration of the fiftieth anniversary of the signing of the Declaration of Independence:

May it be to the world, what I believe it will be, (to some parts sooner, to others later, but finally to all,) the signal of arousing men to burst the chains under which monkish ignorance and superstition had persuaded them to bind themselves, and to assume the blessings and security of self-government. That form we have substituted, restores the free right to the unbounded exercise of reason and freedom in opinion. All eyes are opened, or opening, to the rights of man. The general spread of the light of science has already laid open to every view the palpable truth, that the mass of mankind has not been born with the saddles on their back, nor a favored few booted and spurred, ready to ride legitimately, by the Grace of God. These are the grounds of hope for others. For ourselves, let the annual return of this day forever refresh our recollections of these rights, and an undiminished devotion to them.

Jefferson created a masterwork of the imagination in his successive expressions of the terms on which life in the United States might be enjoyed. Perhaps it takes a great writer, like Lincoln or Frost, to remind us of the power and interest of Jefferson's own manner of political philosophizing. He envisioned the terms in which Americans might think through the contending principles of the republic in sentences that have troubled us for more than two hundred years. If the day ever comes when they cease to trouble us, that day will mark the end of the American experiment.

NOTES

This essay includes material that was previously published as "Thomas Jefferson as a Man of Letters," in *Jefferson: A Reference Biography*, ed. Merrill D. Peterson (New York: Scribner's, 1986), 181–98. Substantially revised, it still reflects my great debt to Merrill Peterson, who gave me the opportunity to write about Jefferson in this way and whose own writings have taught me so much. Helena Wall, Professor of History at Ponoma College, gave me characteristically heartening and steadying advice while I was writing this essay.

1. See "Franklin and Jefferson: Before the Democratic Fact," in Robert Dawidoff, "*History . . . but*" *and Other Essays* (forthcoming from Temple University Press in 1999).

2. Robert Lawson, *Ben and Me: A New and Astonishing Life of Benjamin Franklin As Written by His Good Mouse Amos* (Boston: Little Brown, 1939).

3. Vincent Sheehan, *Thomas Jefferson: Father of Democracy* (New York: Random House "Landmark Book," 1953).

4. *The Howards of Virginia*, Columbia Pictures, 1940. Directed by Frank Lloyd, screenplay by Sidney Buchman based on the novel *The Tree of Liberty* by Elizabeth Page.

5. Merrill D. Peterson's *The Jefferson Image in the American Mind* (New York: Oxford University Press, 1962) remains an indispensable guide to Jefferson's American history and shows how Jefferson's words were used and his spirit invoked by Americans in every generation and from almost every point of view to justify a confusing welter of causes. In this sense, Jefferson amounts almost to an authenticating stamp of the American character.

6. Michael P. Zuckert, *The Natural Rights Republic: Studies in the Foundation of the American Political Tradition* (Notre Dame, Ind.: University of Notre Dame Press, 1996), 1. Zuckert presents this in passing as Jefferson's own view.

7. Robert C. Lautman's remarkable photographs of Monticello convey an invaluable sense of Jefferson's life at home. *Thomas Jefferson's Monticello: A Photographic Portrait* (New York: Monacelli Press in cooperation with the Thomas Jefferson Memorial Foundation, 1997). I am grateful to Jamie Wolf for introducing me to these splendid pictures.

8. Thomas Jefferson to David Rittenhouse, July 19, 1778, in Thomas Jefferson, *Writings*, ed. Merrill D. Peterson, Library of America (New York: Literary Classics of the U.S., 1984), 763.

9. "Thoughts on Prosody" (October 1786), *Writings*, 593–622.

10. One thinks of the story about the time Calhoun wanted to write a love poem but gave up after he was unable to think of any other way to begin it except "whereas . . ."

11. *Writings*, 123–325.

12. Jefferson used this last phrase to describe the Missouri Compromise: "This momentous question, like a fire-bell in the night, awakened and filled me with terror. I considered it at once as the knell of the Union. It is hushed, indeed, for the moment. But this is a reprieve only, not a final sentence." Jefferson to John Holmes, 22 April 1820, *Writings*, 1433–35.

13. This reading of Jefferson comes from an observation David Brion Davis made in passing in a graduate seminar at Cornell, and must stand for the many ways in which his profound understanding of American intellectual history charted the course of my own smaller efforts. Neil Hertz let me attend his seminar at Cornell on the sublime and encouraged me to think about these issues in this way.

14. *Writings*, 866–77.

15. See *The Republic of Letters: The Correspondence between Thomas Jefferson and James Madison 1776–1826*, ed. James Morton Smith (New York: W. W. Norton, 1995).

16. This is not a criticism of the way Monticello is administered. On the contrary, those who care about Jefferson owe Daniel P. Jordan and his staff a debt of gratitude for the way in which they have restored the complexity and variety of Thomas Jefferson to Monticello.

17. Robert Frost, "The Black Cottage," reprinted in Frost, *Collected Poems, Prose, & Plays* (New York: Library of America, 1995), 59–62. I owe my appreciation of this poem to Robert Mezey.

18. *Writings*, 1516–17.

5

Mythologies of a Founder

٭

ROBERT BOOTH FOWLER

In his fine book *The Natural Rights Republic*, based on his Frank M. Covey, Jr., lectures at Loyola University Chicago, Michael Zuckert leads his readers to an appreciation of the intellectual dimensions of the founding of the United States. As Zuckert observes, the founders combined multiple sides of American political thought, including constitutionalism, the theory of natural rights, republicanism, and religious ideas, in a special way to forge the philosophical underpinnings of our nation.[1] Zuckert recognizes that Thomas Jefferson was a figure of undoubted significance in the process, one who is well worth continued efforts to understand his insights and his contributions. I share this judgment and in this spirit offer my own Mr. Jefferson, his political thought, and what I suspect are its foundations.

1. The Fallen Hero

The truth about Thomas Jefferson today is that his image as a founder—and as a person—is in steep decline. His reputation as a political philosopher, moreover, remains modest. While his political thought (or some of his political thoughts) are as popular and perhaps as influential as ever, there is little agreement among scholars with Michael Zuckert's view that Jefferson's political thought was especially creative. The opposite is true, which is just why Jefferson has been so influential. Jefferson was not especially philosophical or creative or unique as a political thinker—and he did not claim to be—but he was a master of uncommonly effective expression of common American ideas, ideas that have changed the world.

In the American pantheon Thomas Jefferson has occupied a place larger than life. This is evident not only on Mt. Rushmore but especially in the serenely beautiful Jefferson Memorial in the nation's capital. Millions each year sightsee in Washington and view the larger-than-life statue of Jefferson at his Memorial. There he stands in his full dignity, surrounded by selections from his political writings that soar above his statue.

As a self-declared Jeffersonian democrat (and Democrat), President Franklin D. Roosevelt dedicated the Jefferson Memorial in 1943. There was a considerable irony in the event, in that FDR by then was no advocate of small government, which was integral to what it meant to be a Jeffersonian and a Jeffersonian democrat (and Democrat). The construction of the Jefferson Memorial did make sense in that era, however, given Jefferson's prominence in the American civic religion. He was as great a figure then as Washington or Lincoln. Some, such as Joseph Ellis in his recent biography, *American Sphinx*, argue that little has changed in recent years. A certain Jefferson remains firmly ensconced in the pantheon of sacred heroes in the United States.[2] In fact, though, a lot has changed. Indeed, I doubt whether the Jefferson Memorial would be built today.

Sanford Levinson has ably explored some of the intriguing meanings of memorials, flags, and other cultural artifacts that exist in this and every age, in this and every land.[3] He recognizes their powerful role in the "realities" people seek to construct or maintain. His analysis helps explain the creation of the Jefferson Memorial, erected during the United States' fight for American democracy and freedoms in World War II. It was a cultural affirmation of these values by honoring a hero from the past who was portrayed as a great exemplar of them.

The monuments to Stalin that have come down in recent years in Eastern Europe mark the fall of a former hero and the fall of the values the hero supposedly embodied. The situation with Jefferson, however, is different. The values celebrated by the Jefferson Memorial have not lost their cultural credibility. What has changed is the confidence that Jefferson is a fitting representative of them. Put another way, Jefferson has fallen victim to contemporary perceptions that "we do indeed live by symbols . . . the tangible . . . marble depictions of those the culture wishes to honor," and in our fractious, cynical, and disillusioned age, "it can occasion no surprise that these symbols have become essentially contested."[4]

In this contest Jefferson's reputation has gone into a steep decline.[5] Despite his having a group of strong admirers, this fate is particularly obvious among intellectual arbiters of the Jeffersonian image, especially historians and political theorists. The consequent conflicts among public intellectuals and scholars in the course of this decline have been as numerous as they have been acrimonious.[6] While Jefferson's overall public standing does not yet seem to have fallen—the visitors to Monticello and the Jefferson Memorial do not decrease—long-run effects in the public eye may surely be expected.

Several observers of Jefferson's standing have traced the steps in his decline; they agree on the considerable contemporary sullying of Jefferson's image and acknowledge that "most recent scholarship on Jefferson . . . is skeptical and, indeed, often critical."[7] Treatments continue to vary somewhat, as reflected, for example, in Joseph Ellis's *American Sphinx: The Character of Thomas Jefferson*, Pauline Maier's *American Scripture: Making the Declaration of Independence*,[8] and Conor Cruise O'Brien's *The Long Affair: Thomas Jefferson and the French Revolution, 1785–1800*,[9] but the hagiographic treatment of Jefferson is now long gone. Even quite sympathetic contemporary considerations on Jefferson—as in Ellis's *American Sphinx*—are far from uncritical.

A crucial step in the decline of Jefferson's reputation came in Leonard Levy's *Jefferson and Civil Liberties: The Darker Side* (1963).[10] Indeed, Gordon Wood judges this work to be the most important opening modern salvo on Jefferson.[11] Levy's approach was not to indulge in nasty gossip about Jefferson. Instead, he relentlessly probed Jefferson's supposedly sterling record on civil liberties and civil rights, especially during his ill-fated presidency. When Levy was finished, he left no heroic Jefferson in his wake. While there have been other views, even recent ones, that are more appreciative of Jefferson's "statecraft" and more sympathetic about his circumstances, they cannot escape Levy's shadow.[12] Levy's open challenge of the author of the Declaration of Independence on his actual record of devotion to liberty left a lasting mark on Jefferson's image.

The 1992 conference, "Jeffersonian Legacies," at Jefferson's University of Virginia crystallized many of the contemporary disputes over Jefferson. In this setting, Jefferson was the object both of warm praise, and of scathing attacks that left no doubt that while "the Jeffersonian image is safely enshrined in the national memory,"[13] it is regarded by many scholars and intellectuals as hopelessly sullied.[14]

The critiques take almost an infinite number of directions. The most frequent ones fault Jefferson as a racist slaveholder. They sternly object to the Jefferson who so often has been celebrated as the herald of American liberty. They see a Jefferson who did oppose slavery in principle, but who always had slaves and depended on them, who held African Americans to be inferior to whites in many ways, and who freed only a handful of his slaves in his will.[15] On this subject the atmosphere is now pretty heated. Historian Paul Finkelman, for instance, castigates Jefferson as an appalling hypocrite on slavery whose convenient perfidy in practice to the antislavery cause he claimed to support was shown in his life. For Jefferson, "the time was never right" to make serious change.[16] Rogers Smith articulates a current orthodoxy when he also brands Jefferson a hypocrite who lived off slave labor, while piously affirming that slavery would and should end someday.[17]

Jefferson's views and practices toward women and Native Americans provide other opportunities for critical judgments about a freedom lover who in fact was not open to a really pluralist society.[18] Smith insists that signs of Jeffersonian concern with Indians are phony. They were merely a part of Jefferson's effort to defend everything American against Europe.[19] Historian Pauline Maier points to Jefferson's dismissal of women as potential citizens and what she considers his equally bad record regarding Native Americans.[20]

Jefferson's sexual behavior also falls under a harsh light. This sphere is, of course, a longtime critics' delight, since the identical charges of today circulated two hundred years ago in Jefferson's time. Critics suspect or simply assert that Jefferson abused his role as master, had sexual relations with some of his slaves, and thereby produced a number of children. Jefferson's denials often get little hearing here, just as do his claims of innocence of liaisons when he was Ambassador to Paris. Fawn Brodie's monument to speculation about Jefferson's sexual behavior, properly entitled *Thomas Jefferson: An Intimate History*, is the most famous example in point.[21] Her salacious treatment of the sexual Jefferson metamorphoses into a more temperate and less speculative form in Annette Gordon-Reed's recent *Thomas Jefferson and Sally Hemings: An American Controversy*.[22] Neither studies burnish Jefferson's image.

These kinds of discussions now regularly meld into broader discussions of Jefferson's psychology, which are often less than flattering. Fawn Brodie's portrayal of Jefferson as weak and dishonest is a notorious example. But it is now routine to suggest that Jefferson was not psychologically whole and to offer, as perfectly serious analyses of Jefferson's life, claims that the young, revolutionary Jefferson was a child in revolt against—whom else?—his mother. Even students sympathetic to Jefferson can be less than helpful when they suggest that Jefferson was at least sincere in all he did, which in less friendly hands means he was incapable of coming to terms psychologically with the contradictions between his life and his values.[23]

Some of the contemporary work on Jefferson concentrates on specialized scholarly analysis of aspects of his career, bypassing most of the more spectacular controversies—or at least not making them their centerpiece. These studies often make a serious contribution to a portion of the Jefferson story, for example, William Howard Adams in his *Paris Years of Thomas Jefferson*[24] and W. S. Randall in his *Thomas Jefferson: A Life*.[25] Other voices expend more effort trying to prop up the image of a fallen Jefferson. The most explicit work devoted to this cause is Thomas G. West's *Vindicating the Founders*. West and others argue that Jefferson believed all people had natural rights, including African Americans and Native Americans; they note Jefferson's consistent opposition to and "eloquent denunciations of slavery,"[26] and argue that Jefferson "refused to flinch before the stark contradiction between slavery" and his own values;[27] they recount Jefferson's faith in progress and therefore the future end of slavery in the United States; and they report his complex and active career that involved so many other good causes that should not now be forgotten.[28]

Another theme of Jefferson's defenders is the folly of the presentism that they judge infects much Jefferson criticism. They do not share the idea that it makes sense to apply moral standards of today to the past—for example, regarding the evil of association with slavery under any circumstances and for any reason. They pose the question: How can Jefferson be judged by our times and terms? The gap between his age and ours, they maintain, is simply too vast.[29]

Nor do defenders have much enthusiasm for what they often regard as an arrogant moralistic judgment of Jefferson that ignores the dilemmas of a real life, where it is easily conceivable that one may fall into traps not so different from Jefferson's when he found himself dependent on the slavery he opposed.[30] Some propose a Jefferson whose ambivalence and complexities (for example, Jefferson as "grieving optimist") make him more attractive than appalling and, in a manner, appropriate for our ambivalent and ironic contemporary age.[31] Still others deny the specific charges that float through the modern literature on Jefferson, such as the claim that he was a sexual libertine, whether in Paris or Monticello.[32]

Joseph Ellis, who is himself ambivalent about Jefferson in a number of ways, offers a different approach. In his psychological analysis he denies that Jefferson was a hypocrite. Jefferson, Ellis argues, allowed his personal optimism and idealism to blur the complexities and contradictions in his life. Ellis suggests this tendency was reinforced by Jefferson's desire to live a kind of courteous, genteel, and conflict-free existence both in his psyche and in his relations with others. This psychological orientation had its costs, Ellis agrees, but making Jefferson a self-conscious hypocrite was not one of them.[33]

2. The Fallen Philosopher

Few would approach Jefferson's political thought today without a sense of Jefferson's standing in the contemporary world of interpretation. To grasp Jefferson's ideas, one must understand how others perceive him.

Michael Zuckert is unusual in that he wants to approach Jefferson—and believes one can understand Jefferson—largely apart from such a discussion. The more vulgar and the more controversial historical disputes about Jefferson apparently do not interest him and, he implies, do not have much of anything to teach us about Jefferson and his thought.

Perhaps this is correct, but I do not think Jefferson can be taken seriously as a political philosopher in anything but the broadest possible conception of philosophy. Jefferson's thought had its greatest importance in the effects of such public documents as the Declaration of Independence, but it does not merit—nor would Jefferson want it to receive—much serious philosophical attention, examination, or analysis.[34] Jefferson was no philosopher even by the definition during his time, despite a sometime but puzzling inclination of some of his admirers to describe him as such.[35]

The significance of this observation needs emphasis in any discussion of Jefferson and his political ideas. Jefferson himself, it must be noted, was always clear that he wanted nothing to do with elaborate philosophical systems or theoretical analyses.[36] He was definitely among those who "distrusted the builders of complicated systems of thought and the glorifiers of abstractions,"[37] and he displayed little interest in the self-consciously philosophical side of the Enlightenment.[38] In good part this is why he could fairly boast that "I never submitted . . . my opinions to the creed of any party . . . whatever, in religion, in philosophy, in politics, or anything else."[39] In his mind, what Jefferson called his "whole system" of thought did not for a minute involve "a new philosophic conception," and with good reason.[40]

Some interpreters read Jefferson as a experientialist and thus not critical of the overly philosophical, schematic, or abstract. This was the fate of Plato, Jefferson's frequent target.[41] Others describe Jefferson's outlook as more "visionary" than experiential, but the conclusion regarding Jefferson's claim to be any kind of a philosopher is the same.[42] Thus it is not clear what value there is in approaching Jefferson's political ideas in a philosophical mode.

Zuckert's views of the nonsystematic, nonphilosophical Jefferson are rare, but one at least exists. It is evidenced in Zuckert's consideration of the origin of Jefferson's ideas. Zuckert understands that here, Jefferson was highly eclectic and "combined thoughts from various and often heterogeneous sources." Indeed, Zuckert joins the lively current debate over which thinkers and traditions had the greatest influence on Jefferson: the Whig tradition of England with its uneasiness regarding government authority, the John Locke so recognizable in the Declaration of Independence, the Scottish Enlightenment, Montesquieu, Adam Smith, Jefferson's own romantic dreams of a utopian society, or an even broader mix whose proportions are now lost forever.[43]

While there is little doubt about the eclectic and diverse range of sources for Jefferson's ideas, it does not follow, of course, that Jefferson's thought was either "very confused or very eclectic." Zuckert certainly warns us away from such a conclusion. He insists this view is quite wrong and argues that it stems from misunderstandings about how to read Jefferson. According to Zuckert, we must read Jefferson's writings with close attention to whom they were written, that is, their intended audience. Once one understands this, then it is possible to unlock the meaning of Jefferson's thought and appreciate its fundamental consistency.[44] At one level this injunction is merely common sense. At another level, it solves little because it forces the texts to disappear into the interpreter's understanding of Jefferson's purpose in writing to different audiences. It does not make the text sovereign at all; it places a speculative interpreter in the role of sovereign.

From some perspectives, there may be no escape from this act of interpretation, but it should induce caution about confidence that one can somehow find the "true" Jeffersonian political ideas by steadily factoring in his intended audience.[45] In fact, this method works only if one is already quite confident of some essential Jefferson. As I shall argue, while Jefferson's political ideas do not deserve dismissal as a mishmash, they hardly constitute a tight, consistent philosophy that somehow a correct reading of Jefferson, his texts, and their audiences can reveal.

3. "The Natural Rights Republic" and the Domesticated Jefferson

While Jefferson may not have been or wanted to be a philosopher, he certainly had plenty of political ideas, drawn from a number of sources. His ideas did amount to a discernable political outlook whose main elements have rarely been in significant dispute. Much more controversial is the priority that Jefferson gave to each of the elements in his political perspective. Michael Zuckert's argument is that Jefferson was a proponent of a "natural rights republicanism," a creative political view in which Jefferson's famous affection for decentralized local government was a prominent feature.[46]

This formulation is plausible as a description of Jefferson's overall political inclinations, though there are others. And it is important to make clear, as Zuckert does, that the term "natural rights republican," while the most felicitous way to express Jefferson's allegiance, can mislead. Jefferson's first loyalty was to natural rights, as revealed, Zuckert points out, in Jefferson's own choice of a legacy: the Declaration of Independence and the Virginia statute for religious freedom. Yet the republican side was also vital for Jefferson, since "no American was more committed to republicanism than Jefferson."[47]

Far more controversial are the claims advanced by Professor Zuckert that Jefferson's views are a unique contribution and that "Jefferson pondered republicanism more seriously than any other American of his age."[48] One may agree that Jefferson was no classical republican in some fifth century BCE sense. In fact, Jefferson did not focus on the classical political world, though he loved aspects of its architecture, arts, and literature. Monticello itself testifies to his affection for aspects of the classical Roman and Greek worlds.[49] Yet, as Zuckert asserts, this did not mean Jefferson was especially interested in classical political philosophies or forms.[50]

This matter aside, however, there is scant discussion by Jefferson of republicanism and even less that is somehow a special contribution. Much of what Jefferson says on the subject is clearly hortatory and nothing more.[51] Much suggests Jefferson's affection for a more democratic and egalitarian republicanism than Zuckert describes. Thus, it is just at this point that the natural rights republican understanding of Jefferson becomes problematic. It drastically domesticates or conservatizes Jefferson, tearing away what many others discern as Jefferson's radical and communitarian democratic program.

Zuckert's view here contrasts with the interpretation of Gordon Wood, the leading contemporary historian of the revolutionary and founding era. Gordon places great emphasis on the radical democratic and communitarian elements of the American Revolution, and he portrays Jefferson as a major voice for these views.[52] Zuckert disagrees, challenging Wood's claim that American republicanism was highly communitarian. Zuckert's understanding of Jeffersonian republicanism concentrates on political community, but not on a broader and more intense societal community as well.[53]

The basic issue is how much Zuckert is willing to acknowledge Jefferson's deep commitment to pervasive community as well as Jefferson's affinity for a high degree of direct democracy. Although Zuckert does not acknowledge this Jefferson, many others do.[54] Zuckert bases his case primarily on the Declaration of Independence and interprets it to show scant commitment by Jefferson to democracy or radically equal political power.[55] For Zuckert the Declaration of Independence "yields up an essentially Lockean teaching," which affirms natural rights, but not any radical or community-oriented society.[56]

For Jefferson, however, popular participation, rule, and control were essential to a proper outlook—"his commitment to democratic politics was firm and enduring"[57]—and this is why Jefferson supported a host of strongly democratic ideas and measures to ensure that government was as close to the people as possible, including public election of judges, a free press, and annual terms for officeholders. The list is long, but its existence is crucial. It is the practical evidence (something that matters to Jefferson) of his commitment to a radical democracy.[58]

Yes, Jefferson recognized the dangers posed by a corrupted human nature, whether the corruption came from Europe or from bad leaders. But far more than most of Jefferson's fellow "republicans," Jefferson was a democrat. He did indeed have an authentic "faith in the people."[59] He rarely doubted that "the good sense of the people will always be found to be the best army."[60] Jefferson meant it when he said, "I consider the people who constitute a society or nation as the source of all authority in the nation," and he was absolutely confident that "no government can continue good but under the control of the people."[61] Gordon Wood best defends the spirit of Jefferson, despite Jefferson's warts, by observing that Jefferson above all championed democratic commitment to the people. Wood contrasts Jefferson with Madison, who lacked this commitment, and Wood concludes that this "is why we remember Jefferson, and not Madison."[62]

4. Jefferson and Natural Rights

Jefferson's profound interest in nature is justly famous. His breadth of interest ranged from human nature to nature in the wild or in the gardens on his plantation. Jefferson's fascination with nature was more empirical than romantic. His careful, descriptive garden books, rather than any romantic poetry of nature, characterize his interest.[63] Jefferson strove to understand nature rationally and to organize and classify it.[64] This enterprise was a life-long journey for Jefferson. In its course, he was often able to distinguish the conventional and the natural so that nature was not simply reducible to his prejudices.

Perhaps this ability was present when Jefferson argued that there was no right to property in nature.[65] At other junctures, like many other celebrants of "nature," Jefferson constructed a nature that embodied his values and employed it as a force against much in his own society—and many other societies—that he disliked. He was, for example, especially fond of aligning the "natural" human mind and its "natural" development with his preferences in this pleasant, self-justifying manner.[66]

Obviously, in the context of his political thought, the topic of Jefferson and nature quickly leads us to Jefferson's doctrine of natural rights, which, as has long been clear, follows John Locke. Indeed, over the course of his

long career, Jefferson repeatedly identified Locke as his most highly rec-
ommended political theorist, and he followed his own advice with that
part of his political thought that addressed natural rights.[67]

In his discussions of Jefferson and nature, Zuckert makes the case that
Jefferson had a fairly complex understanding of nature and its connec-
tion with rights. Once again, Zuckert relies on Jefferson's Declaration of
Independence, and also on his most thoughtful, sustained piece of writing,
"Notes on the State of Virginia," to make his argument. While Profes-
sor Zuckert's view is hardly self-evident, it shows how much a skilled an-
alyst can get from the works of the only faintly politically philosophical
Jefferson.

In particular Zuckert contends that Jefferson's rather complex understanding of nature had little to do with simple-minded worship of nature.
Jefferson conceived of nature as deeply intertwined with issues of security
as well as with truth and rights. Jefferson's nature offered great security in
one sense, but it could also threaten human security, and thus was no un-
qualified good in Jefferson's vision. After all, the argument goes, Jefferson
realized that the natural passions of human beings could be dangerously
selfish. While he was no skeptic of people to the degree that James Madison was, he knew about excessive human selfishness.

Yet nature also could and did assist people to overcome this unfortunate side of itself, according to Zuckert, by helping them create a secure
world within the context of the natural. The key instrument was the ac-
knowledgment and enforcement of another and good part of nature: natural rights, so dramatically affirmed by Jefferson in the Declaration of
Independence.[68] Thus, natural rights were not only true for Jefferson but
were essential for the realization of nature at its best. One might suggest
that this is why, from the beginning to the end of his life, Jefferson insisted that "nothing then is unchangeable but the inherent and unalien-
able rights of man."[69]

While skeptics may well wonder if this Jefferson on nature does not
sometimes confuse Thomas Jefferson with Thomas Hobbes, Zuckert's
consideration of Jefferson and natural rights does slay several dragons
whose death should not be mourned. Thus, Zuckert deals firmly with the
bizarre analysis of Morton White that Jefferson's Declaration of Independence must be understood within the framework of the obscure European
theorist Jacques Burlamaqui.[70] As Zuckert observes, there simply is no
evidence for this supposition.[71] Zuckert shows an equal disinterest in
Garry Wills's determined effort to make Jefferson and his Declaration of
Independence an expression of the Scottish Enlightenment.[72] Much of
Zuckert's objection to Wills's reading of Jefferson proceeds from his correct suspicion that Wills wants to promote a radically egalitarian Jefferson,
which, as we know, Zuckert decidedly does not.[73]

Zuckert, however, offers his own controversial interpretations of Jefferson and natural rights. "We hold these truths to be self-evident," for example, might seem to be a straightforward proclamation of the fundamental and universal truth of the natural rights proclaimed in the Declaration of Independence, but Zuckert's reading is quite different. He argues that this phrase means "truths" understood as what is appropriate within the practice of a given society. "We" becomes the key word, and it means the "we" of each particular culture. This interpretation fits nicely with Professor Zuckert's broader objective of domesticating Jefferson and stripping his doctrine of natural rights of its radical, universal edge. The problem in my view is that this edge is exactly what Jefferson sought and meant regarding his natural rights. They applied to any and every society and were universal truths, which is why Jefferson supported natural rights so strongly.[74] Any other view of his position would have stunned him.

Zuckert also argues that there is nothing "self-evident" about Jefferson's natural rights and that he did not mean there to be. After all, if natural rights are not actually universal but conceived in terms of a given culture's understanding, they can hardly be self-evident in some universal sense. Thus "the language, the logic, and the historic connections of the Declaration all point to the same conclusion: the truths announced in the Declaration are not self-evident, nor are they pronounced to be."[75] Once again, the problem is that Jefferson in the Declaration does not agree. Jefferson did not want his truths domesticated; he self-consciously proclaimed that they are "self-evident" to all humankind.

Jefferson can be fuzzy about rights. He sometimes speaks of group, or institutional, or—in the instance of his draft of the Kentucky Resolution—of states' rights as often as he asserts the existence of individual natural rights. The particular rights vary and so does his answer to whether all people have rights in theory (only the living?) or in practice (all people or just male farmers?). One way to resolve these conundrums is to suggest that Jefferson's thought about rights was always in process; another way is to suggest that Jefferson's views on rights pitched according to personal and political swells as does any ship.[76]

One of the best sides of Zuckert's Jefferson lies in his recognition that Jefferson had little spiritual or religious dimension to his conception of nature or natural rights (or anything else, for that matter).[77] This perspective is finally gaining hegemony, despite the efforts of some analysts and, more recently, of particular political activists somehow to transform all the founders into exemplars of Christian piety. In Jefferson's case the issue is not whether he was a Christian (he was not), but whether he was spiritual in any recognizable manner (he was not). Despite some efforts to find a different Jefferson, the truth is that he was tone deaf to the spiritual in life. Jefferson claimed his natural rights position was "supported by faith in a benevolent God whose design had made the claims of individual men harmonious."[78] But Jefferson's commitment to such a view was at best perfunctory.

Zuckert is anxious to separate rights and religion in American history and especially at the founding. He cites his fellow neo-Straussian Thomas Pangle as an authority and insists that "rights are a terrible stumbling block" for interpreters who want rights and religion to be firmly connected in the American story from the beginning. There was plenty of religion on the Mayflower and in the soul of John Winthrop, but there was no talk of rights there. The Pilgrims' famous original contract was between the people and God and not, like Jefferson's, among the citizens themselves.[79] The point here is that natural rights in the American colonial experience, for the founders and especially Jefferson, had little central connection with religion (and, implicitly, needed little connection).

This does not mean that Jefferson had no use for religion. According to Zuckert, Jefferson used religion in a Tocquevillian manner, that is, religion was vital as a restraint on liberty in order to preserve liberty. Perhaps there is a case to be made for a strain of Jeffersonian religion conceived for this purpose, yet he and Tocqueville are far apart here. Tocqueville did see religion in largely utilitarian terms. But because its social stabilizing role was important, he thought religion was absolutely central for U.S. society, a conviction Jefferson did not share.[80]

One major problem for all the efforts to grasp Jefferson as a natural rights thinker is that he was so highly eclectic in his political argument and justification. Certainly Jefferson made plenty of appeals to natural rights, as he also made abundant appeals to other bases for values, such as his radical democratic ethos. Moreover, Jefferson appealed to natural rights at least as often for their pragmatic advantages as for a deontological moral grounding. Indeed, his usual theme regarding natural rights was praise of their value due to the social and human benefits of their invocation.[81]

It is not really clear that Jefferson cared much about natural rights, except as a lever to promote his understanding of the good society. This is evident in all the famous Jefferson proclamations, and it casts doubt on the validity of dressing Jefferson largely in natural rights clothes. For instance, consider his "Act for Establishing Religious Freedom," first proposed in 1777 and adopted by Virginia in 1786, an act which meant the world to Jefferson. It defended religious freedom, but the question is why. The act defends religious liberty because of its social benefits: helping truth triumph, lowering the cost of government (regulating religions), and the like. The heart of his argument is utilitarian.[82]

This is exactly why Jefferson has so much to say about education—much more than he does about natural rights. As is well understood,

Jefferson thought education was the way to achieve the social advancement and general happiness (as he understood both) that he as a kind of nonphilosophical utilitarian so sincerely sought. Natural rights were not the issue. Education was needed, Jefferson fondly believed, because it could make such a difference in the practical terms that moved him.[83]

5. The Pragmatic Jefferson

Despite his grand declarations of principle, Jefferson was quite often more a pragmatist as a thinker and as a politician than anything else. This is a Jefferson that merits emphasis. Jefferson engaged in a lifetime of political maneuvering and manipulation, and he was often quite successful in these activities. This Jefferson does provide evidence for Zuckert's view that the Jeffersonian audience must be understood before Jefferson's arguments are taken too seriously on their own terms. Thus, Jefferson's strenuous critiques of the Alien and Sedition Acts mostly took the form of complaints that they violated the Constitution, not natural rights. Jefferson made this argument recognizing its pragmatic and broader appeal. It certainly was no monument to his consistency, given his long-term skepticism of constitutions, including that of the United States.[84]

Jefferson's pragmatic disposition was, in fact, integral to his political thought. He was also a pragmatist in other areas of his life. This was most famously—or notoriously—true in his self-conscious choice to own and live off slaves in denial of his natural rights philosophy. This situation painfully but fairly illustrates why one must look closely at Jefferson's life to grasp his basic thought.[85] Jefferson was also a self-conscious pragmatist of sorts in that he held that life experience was ultimately the basis for every individual's and every society's best development. Thus, what Jefferson actually offered in his political and social thought was no "new philosophic conception," but rather an informal and experience-tested outlook, an approach that he thought inescapable.[86]

In all this Jefferson of course affirmed the importance of empirical reason and the growth of science in good Enlightenment fashion. Empirical reason was his epistemology. Yet matters are more complicated here than they may at first appear. Zuckert rightly observes that Jefferson was not fully "the Enlightenment rationalist he is most often taken to be" and his epistemology cannot really be summed up as "pursuit of reason."[87] For when it came to morality, it was "moral instinct," as Jefferson put it, that was central to understanding of human beings and human life. It was hardly just another function or dimension of reason. Feelings and desires and intimations mattered greatly to Jefferson and his moral and political vision.[88]

6. The Epicurean Jefferson

Michael Zuckert perceives very well that nature was not the ground of all Jefferson's thought, though he does not think the pragmatic Jefferson was dominant either. He argues that for Jefferson nature "is not unequivocally the home of natural rights" and it cannot be, since Jefferson opts for civilization over a natural state of existence.[89] As Zuckert puts it, for Jefferson it is only in social life that people develop their natural rights fully and recognize and honor those rights in all that they have perceived in themselves from the start.[90]

I want to argue, though, that all earnest discussion of Jefferson and natural rights, republicanism, and democracy speaks only to one, albeit central, side of Jefferson's outlook regarding politics and society. This dimension receives far too much discussion from politically-oriented intellectuals and has for a long time. It results in a much too political Jefferson, and it miscasts Jefferson as a political thinker above all else. There is another side to Jefferson, a dimension of equal or greater importance, and it is Jefferson's Epicureanism. "I too am an Epicurean," Jefferson wrote. [91] This Jefferson may not be ignored, and he matters enormously in terms of Jefferson's political thought.

Jefferson's Epicureanism included such "philosophical" positions as materialism and such personal attitudes as deep respect for those who achieved balance in their lives as well as a yearning for balance in his own life, in which he was, indeed, an Epicurean "grieving optimist."[92] Above all, though, Jefferson's Epicureanism was about how to live life. What Jefferson had in mind—and what he sometimes succeeded in practicing—were the lessons of Epicurus, the master, on the value of a good existence lived out of the public eye in the quiet of one's mental and spatial garden.[93] It was certainly what lay behind what an unfriendly voice terms his "obsessive concerns with privacy."[94] This Jefferson did not focus on natural rights, pragmatism, republicanism, or democracy, though he supported and practiced each of them also.

The idea that Jefferson was an Epicurean in this sense obviously clashes with Jefferson's long and active political career. Although the Epicurean side has been neglected, it has attracted attention in some quarters, usually in the form of disapproval, such as pointing out Jefferson's "reclusive pattern of behavior."[95] The truth is that the Epicurean Jefferson constantly sought relief from his political undertakings and returned to Monticello and his Epicurean garden again and again with the greatest joy. There is no denying that he was involved in politics and that he wanted to be, nor that he was a busy political thinker and that he wanted to be. But at the same time, Jefferson's Epicureanism showed in the many other activities that gave him intense pleasure and were important to him because they gave him that pleasure. Jefferson was just as multidimensional as most portraits describe him.[96] After all, there was Jefferson the bibliophile, architect, inventor, wine connoisseur, student of coins and coinages, European capitals, the gardens of England, walnut trees, and ploughs; expert in elevators, patents, and standards of weights and measures. The list knows no end.

This was a man for whom there were pleasures to be found everywhere in the natural and human worlds, and he reached out to enjoy a great many of them.[97] One of the most important expressions of this Jefferson was his devotion to friendship and to his friends, to whom he wrote innumerable letters. As with Epicurus in his garden, so for Jefferson his friends (often through the mail) were fundamental to his untiring pursuit of happiness. The pleasure was distinctly mutual, since Jefferson was "an engaging and considerate friend," just as he wanted to be.[98]

Looking at Jefferson as an Epicurean warns us away from too much stress on Jefferson as a political thinker—without denying this Jefferson either. It equally warns us away from expecting or believing we can encounter a Jefferson who was particularly philosophical. Jefferson was no professional political theorist or philosopher and had no interest in such roles. He was an Epicurean fascinated with innumerable aspects of life and the pleasures that he experienced with each. Politics, natural rights, education, republicanism, and all the rest were but the means to the Epicurean freedom required to pursue his (and others') chosen pleasures, desires, and life objectives. He called on these political values when he judged them helpful toward his Epicurean model, no more and no less.

Granted this Jefferson is not the only Jefferson. Far from it, though the Epicurean Jefferson's disposition was integral to the other Jeffersons. This understanding also leads us away from the idea that there is some "essential" Jefferson, which reduces all other dimensions of this fascinating figure to very little. The truth is that "the search for a single definitive, 'real' Jefferson is a fool's errand, a hopeless search."[99]

Such a view hardly denigrates Thomas Jefferson. It is not another effort to tear down the monuments to Jefferson. Rather, it is an attempt to help free Jefferson (and the Jeffersonian image) from the status of a monument—to be celebrated or attacked—and let him be what he was. Thomas Jefferson was an extraordinary but very real human being, in love with life and its endless dimensions, flawed as we all are, and always a restless, pragmatic, reflective, many-sided Epicurean.

NOTES

1. Michael P. Zuckert, *The Natural Rights Republic: Studies in the Foundation of the American Political Tradition* (Notre Dame, Ind.: University of Notre Dame Press, 1996).

2. Joseph J. Ellis, *American Sphinx: The Character of Thomas Jefferson* (New York: Knopf, 1997).

3. Sanford Levinson, "They Whisper: Reflections on Flags, Monuments, and State Holidays, and the Construction of Social Meaning in a Multicultural Society," *Chicago Kent Law Review* 70 (1995): 1079–1119.

4. Sanford Levinson, "Written in Stone: Public Monuments in Changing Societies," *Duke University Law Review* (1998): 82.

5. To a lesser extent, so has that of some other founders; see the discussion in Thomas G. West, *Vindicating the Founders: Race, Sex, Class, and Justice in the Origins of America* (Lanham, Md.: Rowman and Littlefield, 1997).

6. Scot A. French and Edward L. Ayers, "The Strange Career of Thomas Jefferson," in *Jeffersonian Legacies*, ed. Peter S. Onuf (Charlottesville: University Press of Virginia, 1993), 418–56.

7. Jan Lewis and Peter S. Onuf, "American Synecdoche: Thomas Jefferson as Image, Icon, Character, and Self," *American Historical Review* 103 (February 1988): 127. I thank my friend James Baughman for bringing this article to my attention.

8. Pauline Maier, *American Scripture: Making the Declaration of Independence* (New York: Knopf, 1997), introduction.

9. Conor Cruise O'Brien, *The Long Affair: Thomas Jefferson and the French Revolution, 1785–1800* (Chicago: University of Chicago Press, 1996).

10. Leonard Levy, *Jefferson and Civil Liberties: The Darker Side* (Cambridge: Harvard University Press, 1963).

11. Gordon S. Wood, "The Trials and Tribulations of Thomas Jefferson," in *Jeffersonian Legacies*, ed. Onuf, 395–417.

12. Robert W. Tucker, *Empire of Liberty: The Statecraft of Thomas Jefferson* (New York: Oxford University Press, 1990), or Forrest McDonald, *The Presidency of Thomas Jefferson* (Lawrence: University Press of Kansas, 1976).

13. Onuf, *Jeffersonian Legacies*, 23.

14. Ibid., prologue.

15. Some examples: Paul Finkelman, "Jefferson and Slavery," in Onuf, *Jeffersonian Legacies*, chap. 6; John Chester Miller, *The Wolf by the Ears: Thomas Jefferson and Slavery* (New York: Free Press, 1977), chap. 7; O'Brien, *The Long Affair*.

16. Finkelman, "Jefferson and Slavery."

17. Rogers Smith, *Civic Ideals: Conflicting Visions of Citizenship in U.S. History* (New Haven: Yale University Press, 1997), 105 and chap. 7.

18. Ellis, *American Sphinx*, 200–202.

19. Smith, *Civic Ideals*, 110.

20. Maier, *American Scripture*, 193, 197.

21. Fawn Brodie, *Thomas Jefferson: An Intimate History* (New York: Bantam, 1974).

22. Annette Gordon-Reed, *Thomas Jefferson and Sally Hemings: An American Controversy* (Charlottesville: University Press of Virginia, 1997).

23. This is the main defense, so to speak, offered by Ellis in *American Sphinx*.

24. William Howard Adams, *Paris Years of Thomas Jefferson* (New Haven: Yale University Press, 1997).

25. W. S. Randall, *Thomas Jefferson: A Life* (New York: Holt, 1993).

26. West, *Vindicating*, 175.

27. Ibid., 10.

28. Miller, *Wolf by the Ears*, 248, 122, and passim; West, *Vindicating*, 1–4, 30, and 72.

29. Ellis, *American Sphinx*, epilogue.

30. Ibid., 148–49.

31. Andrew Burstein, *The Inner Jefferson: Portrait of a Grieving Optimist* (Charlottesville: University Press of Virginia, 1995).

32. For example, see ibid., 93–97, and Miller, *Wolf by the Ears*, chaps. 20–21.

33. Ellis, *American Sphinx*, 86–89.

34. Some admirers reach this conclusion with apologies, but reach it firmly nonetheless. See, for example, James W. Ceasar's *Reconstructing America* (New Haven: Yale University Press, 1997).

35. Adrienne Koch, *Jefferson and Madison: the Great Collaboration* (New York: Oxford University Press, 1964).

36. Karl Lehmann, *Thomas Jefferson, American Humanist* (Chicago: University of Chicago Press, 1965), xii and 77.

37. Ibid., xii.

38. Ibid., 79.

39. Jefferson to Francis Hopkinson, March 13, 1789, in *The Political Writings of Thomas Jefferson*, ed. Edward Dumbauld (Indianapolis: Bobbs-Merrill, 1955), 46.

40. Daniel Boorstin, *The Lost World of Thomas Jefferson* (Boston: Beacon, 1948), 237.

41. Ibid.; Lehmann, *Thomas Jefferson*, 83–84.

42. Ellis, *American Sphinx*, 275.

43. Some places to look: Lehmann, *Thomas Jefferson*, 73; Ellis, *American Sphinx*, 42–43 and 58–59; Garry Wills, *Inventing America: Jefferson's Declaration of Independence* (New York: Doubleday, 1978).

44. Zuckert, *Natural Rights Republic*, 87–89.

45. Of course, in this proposed methodology, as elsewhere, Zuckert's fidelity to neo-Straussian tenets is evident.

46. Zuckert, *Natural Rights Republic*, chap. 7.

47. Ibid., 211.

48. Ibid.

49. Lehmann, *Thomas Jefferson*, chap. 4.

50. Zuckert, *Natural Rights Republic*, 212.

51. Consider, for example, Jefferson to Thomas Lomas, March 12, 1799, in Dumbauld, *Political Writings*, 78.

52. Gordon Wood, *The Creation of the American Republic* (Chapel Hill: University of North Carolina Press, 1969) and *The Radicalism of the American Revolution* (New York: Knopf, 1992).

53. Zuckert, *Natural Rights Republic*, 21–22 and 204–209.

54. The most vigorous effort to argue this in a position diametrically opposed to Zuckert may be found in Richard K. Matthews, *The Radical Politics of Thomas Jefferson* (Lawrence: University Press of Kansas, 1984).

55. Zuckert, *Natural Rights Republic*, 16–20 and 29–30.

56. Ibid., 16.

57. Michael Lienesch, "Thomas Jefferson and the American Democratic Experience," in Onuf, *Jeffersonian Legacies*, 318.

58. For example, ibid., 336; Jefferson to John Taylor, May 28, 1816, in Dumbauld, *Political Writings*, 51–53; Jefferson to Samuel Kercheval, July 12, 1816, in ibid., 118; also see Dumbauld, *Political Writings*, 101.

59. Dumbauld, *Political Writings*, xxxv.

60. Jefferson to Edward Carrington, January 16, 1787, in *Basic Writings of Thomas Jefferson*, ed. Philip S. Foner (New York: Wiley, 1944), 549–50.

61. "Cabinet Opinion," in Dumbauld, *Political Writings*, 79; Jefferson to John Adams, December 10, 1819, in Dumbauld, *Political Writings*, 92.

62. Wood, "Trials and Tribulations," 415.

63. Thomas Jefferson, *The Garden and Farm Books*, ed. Robert C. Baron (Golden, Colo.: Fulcrum, 1987).

64. Jefferson to Dr. John Manners, February 22, 1814, in Foner, *Basic Writings*, 726–29.

65. Matthews, *Radical Politics*, chap. 2.

66. Foner, *Basic Writings*, 675.

67. Jefferson to Bernard Moore, 1767, and to John Minor, August 1814, in ibid., 499–503.

68. Zuckert, *Natural Rights Republic*, 69–70.

69. Jefferson to John Cartwright, June 5, 1824, in Dumbauld, *Political Writings*, 126.

70. See Morton White, *The Philosophy of the American Revolution* (New York: Oxford University Press, 1981).

71. Zuckert, *Natural Rights Republic*, 34–40.

72. Wills, *Inventing America*.

73. Zuckert, *Natural Rights Republic*, 32–34.

74. Ibid., chap. 2.

75. Ibid., 49.

76. Stephen A. Conrad, "Putting Rights Talk in Its Place," in Onuf, *Jeffersonian Legacies*, chap. 8; Dumbauld, *Political Writings*, 156–62; Koch, *Jefferson and Madison*, chap. 4.

77. Paul K. Conklin, "The Religious Pilgrimage of Thomas Jefferson," in Onuf, *Jeffersonian Legacies*, 19–49.

78. Boorstin, *Lost World*, 245.

79. Zuckert, *Natural Rights Republic*, 132–46.

80. For Zuckert's view, ibid., 201; for a thorough and sympathetic religious biography of Jefferson, see Edwin A. Gaustad, *Sworn on the Altar of God: A Religious Biography of Thomas Jefferson* (Grand Rapids, Mich.: Eerdmans, 1996).

81. For example, see Thomas Jefferson, "Autobiography" 1821, in Foner, *Basic Writings*, 482.

82. Thomas Jefferson, "An Act for Establishing Religious Freedom," in *Thomas Jefferson: Selected Writings*, ed. Harvey Mansfield, Jr. (Arlington Heights, Ill.: Harlan Davidson, 1979), 13–15.

83. Jefferson to George Wythe, August 13, 1786, in Foner, *Basic Writings*, 534–35; Jefferson to Pierre Dupont, April 24, 1816, in Dumbauld, *Political Writings*, 50.

84. Jefferson to John Taylor, November 26, 1798, in Dumbauld, *Political Writings*, 155; Jefferson to Abigail Adams, September 11, 1804, in Foner, *Basic Writings*, 669–71.

85. Brodie, *Thomas Jefferson*, chaps. 2 and 3; Miller, *The Wolf by the Ears*, chap. 13.

86. See, for example, Boorstin, *Lost World*.

87. The first quote is Zuckert, *Natural Rights Republic*, 66, and the second is from the title of Noble E. Cunningham, *In Pursuit of Reason: The Life of Thomas Jefferson* (New York: Ballantine, 1988).

88. For example, see Jefferson to Thomas Low, June 3, 1814, in Mansfield, *Selected Writings*, 79–81.

89. Zuckert, *Natural Rights Republic*, 73.

90. Ibid., chap. 3 contains a full discussion of Zuckert's intriguing argument.

91. Jefferson to William Short, October 31, 1819, in Foner, *Basic Writings*, 764–66.

92. Lehmann, *Thomas Jefferson*, 141–42; Burstein, *The Inner Jefferson*.

93. Epicurus, *Letters, Principal Doctrines, and Vatican Sayings* (Indianapolis: Bobbs-Merrill, 1964).

94. Lewis and Onuf, "American Synecdoche," 133.

95. The quote is from Ellis, *American Sphinx*, 27; for another view, see Matthews, *Radical Politics*, 92.

96. Brodie, *Thomas Jefferson*.

97. Some relevant citations: Jefferson to George Watterson, May 7, 1815, in Foner, *Basic Writings*, 740–41; to John Taylor, December 29, 1794, Foner, 632–33; to Isaac McPherson, August 13, 1813, Foner, 708–14; to Dr. Robert Patterson, October 10, 1811, Foner, 694–701; "A Tour of Some of the Gardens of England 1786," Foner, 281–85; "Notes on the Establishment of a Money Unit and of a Coinage for the United States 1784," Foner, 194–203; "Memoranda Taken on a Journey from Paris into the Southern Parts of France, and Northern Parts of Italy, in the Year 1787," Foner, 240–81; "Memoranda on a Tour From Paris to Amsterdam, Strasbourg, and Back to Paris 1788," Foner, 285–309; Dumas Malone, "Forward," in Lehmann, *Thomas Jefferson*, vii–xiv.

98. Lewis and Onuf, "American Synecdoche," 134.

99. Ibid., 132.

6

Economics:
The Agrarian Republic

✻

JOYCE APPLEBY

Nineteen forty-three marked the two-hundredth anniversary of the birth of Thomas Jefferson and the occasion for bestowing yet another honor on the Sage of Monticello. Amid salutes to Jefferson's politics and philosophy, historians and agronomists seized the opportunity to herald his contributions to scientific agriculture. Quoting from Vice-President Henry A. Wallace, M. L. Wilson claimed that farmers identified Jefferson with "the application of science to agriculture," and he then admiringly listed Jefferson's scientific achievements: the invention of a threshing machine, the improvement of the plow, the introduction of Merino sheep, and the advocacy of soil conservation.[1] August C. Miller, Jr., called Jefferson the father of American democracy and "a scientific farmer and agriculturist in the most comprehensive sense" of the term.[2] On this bicentennial anniversary, according to A. Whitney Griswold, people paid tribute to Jefferson as "preeminently and above all a farmer." Noting that Jefferson's enthusiasm for farming had always included commerce, Griswold agreed with William D. Grampp that Jefferson's concern about marketing farm commodities had made him an ardent proponent of international free trade.[3] Thus, like the Department of Agriculture experts who gathered in the auditorium that bore his name, Jefferson in 1943 was depicted as an early-day New Dealer, a modernizer dedicated to helping ordinary farmers become efficient producers.

In 1955—just twelve years later—Richard Hofstadter published *The Age of Reform*, and Jefferson was captured for an altogether different historiographical tradition. Looking for the roots of the nostalgia that flowered with the Populists, Hofstadter described how Jefferson and other eighteenth-century writers had been drawn irresistibly to the "noncommercial, nonpecuniary, self-sufficient aspects of American farm life." The Jeffersonians, Hofstadter said, had created an "agrarian myth" and fashioned for the new nation a folk hero, the yeoman farmer, who was admired "not for his capacity to exploit opportunities and make money," but rather for his ability to produce a simple abundance. Underlining the mythic aspect of this literary creation, Hofstadter noted the actual profit orientation of the farmers who, he said, accepted the views of their social superiors as harmless flattery.[4]

The instantaneous popularity of Hofstadter's "agrarian myth" owes a good deal more to trends in the writing of history than to the evidentiary base upon which it rested. That, in fact, was very shaky. Hofstadter directed his readers to two writers, neither of whom drew the distinction he had made between the romantic myth of rural self-sufficiency created by writers and the reality of farming for profit acted upon by ordinary men. Griswold, whom Hofstadter claimed had produced "a full statement of the agrarian myth as it was formulated by Jefferson," in fact explored Jefferson's views on agricultural improvements and commercial expansion in order to point out that what had made sense in Jefferson's day no longer held true in the twentieth century.[5] The second writer to whom Hofstadter referred, Chester E. Eisinger, addressed Hofstadter's theme of national symbols, but his freehold concept can be readily differentiated from Hofstadter's agrarian myth. Tracing the appearance of independent freehold farmers to the destruction of feudal tenures, Eisinger explained how in England the same commercial forces that destroyed the manorial system had also worked to eliminate the small, freeholding producer. In America the reality of vacant land gave substance to a vision of a society of independent farmers; so the freehold concept, like so many other ideas, got a new lease on life by crossing the Atlantic. Where Hofstadter stressed the appeal of yeoman self-sufficiency, however, Eisinger linked the freehold concept to the emerging capitalistic economy. In the era of commercial agriculture, Eisinger wrote, "not only could a man possess his own farm, but he was his own master, rising and falling by his own efforts, bargaining in a free market."[6] Thus where Hofstadter's introductory chapter juxtaposed the agrarian myth and commercial realities, Eisinger distinguished between the poetic yearning for a bygone age of peasants and the modern reality of market-oriented farmers. All of Hofstadter's sources had traced the eighteenth-century literary preoccupation with farming to the rising population and the consequent importance of food production, but Hofstadter snapped this connection between material reality and intellectual response by stressing the purely mythic power of what two of his students have recently characterized as the ideal of "'the self-sufficient' yeoman dwelling in a rural arcadia of unspoiled virtue, honest toil and rude plenty."[7]

Without looking firsthand at the literature of the 1790s, Hofstadter wrote his thesis about the nostalgic politics of the Populist era back into the earlier period. His indifference to a time that provided only a backdrop to the central drama in the age of reform is understandable. Indeed, what sustained the attractiveness of the yeoman ideal was not Hofstadter's book but a much stronger tide coursing through scholarship on eighteenth-century America. As a quick survey of titles and expository prose produced in the last twenty years will reveal, *yeoman* has become a favorite designation for the ordinary farmer of postrevolutionary America. Losing its definition as a rank in a hierarchical society of tenants, yeoman, gentlemen, and lords, it has become instead a code word for a man of simple tastes, sturdy independence, and admirable disdain for all things newfangled. In this form the yeoman archetype has become particularly congruent with the recent work of social historians, who have sought to reconstruct the basic character and structure of colonial society.

Using continuous records on family formation and landholding patterns, these scholars have given special attention to the collective experience of whole communities. The models of the social scientists that they have employed, moreover, have encouraged them to look for the similarities between early American society and its counterpart in Europe. Where earlier historians had emphasized the idea of an America born free and modern, the new practitioners of social history have been more open to the possibility that America, too, had once been a traditional society. Indeed, they have found that, like traditional men and women of sociological theory, colonial Americans created the community solidarity and familial networks that encouraged resistance to change.[8] Instead of the contrast between old-fashioned and up-to-date that had been employed to describe the essentially external transformation from rural to industrial America, recent writings have concentrated on the connection between visible social action and invisible cultural influences. Traditional society as an abstract concept has been invested with the normative values of stability, cohesion, and neighborly concern, while the changes that came with economic development have been characterized as intrusive, exploitive, and class-biased. Where Hofstadter played off myth against reality, the new interpreters of early America are more likely to insist that a genuine conflict existed between farm communities and the modern world of money, markets, and merchants.

It is this more refined and subtle model of rural life that has turned the Jeffersonians into nostalgic men fighting a rearguard action against the forces of modernity. Thus J. G. A. Pocock has named Jefferson as the conduit through which a civic concept of virtue entered "the whole tradition of American agrarian and populist messianism."[9] Less concerned with political issues, James A. Henretta has stressed the farmers' concern with protecting the lineal family from the centrifugal forces of individual enterprise and economic competition.[10] According to Lance Banning, the Republican party appealed to "the hesitations of agrarian conservatives as they experienced the stirrings of a more commercial age," while John M. Murrin has concluded that the Jeffersonians were like the English Country opposition on political and economic questions because "they idealized the past more than the future and feared significant change, especially major economic change, as corruption and degeneration."[11] For Drew McCoy the tension between tradition and innovation is more explicit. The Jeffersonians, he has said, were forced to reconcile classical ideals with social realities; their ambiguities and contradictions reflected "an attempt to cling to the traditional republican spirit of classical antiquity without disregarding the new imperatives of a more modern commercial society."[12] In *The Elusive Republic* McCoy has recovered the centrality of commercial policy in the Jeffersonians' program, but he has assumed that the values of civic humanism gave shape and direction to their recommendations.

In contrast to these characterizations of early national attitudes, I shall argue that the new European demand for American grains—the crops produced by most farm families from Virginia through Maryland, Pennsylvania, Delaware, New Jersey, New York, and up the Connecticut River Valley—created an unusually favorable opportunity for ordinary men to produce for the Atlantic trade world. Far from being viewed apprehensively, this prospect during the thirty years following the adoption of the Constitution undergirded Jefferson's optimism about America's future as a progressive, prosperous, democratic nation. Indeed, this anticipated participation in an expanding international commerce in foodstuffs created the material base for a new social vision owing little conceptually or practically to antiquity, the Renaissance, or the mercantilists of eighteenth-century England. From this perspective the battle between the Jeffersonians and Federalists appears not as a conflict between the patrons of agrarian self-sufficiency and the proponents of modern commerce, but rather as a struggle between two different elaborations of capitalistic development in America. Jefferson becomes, not the heroic loser in a battle against modernity, but the conspicuous winner in a contest over how the government should serve its citizens in the first generation of the nation's territorial expansion.

Anyone searching for the word *yeoman* in the writings of the 1790s will be disappointed. A canvass of titles in Charles Evans's *American Bibliography* failed to turn up the designation *yeoman* in more than thirty thousand works published in the United States between 1760 and 1800. The word *yeomanry* appeared only three times, all in works by a single author, George Logan.[13] Noah Webster, America's first lexicographer, defined *yeoman* as "a common man, or one of the plebeians, of the first or most respectable class; a free-holder, a man free born," but went on to explain that "the word is little used in the United States, unless as a title in law proceedings . . . and this only in particular states." *Yeomanry*, on the other hand, was much used, according to Webster, and referred to the collective body of freeholders. "Thus the common people in America are called the yeomanry."[14] For Webster, an ardent Federalist, the word retained the social distinction of its British provenance but conveyed nothing as such about farming. I have never found the word *yeoman* in Jefferson's writings; it certainly does not appear in his one book, *Notes on the State of Virginia*, where undifferentiated people in political contexts are called "citizens," "tax-payers," or "electors"; in economic references, "husbandmen," "farmers," or "laborers"; and in social commentary, "the poor," "the most discreet and honest inhabitants," or "respectable merchants and farmers." When Jefferson spoke in theoretical terms, ordinary persons were often discussed as "individuals," as in a passage where he says the dissolution of power would leave people "as individuals to shift for themselves."[15] Like Jefferson, the writers who filled Evans's bibliography with titles chose such socially neutral nouns as *farmers, planters, husbandmen, growers, inhabitants, landowners*, or more frequently, simply *countrymen*, a term whose double meaning reflected accurately the rural location of the preponderance of American citizens.

The absence of the word *yeoman* is negative evidence only, although its occasional use by contemporary Englishmen and New Englanders suggests a lingering reference to a status designation.[16] The error in current scholarly usage, however, is not lexical, but conceptual; it points Jefferson and his party in the wrong direction. Despite Jefferson's repeated assertions that his party was animated by bold new expectations for the human condition, the agrarian myth makes him a traditional, republican visionary, socially radical perhaps, but economically conservative. The assumed contradiction between democratic aspirations and economic romanticism explains why his plans were doomed to failure in competition with the hard-headed realism of an Alexander Hamilton. To this form of the argument, interpretive schemes much older than Hofstadter's have contributed a great deal. Viewed retrospectively by historians living in an industrial age, Jefferson's enthusiasm for agriculture has long been misinterpreted as an attachment to the past. So dazzling were the technological triumphs of railroad building and steam power that the age of the marvelous machines came to appear as the great divide in human history.

Henry Adams offers a splendid example of this distorting perspective. Describing America in 1800, Adams said that "down to the close of the eighteenth century no change had occurred in the world which warranted practical men in assuming that great changes were to come." The connection between industrial technology and a modern mentality for him was complete, for he then went on to say, "as time passed, and as science developed man's capacity to control Nature's forces, old-fashioned conservatism vanished from society."[17] In fact, an American who was forty years old in 1800 would have seen every fixed point in his or her world dramatically transformed through violent political agitation, protracted warfare, galloping inflation, and republican revolutions. Yet for Adams the speed of travel held the human imagination in a thrall that the toppling of kings could not affect.

Two interpretative tendencies have followed from this point of view. One has been to treat proponents of agricultural development as conservative and to construe as progressive those who favored manufacturing and banking. The contrast between Jefferson cast as an agrarian romantic and Hamilton as the far-seeing capitalist comes readily to mind. The other retrospective bias has been the characterization of industrialization as an end toward which prior economic changes were inexorably moving. Both classical economic and Marxist theory have contributed to this determinism which recasts historical events as parts of a process, as stages in a sequential morphology. Under this influence, the actual human encounter with time is reversed; instead of interpreting social change as the result of particular responses to a knowable past, the decisions men and women made are examined in relation to future developments unknown to them.[18] The situation in America at the end of the eighteenth century is exemplary.

Ignorant of the industrial future, Americans were nonetheless aware that their economy was being reshaped by the most important material change of the era: the rise of European population and the consequent inability of European agriculture to meet the new demand for foodstuffs. After 1755 the terms of trade between grain and all other commodities turned decisively in favor of the grains and stayed that way until the third decade of the nineteenth century.[19] In *Common Sense*, Thomas Paine dismissed colonial fears about leaving the security of the English navigation system by saying that American commerce would flourish so long as "eating is the custom of Europe."[20] Eating, of course, has long been the custom of Europeans. What made their eating habit newly relevant to Americans was their declining capacity to feed themselves. More fortunate than most of her neighbors, England benefited from a century and a half of previous agricultural improvements so that pressure from her growing population meant that harvest surpluses, which had once been exported, after mid-century were consumed at home. The withdrawal of English grains, however, created major food deficits on the Iberian peninsula. No longer able to rely upon Britain's bounteous harvests, the Spanish and Portuguese began looking anxiously across the Atlantic to North America. The impact of food shortages had a differential impact upon European nations, but for Americans the consequences, particularly after 1788, were salubrious. The long upward climb of prices enhanced the value of those crops that ordinary farmers could easily grow.[21] Combined with the strong markets in the West Indies for corn and meat products, the growth of European markets for American foodstuffs had the greatest impact on the ordinary farmer who pursued a mixed husbandry.

The first and most conspicuous response to these economic changes came in the prerevolutionary South where large planters and small farmers alike began planting wheat instead of tobacco. While soil exhaustion offered an incentive to make the switch, rising prices for grains financed the conversion. In the frontier areas of the Piedmont and Shenandoah Valley, selling grain and livestock surpluses offered a speedy avenue of integration into the Atlantic trade world.[22] As historians have recently made clear, this changeover to grains in the Upper South involved more than agricultural techniques, for the marketing of wheat and corn had a decisive influence upon the area's urban growth. The switch to grains and livestock along the Eastern Shore, the lower James, the upper Potomac, and in the Piedmont promoted in two decades the cities, towns, and hamlets that had eluded the Chesapeake region during the previous century of tobacco production. Equally important to the character of these new urban networks was capturing what Jacob M. Price has termed "the entrepreneurial headquarters" of the grain trade. Unlike tobacco, the capital and marketing profits for the commerce in food remained in American hands.[23] For planters and farmers the switch to wheat could mean liberation from British factors and merchants who controlled both the sales and purchases of Tidewater tobacco planters. Such a possibility can be read in more personal terms in the writings of the young planter George Washington, who pledged himself to economic freedom by raising wheat.[24] Fanning out from Baltimore, Norfolk, and later Richmond, an array of market towns sprang up to handle the inspection, storage, processing, and shipping of the grains and livestock being pulled into the Atlantic trade from the rural areas of North Carolina, Virginia, Maryland, and Pennsylvania. During these same years, Philadelphia and New York, both drawing on a grain-raising hinterland, surpassed Boston in population, wealth, and shipping.[25]

The dislocations of the American Revolution were followed by a five-year depression, but in 1788 a new upward surge in grain and livestock prices ushered in a thirty-year period of prosperity. Even in England the shortfall between grain production and domestic demand led to net grain imports for twenty-seven out of these thirty years. Southern European demand remained strong. A printed solicitation for American business sent from a Barcelona firm in 1796 described American wheat and flour as much esteemed and constantly in demand "in this Place & Province, which," as the handbill explained, "in years of abundance never produces more than for four Months provisions."[26] In the longer run, sustained profits in grain-raising encouraged investments in agricultural improvements and prompted heroic efforts to increase output. By 1820, especially in England, Belgium, and the Netherlands, food production again had caught up with population growth, and prices returned to the levels of the mid-1790s.[27] Higher yields abroad, not the end of the Napoleonic wars, curbed demand for American farm products.

Coinciding as it did with the adoption of the United States Constitution, the new climb of food prices meant not only that the market could penetrate further into the countryside but also that the national government could extend its reach with improvements in communication and transportation systems. In the single decade of the 1790s, America's 75 post offices increased to 903 while the mileage of post routes went from 1,875 to 20,817. The number of newspapers more than doubled; circulation itself increased threefold. In the middle of the decade turnpike construction began.[28] With each decadal increase in grain prices the distance wheat and flour could be carted profitably to market increased dramatically. At 1772 price levels, farmers and grain merchants could afford to ship flour 121 miles and wheat 64 to reach the grain-exporting seaports of Norfolk, Baltimore, Richmond, Philadelphia, and New York. Between 1800 and 1819 the range had extended to 201 miles for flour and 243 for wheat. For the farmer who wished to earn his own teamster's wage, the distance could be extended further.[29] The population doubled during the first twenty-three years of the new national government, but even more important to the burgeoning trade in American foodstuffs, the preponderance of American farmers lived within marketing range of the inland waterways that flowed into the sea-lanes of the great Atlantic commerce. As the volume of grain exports grew, country stores replaced rural fairs, and millers, bakers, butchers, brewers, and tanners turned from the custom trade of their neighbors to the commercial processing of the farmer's surpluses.

For the gentlemen planters of the Upper South, the switch to wheat represented a calculated response to new market opportunities, but for the mass of ordinary farmers the growing demand for foodstuffs abroad offered an inducement to increase surpluses without giving up the basic structure of the family farm. The man with seventy-five to one hundred acres who relied principally upon his own and his family's labor to grow

Indian corn and wheat and to tend his livestock and draft animals could participate in the market with increasing profits without taking the risks associated with cash crops.[30] European population growth had enhanced the value of the little man's harvests, not that of the rich man's staples. It also blurred the old textbook distinction between the commercial agriculture of the South and the subsistence farming of the North. The wheat farmer's replication of European crops was no longer a commercial liability, for it was exactly the foods and fibers indigenous to Europe that were in demand. Published prices current of American produce in Liverpool, Amsterdam, LeHavre, Bordeaux, Barcelona, Saint-Domingue, and Havana convey the situation: Wheat, flour, Indian corn, clover seed, flax seed, hemp, deerskins, beeswax, staves, and timber all commanded good prices, while West Indian markets took beef, pork, fish, cider, apples, potatoes, peas, bread, lard, onions, cheese, and butter as well. The mixed husbandry through which the farmer supplied his family also fed into the stream of commerce that linked rural stores and backcountry millers to the Atlantic commerce. To be sure, as Diane Lindstrom has pointed out, the farmer's family remained his best customer, but this held true well into the nineteenth century.[31]

The diversity of demand for American farm commodities in the generation after 1788 encouraged the adoption of the up-and-down husbandry that had revolutionized English and Dutch agriculture a century earlier. Here diversification, not specialization, held the key to raising crop yields and maintaining soil fertility in an age without chemical fertilizers.[32] Livestock and wheat raising required dividing land among meadows, pastures, and fields. When these were rotated, yields could be increased and fertility maintained. Livestock fed with soil-enriching grasses could also produce manure for fields of wheat and corn. While foreign visitors judged American farmers improvident and wasteful, American writers insisted that European practices had been adapted to American needs. Fertility in the grain- and livestock-producing areas evidently held up.[33]

Economies of scale had practically no bearing on the enhancement of the harvests that produced the food surpluses of the eighteenth and early nineteenth centuries. Attention to detail was the key. As the agricultural writer John Dabney explained, the farmer who does not "cart out his summer dung, nor plough those lands in the fall which he means to feed in the following spring" could not grow rich.[34] In no other husbandry was it more true that the best manure was the tread of the master's foot. Moreover, the capital investments that could improve output—folding animals, bringing uncultivated land under the plow, laying down new pastures—could be made by the ordinary farmer willing to exchange leisure for off-season labors.[35] Increasing surpluses required, above all, a better management of time and a close watch on the market. Here too the range of farm commodities in demand redounded to the benefit of the small farmer, for each nook and cranny had a potential use. Hemp, according to John Alexander Binns, could be raised on every conceivable hollow just as bee hives, whose wax commanded good prices in England, could be lodged near the ubiquitous stands of white clover.[36] The relative success of the farmers who harvested wheat in the Middle Atlantic states can be gauged by Stanley L. Engerman's findings that the wealth of the North surpassed that of the South for the first time in the period from 1774 to 1798.[37] Without any of the qualities that characterized commercial agriculture in the colonial period—slave labor, specialization, large holdings—northern farmers had been brought into the thriving trade in foodstuffs.

Although high food prices greatly increased the ambit of the market, soil and climate more rigidly delimited the domain of up-and-down husbandry. The optimal mix of livestock and grain raising depended on crops of timothy, alfalfa, and clover, which were not easily grown in the lower South where heavy rains leached the land, leaving severe lime deficiencies. Hot, humid summers exposed cattle to ticks and mosquitos which kept herds small. Agricultural improvements in these areas had to await later developments in fertilizers and soil amendments.[38] In New England the thin soils and rocky terrain also barred farmers from effectively competing with the rich farmlands of the South and West. Even before the Revolution, Massachusetts had become an importer of wheat.[39] The New England situation did not encourage the embrace of an expansive, market-oriented, food-raising economy. In time the reexport trade breathed new life into the mercantile sector, but manufacturing, with its very different cultural imperatives, held out the long-range prospect for development.[40] Thus, despite the easy entry into the mixed husbandry of grain and livestock raising, climate and topography drew the borders around the wheat belt that passed through Virginia, Maryland, Delaware, Pennsylvania, New Jersey, and New York. As long as food prices remained high, the conventional divisions of North and South, subsistence and commercial, yielded to a core of common interests among American farmers, food processors, and merchants in this favored region.[41]

The acknowledged novelty of the new American nation's political experiments has too often obscured the equally strong sense contemporaries had that they were entering a new economic era as well. Gouverneur Morris, for instance, called his fellow countrymen of 1782 "the first born children of extended Commerce in modern Times."[42] Americans were repeatedly characterized as eager market participants—certainly when it came to spending and borrowing—and commerce itself was associated with a remarkable augmentation of wealth-producing possibilities. "The spirit for Trade which pervades these States is not to be restrained," George Washington wrote to James Warren in 1784. Jefferson, eager to build canals linking the Chesapeake to the interior valleys of Virginia, wrote Washington that since all the world was becoming commercial, America too must get as much as possible of this modern source of wealth and power.[43] Timothy Matlack predicted for an audience in Philadelphia the rise of America to a "Height of Riches, Strength and Glory, which the fondest Imagination cannot readily conceive," going on to specify that the "Star-bespangled Genius of America . . . points to Agriculture as the stable Foundation of this rising mighty Empire."[44] Without any major technological breakthrough, the late-eighteenth-century economy nonetheless suggested to men that they stood on the threshold of major advances.

By isolating in time and space the golden era of grain growing in the early national period, one can see more clearly the material base upon which Jefferson built his vision of America, a vision that was both democratic and capitalistic, agrarian and commercial. It is especially the commercial component of Jefferson's program that sinks periodically from scholarly view, a submersion that can be traced to the failure to connect Jefferson's interpretation of economic developments to his political goal. Agriculture did not figure in his plans as a venerable form of production giving shelter to a traditional way of life; rather,he was responsive to every possible change in cultivation, processing, and marketing that would enhance its profitability. It was exactly the promise of progressive agricultural development that fueled his hopes that ordinary men might escape the tyranny of their social superiors both as employers and magistrates. More than most democratic reformers, he recognized that hierarchy rested on economic relations and a deference to the past as well as formal privilege and social custom.

The Upper South's conversion from tobacco to wheat provided the central focus for Jefferson's discussion of commerce and manufacturing in his *Notes on the State of Virginia*. Throughout the Tidewater, planters were shifting from the old staple, tobacco, to the production of cereals. Made profitable by the sharp prices occasioned by European and American population growth, foodstuffs were much less labor-intensive than tobacco and were therefore suitable for family farms. Large and small Virginia planters became integrated into the new grain-marketing network that connected American producers from the James to the Hudson with buyers throughout the Atlantic world. As Jefferson wrote, wheat raising "diffuses plenty and happiness among the whole," and it did so, he noted, with only moderate toil, an observation that evokes the unstated, invidious comparison with slave labor.[45] Whether talking about consumption or

production, he took for granted the importance of the market in influencing developments. For instance, he predicted that wheat would continue to
replace tobacco because growers in Georgia and the Mississippi Territory
would be able to undersell their Chesapeake competitors. Similarly the
weevil might threaten the profits of the Virginia wheat grower, for the expense of combating the infestation would "enable other countries to undersell him." Looking to the future Jefferson hailed the "immensity of land
courting the industry of the husbandman," but he assumed that the husbandman would participate in international trade. Popular taste, that final
arbiter for Jefferson, guaranteed that Americans would "return as soon as
they can, to the raising [of] raw materials, and exchanging them for finer
manufactures than they are able to execute themselves." The country's
interest, therefore, would be to "throw open the doors of commerce, and
to knock off all its shackles." At the same time it was entirely natural to
Jefferson to mix shrewd assessment of market realities with homiletic commentary. Thus, he said, relying on European manufacturing would fore-
stall the corruption of "the mass of cultivators," and he condemned tobacco raising as "a culture productive of infinite wretchedness."[46]

Working with a completely commercial mode of agriculture, Jefferson
projected for America a dynamic food-producing and food-selling economy which promised the best of two worlds: economic independence for
the bulk of the population and a rising standard of living. Even the word
farmer captured some of the novelty of the new prospect. As William
Tatham explained to his English readers, the cultivator "who follows the
ancient track of his ancestors, is called a *planter*" while he "who sows wheat,
and waters meadows, is a *farmer*.[47] The concrete policy measures that ema-
nated from this prescription for American growth were both political and
economic: making new land in the national domain accessible to the individual farmer-owner, using diplomatic initiatives to open markets around
the world, committing public funds to internal improvements, and, negatively, opposing fiscal measures that bore heavily upon the ordinary,
rural taxpayers.[48] William N. Parker has described just what these policies
meant to mid-nineteenth-century agriculture: "an ambitious farmer might
buy more farms, but he gained no economies by consolidating them" because "enterprise was too vigorous and too widely diffused, competition
for finance, land, and labor too intense to permit large concentrations of
wealth inland." The larger farmer, moreover, "suffered the disadvantages of
the liberal land policy and the prevailing sentiment in favor of the settler."[49]

Jefferson was not alone in joining political democracy to economic freedom; these themes coalesced in a number of local movements that in time
found a national base in the opposition to Hamilton's program. Typical of
this new view was Logan's declaration that the sacred rights of mankind in-

cluded farmers deriving "all the advantages they can from every part of the produce of their farms," a goal that required "a perfectly free commerce" and "a free unrestricted sale for the produce of their own industry."[50] In a similar spirit John Spurrier dedicated *The Practical Farmer* to Jefferson because of his interest in agricultural science and his efforts "to promote the real strength and wealth of this commonwealth" on rational principles.[51] Writing at the same time Tench Coxe described the overwhelming importance of farming to America. Capital and labor investments in agriculture were eight times those in any other pursuit, Coxe estimated. More pertinently, he gave almost exclusive attention to the range of foodstuffs produced by family labor from Virginia to Connecticut.[52]

The nationalism implicit in these descriptions of America's economic future helps explain the breadth of the Republican movement, and the emphasis upon the commercial value of the grains, livestock, and beverages produced on family farms indicates how market changes affected early national politics. Jefferson's own nationalism was closely tied to the issues of international free trade and the disposition of the national domain. In this he was representative of the Virginia nationalists who dominated American politics after 1783 and led the campaign to establish "a more perfect union" four years later. With peace and the failure of William Morris's impost scheme, attention in the Continental Congress passed to matters of vital concern to Virginians—the taking-up of western land and the marketing of America's bounteous harvests. Both goals encouraged a national perspective. To expel the British from the Northwest, to ease the Indians out of Ohio territory, to negotiate new commercial treaties abroad—these things required more than confederal cooperation. Just how long-range their view was can be gauged by the passions aroused by the idea of closing the port of New Orleans at a time when settlers had reached Kentucky. The implicit social values of this southern program, as H. James Henderson has pointed out, were secular rather than religious, anticipatory rather than regressive, individualistic rather than corporate. The leaders of the Old Dominion "looked forward to continental grandeur rather than back to ancestral virtue."[53] East of the Hudson there was little support for an expansive American republic. The stagnating Massachusetts economy made the past a more reliable guide to the future than dreams of a new age of prosperity and progress. In the middle and southern states, however, the depressed 1780s reflected less the limits of growth than the failure to unlock America's rich resources.

From Georgia to New York a hinterland ran westward that gave the new American nation what no other people had ever possessed: the material base for a citizenry of independent, industrious property holders. And Virginia, the largest and wealthiest state, produced the leaders who turned this prospect into a political program. Most national leaders recognized the economic potential in America; the question that emerged was how and in deference to which values would this potential be realized. The issues that clustered around the opening of the national domain reveal very well how choices would affect the character of American society. Manufacturing, proponents argued, would provide jobs for sons and daughters at home; uncontrolled movement in the west would scatter families.[54] Recognizing the class difference in migration rates, an article addressed to the working people of Maryland urged support for the Constitution on the grounds that the common people were more properly citizens of America than of any particular state, for many of them died far away from where they were born.[55] The congressional debates on the Land Act of 1796 swirled around the question whether these sons and daughters who moved west would become independent farmers or the tenants of land speculators. The geographic base of the Jeffersonian Republicans can be traced in the votes for 160–acre sales.[56] Because grains were raised throughout the United States and required ancillary industries for their processing and sale, the Republican program was neither regional nor, strictly speaking, agrarian. It should be emphasized that it involved neither American isolation nor a slowed pace of growth. It was in fact a form of capitalism that Jefferson seized as the ax to fell Old World institutions because free trade offered the integrative network that social authority supplied elsewhere. Hamilton's response to the Louisiana Purchase makes this point negatively: the extension of America's agricultural frontier, he maintained, threatened to remove citizens from the coercive power of the state.[57]

The Revolution had made possible Jefferson's vision of a great progressive republic, but developments during the first years of independence brought to light two different threats to its fulfillment. The one was old and predictable: the tendency of the rich and mighty to control the avenues to profit and preferment. The other came from the very strength of common voters in revolutionary America. The war effort itself had democratized politics, and without royal government, the broad prerevolutionary suffrage was translated into comprehensive popular power.[58] Emboldened by the natural rights rhetoric of the resistance movement, political newcomers began to challenge the old merchant oligarchies in the cities, while their counterparts in state legislatures pushed through radical measures affecting taxation, inheritance, insolvency, debt retirement, and land sales.[59] The ensuing conflicts, which Progressive historians made familiar as part of the struggle between rich and poor, aroused fears that cannot be categorized so easily. The new aggregate power of the people channeled through popularly elected legislatures alarmed men as philosophically different as Jefferson and Hamilton, as unlike temperamentally as Benjamin Rush and Robert Livingston. When ordinary Americans used their new voting power to push for legislation favorable to themselves, they made committed democrats as well as conservatives apprehensive. The anxieties expressed during the late 1780s cannot be ascribed solely to an elitist distrust of the poor, the ill-born, and the untalented many. Men destined to become the champions of political equality found the augmentation of power in the first state governments a genuine threat. A historiographical tradition that reads all fears of popular, unrestricted governmental power as evidence of upper-class sympathies is in danger of missing the most compelling political goal to emerge in late-eighteenth-century America—the limitation of formal authority in deference to individual freedom. Disaggregating society, the Jeffersonians redirected the sovereign people away from exercising power as a body and toward enjoying free choice as private persons. Leaders of both the Federalist and Republican parties had cooperated in 1787 because a national political framework and a unified economy were essential to their differing conceptions of America's future. The new government created by the Constitution, however, proved to be a double-edged sword for the democratic nationalists. Strong enough to provide the conditions for freedom and growth, it could be used to concentrate power and thereby raise a new national elite.

In resisting Hamilton's policies the Republicans eschewed the very divisions that historians have dwelt upon in explaining party formation. Far from pitting merchants against farmers, rich against poor, or the commercially inclined against the self-sufficient, the Jeffersonians assumed that a freely developing economy would benefit all. The eradication of privilege and the limitation of formal power would stimulate the natural harmony of interests. Thomas Paine with his usual directness gave expression to this liberal view in the fight over Robert Morris's bank. In a republican form of government, he wrote, "public good is not a term opposed to the good of individuals; on the contrary, it is the good of every individual collected. . . . the farmer understands farming, and the merchant understands commerce; and as riches are equally the object of both, there is no occasion that either should fear that the other will seek to be poor."[60] Making a slightly different point, the Jeffersonian congressional leader, Albert Gallatin, opposed the Federalists' 1800 bankruptcy bill because its provisions could not be restricted to merchants. In America, he argued, "the different professions and trades are blended together in the same persons; the same man being frequently a farmer and a merchant, and perhaps a manufacturer."[61] What was distinctive about the Jeffersonian economic policy was not anticommercial bias, but a commitment to growth through the unimpeded exertions of individuals whose access to economic opportunity was both protected and facilitated by government.

Treated for so long as a set of self-evident truths, the flowering of liberal thought in America owed much to specific developments. The advantageous terms of trade for American farm commodities, the expulsion of Europeans and Native Americans from the trans-Appalachian west, the people's commercial tendencies that Jefferson described—all these made men and women receptive to a new conception of human nature that affirmed the reciprocal influences of freedom and prosperity. What had given a sacred underpinning to Locke's contract theory was his assumption that men living under God's law were enjoined to protect the life, liberty, and property of others as well as their own. Jefferson perceived that Locke's identity of interests among the propertied could be universalized in America and thereby acquire a moral base in natural design. It was indeed a *novus ordo seclorum*.

NOTES

1. M. L. Wilson, "Thomas Jefferson—Farmer," *Proceedings of the American Philosophical Society* 87 (1944): 217–19.

2. August C. Miller, Jr., "Jefferson as an Agriculturist," *Agricultural History* 16 (April 1942): 65.

3. A. Whitney Griswold, *Farming and Democracy* (New York, 1948), 18–19, 26–32; William D. Grampp, "A Re-examination of Jeffersonian Economics," *Southern Economic Journal* 12 (January 1946): 263–82.

4. Richard Hofstadter, *The Age of Reform: From Bryan to F. D. R.* (New York, 1955), 23–24, 30.

5. Ibid., 25; Griswold, *Farming and Democracy,* 12–15.

6. Chester E. Eisinger, "The Freehold Concept in Eighteenth-Century American Letters," *William and Mary Quarterly* 4 (January 1947): 46–47. See also Chester E. Eisinger, "Land and Loyalty: Literary Expressions of Agrarian Nationalism in the Seventeenth and Eighteenth Centuries," *American Literature* 21 (May 1949): 160–78; and Chester E. Eisinger, "The Farmer in the Eighteenth Century Almanac," *Agricultural History* 28 (July 1954): 107–12.

7. Stanley Elkins and Eric McKitrick, "Richard Hofstadter: A Progress," in *The Hofstadter Aegis: A Memorial,* ed. Stanley Elkins and Eric McKitrick (New York, 1975), 316.

8. For a review of this literature, see John J. Waters, "From Democracy to Demography: Recent Historiography on the New England Town," in *Perspectives on Early American History: Essays in Honor of Richard B. Morris,* ed. Alden T. Vaughan and George Athan Billias (New York, 1973), 222–49.

9. J. G. A. Pocock, "Virtue and Commerce in the Eighteenth Century," *Journal of Interdisciplinary History* 3 (Summer 1972): 134. See also J. G. A. Pocock, *The Machiavellian Moment: Florentine Political Thought and the Atlantic Republican Tradition* (Princeton, 1975), ix, 529–33.

10. James A. Henretta, "Families and Farms: *Mentalité* in Pre-Industrial America," *William and Mary Quarterly* 35 (January 1978): 3–32.

11. Lance Banning, *The Jeffersonian Persuasion: Evolution of a Party Ideology* (Ithaca, 1978), 269; John M. Murrin, "The Great Inversion, or Court versus Country: A Comparison of the Revolution Settlements in England (1688–1721) and America (1776–1815)," in *Three British Revolutions: 1641, 1688, 1776*, ed. J. G. A. Pocock (Princeton, 1980), 406.

12. Drew McCoy, *The Elusive Republic: Political Economy in Jeffersonian America* (Chapel Hill, 1980), 10.

13. Charles Evans, C. K. Shipton, R. P. Bristol, comps., *American Bibliography* (14 vols., New York, 1959); George Logan, *Letters Addressed to the Yeomanry of the United States* (Philadelphia, 1791); George Logan, *Five Letters Addressed to the Yeomanry of the United States Containing Some Observations on the Dangerous Scheme of Governor Duer and Mr. Secretary Hamilton* (Philadelphia, 1792); George Logan, *Letters Addressed to the Yeomanry of the United States Containing Some Observations on Funding and Bank Systems* (Philadelphia, 1793).

14. Noah Webster, *An American Dictionary of the English Language* (2 vols., New York, 1828), s.v. "Yeoman" and "Yeomanry." See also Noah Webster, *A Compendious Dictionary of the English Language* (Hartford, 1806), where *yeoman* is defined as "a gentleman-farmer, freeholder, officer."

15. Thomas Jefferson, *Notes on the State of Virginia*, ed. William Peden (Chapel Hill, 1955), 125, 127, 130, 164–65, 213.

16. For the use of *yeoman* in this period, see *Boston Gazette*, April 15, 1790, March 3, 1794, May 25, 1796; *Independent Chronicle* (Boston), December 15, 1786, April 9, 1789.

17. Henry Adams, *The United States in 1800* (Ithaca, 1955), 42. Contrast this with Duc Francois de La Rochefoucauld-Liancourt's firsthand observation that America was "a country in flux; that which is true today as regards its population, its establishments, its prices, its commerce will not be true six months from now." David J. Brandenburg, "A French Aristocrat Looks at American Farming: La Rochefoucauld-Liancourt's *Voyages dans les Etats-Unis,*" *Agricultural History* 32 (1958): 163.

18. For a critique of this tendency in economic history, see Robert E. Mutch, "Yeoman and Merchant in Pre-Industrial America: Eighteenth-Century Massachusetts as a Case Study," *Societas* 7 (Autumn 1977): 279–302.

19. B. H. Slicher Van Bath, "Eighteenth-Century Agriculture on the Continent of Europe: Evolution or Revolution?" *Agricultural History* 43 (January 1969): 173–75.

20. [Thomas Paine], *Common Sense, Addressed to the Inhabitants of America*, in *The Writings of Thomas Paine*, ed. Moncure Daniel Conway (4 vols., New York, 1894–1896), 1:86.

21. For some important interpretative points in regard to agricultural productivity and to exports as its measure, see Claudia D. Goldin and Frank D. Lewis, "The Role of Exports in American Economic Growth during the Napoleonic Wars, 1793 to 1807," *Explorations in Economic History* 17 (January 1980): 6–25; William N. Parker, "Sources of Agricultural Productivity in the Nineteenth Century," *Journal of Farm Economics* 49 (December 1967): 1455–68; and Andrew Hill

Clark, "Suggestions for the Geographical Study of Agricultural Change in the United States, 1790–1840," in *Farming in the New Nation: Interpreting American Agriculture, 1790–1840*, ed. Darwin P. Kelsey (Washington, 1972), 155–72.

22. Robert D. Mitchell, *Commercialism and Frontier: Perspectives on the Early Shenandoah Valley* (Charlottesville, 1977), 40, 173–78; Malcolm J. Rohrbough, *The Trans-Appalachian Frontier: People, Societies and Institutions, 1775–1850* (New York, 1978), 99–106.

23. Carville Earle and Ronald Hoffman, "Staple Crops and Urban Development in the Eighteenth-Century South," *Perspectives in American History* 10 (1976): 5–78; Jacob M. Price, "Economic Function and the Growth of American Port Towns in the Eighteenth Century," ibid. 8 (1974): 121–86.

24. James Thomas Flexner, *George Washington: The Forge of Experience, 1732–1775* (Boston, 1965), 279–84.

25. Price, "Economic Function and the Growth of American Port Towns," 151–60.

26. Arabet, Gautier & Manning handbill, Barcelona, May 18, 1796, file 1215, Miscellaneous Material Regarding Philadelphia Business Concerns, 1784–1824 (Eleutherian Mills Historical Library, Wilmington, Del.). British imports of American grain can be followed in Great Britain, *Parliamentary Papers* (Commons), "An Account of the Grain of All Sorts, Meal, and Flour, Stated in Quarters, Imported into Great Britain in Each Year from January 5, 1800 to January 5, 1825" (no. 227), 1825, 20:233–67. For the earlier period, see Great Britain, *Parliamentary Papers* (Commons), "Accounts Relating to Corn, Etc." (no. 50), 1826–1827, 16:487–501.

27. Slicher Van Bath, "Eighteenth-Century Agriculture," 175.

28. Allan R. Pred, *Urban Growth and the Circulation of Information: The United States System of Cities, 1790–1840* (Cambridge, 1973), 58–59, 80, 153.

29. Ibid., 114. Max G. Schumacher has calculated the "approximate maximum commercial range from Baltimore and Philadelphia of wheat and flour dependent on land-carriage" for price levels in 1755 and 1772. I extended Schumacher's ratios to the price range from 1800 to 1819. Max G. Schumacher, *The Northern Farmer and His Markets during the Late Colonial Period* (New York, 1975), 63.

30. As this relates to Maryland, see Paul G. E. Clemens, *The Atlantic Economy and Colonial Maryland's Eastern Shore: From Tobacco to Grain* (Ithaca, 1980). See also Mitchell, *Commercialism and Frontier*, 234; David Maldwyn Ellis, *Landlords and Farmers in the Hudson-Mohawk Region, 1790–1850* (New York, 1967), 76–82; Sarah Shaver Hughes, "Elizabeth City County, Virginia, 1782–1810: The Economic and Social Structure of a Tidewater County in the Early National Years," (Ph.D. diss., College of William and Mary, 1975), 406–7; and David C. Klingaman, *Colonial Virginia's Coastwise and Grain Trade* (New York, 1975). For some of the theoretical implications of the market involvement of self-sufficient family farms, see Mutch, "Yeoman and Merchant," 279–302.

31. Diane Lindstrom, "Southern Dependence upon Western Grain Supplies," (M.A. thesis, University of Delaware, 1969), 10. Printed prices current and merchant handbills can be sampled in manuscript files 1303, 667, 1097, 1144, 1215,

and 1457 (Eleutherian Mills Historical Library). Comparisons were made between advertised export items and farm account books in the collections at the Delaware State Archives (Dover, Del.); the University of Delaware Library Special Collections (Newark, Del.), and the Historical Society of Delaware (Wilmington, Del.).

32. Eric Kerridge, *The Agricultural Revolution* (London, 1967), 39–40, 107, 214–15, 299, 347–48.

33. For a foreign view of American agriculture based on a tour in 1794–95, see William Strickland, *Observations on the Agriculture of the United States of America* (London, 1801). A rebuttal is provided by William Tatham, *Communications Concerning the Agriculture and Commerce of America* (London, 1800). The controversy over William Strickland's report to the English Board of Agriculture is covered by G. Melvin Herndon, "Agriculture in America in the 1790s: An Englishman's View," *Agricultural History* 49 (July 1975): 505–16. Other contemporary writers who stressed both the differences and the profitability of American agriculture were Timothy Matlack, *An Oration Delivered March 16, 1780* (Philadelphia, 1780), 14–16; Francois Alexandre Frederick, duc de La Rochefoucauld-Liancourt, *Voyages dans les Etats Unis d'Amerique Fait en 1795, 1796, et 1797* (8 vols., Paris [1799]), 1:101–17, 2:325, 3:50; John Spurrier, *The Practical Farmer* (Wilmington, Del., 1793); John A. Binns, *A Treatise on Practical Farming* (Frederick-town, Md., 1803); George Logan, *Fourteen Experiments on Agriculture* (Philadelphia, 1797); and J. B. Bordley, *Essays and Notes on Husbandry and Rural Affairs* (Philadelphia, 1801). Estimates on yields very widely. William Guthrie estimated that yields in Delaware after fifty years of planting continued at levels of fifteen to twenty-five bushels per acre for wheat and barley and two hundred for Indian corn. William Guthrie, *A New System of Modern Geography* (2 vols., Philadelphia, 1795), 2:458. Sarah Shaver Hughes has confirmed Guthrie's conclusion that fertility held up. Hughes, "Elizabeth City County, Virginia," 90–91. An elaborate tabular computation of wages, prices, and yields done by La Rochefoucauld-Liancourt indicates yields ranging from eight to twenty-five bushels per acre for various areas in the Delaware, Maryland, and Pennsylvania wheat-raising belt. "Tabulation of Commerce in the United States, 1795–97," file 501, P. S. DuPont Office Collection (Eleutherian Mills Historical Library).

34. [John Dabney], *An Address to Farmers* (Newburyport, 1796), 5. John Dabney continued: "A complete Farmer is also a man of great carefulness and solicitude; without care, the severest labor on the best of Farms, will never produce riches nor plenty."

35. For theoretical discussion of this point, see Stephen Hymer and Stephen Resnick, "A Model of an Agrarian Economy with Nonagricultural Activities," *American Economic Review* 59 (September 1969): 493–506.

36. John A. Binns, *A Treatise of Practical Farming* (Richmond, 1804), 63. Dabney maintained that a farmer could clear £6 profit from an acre of flax. Dabney, *Address to Farmers*, 51. Substantial British imports of American beeswax are reported in Edmund C. Burnett, "Observations of London Merchants on American Trade, 1783," *American Historical Review* 18 (July 1913): 776.

37. Stanley L. Engerman, "A Reconsideration of Southern Economic Growth, 1770–1860," *Agricultural History* 49 (April 1975): 348–49.

38. Julius Rubin, "The Limits of Agricultural Progress in the Nineteenth-Century South," *Agricultural History* 49 (April 1975): 362–73.

39. Klingaman, *Colonial Virginia's Coastwise and Grain Trade*, 38.

40. Charles L. Sanford, "The Intellectual Origins and New-Worldliness of American Industry," *Journal of Economic History* 18 (March 1958): 1–16.

41. For discussion of the problem of discriminating between a subsistence and a commercial agriculture, see Clark, "Suggestions," 166.

42. Gouverneur Morris to Matthew Ridley, August 6, 1782, quoted in Clarence Ver Steeg, *Robert Morris: Revolutionary Financier* (Philadelphia, 1954), 166–67.

43. George Washington to James Warren, October 7, 1785, *The Writings of George Washington, from the Original Manuscript Sources, 1745–1799*, ed. John C. Fitzpatrick (39 vols., Washington, 1931–1944), 28:290–91; Thomas Jefferson to Washington, March 15, 1784, *The Papers of Thomas Jefferson*, ed. Julian P. Boyd et al. (19 vols., Princeton, 1950–1974), 7:26.

44. Matlack, *Oration*, 25.

45. Jefferson, *Notes on the State of Virginia*, 168.

46. Ibid., 164–68, 174. For a description of the founding fathers as having "commerce-phobia," citing Jefferson's expressions of enthusiasm for free trade as the result of his years in France, see James H. Hutson, "Intellectual Foundations of Early American Diplomacy," *Diplomatic History* 1 (Winter 1977): 6, 8.

47. Tatham, *Communications Concerning the Agriculture and Commerce of the United States*, 46.

48. For excellent discussions of Thomas Jefferson's commercial policies, see Merrill Peterson, "Thomas Jefferson and Commercial Policy, 1783–1793," *William and Mary Quarterly* 22 (October 1965); Richard E. Ellis, "The Political Economy of Thomas Jefferson," in *Thomas Jefferson: The Man, His World, His Influence*, ed. Lally Waymouth (New York, 1973), 81–95.

49. William N. Parker, "Productivity Growth in American Grain Farming: An Analysis of Its 19th Century Sources," in *Reinterpretation of American Economic History*, ed. Robert Fogel and Stanley L. Engerman (New York, 1971), 178.

50. Logan, *Five Letters*, 25, 28.

51. Spurrier, *Practical Farmer*, iii.

52. Tench Coxe, *A View of the United States of America* (Philadelphia, 1794), 8–9, 87–99.

53. H. James Henderson, "The Structure of Politics in the Continental Congress," in *Essays on the American Revolution*, ed. Stephen G. Kurtz and James H. Hutson (Chapel Hill, 1973), 188.

54. "On American Manufactures," *American Museum or Repository of Ancient and Modern Pieces, Prose and Poetical* 1 (January 1787): 18.

55. *Pennsylvania Gazette*, April 2, 1788, p. 3.

56. Rudolph M. Bell, *Party and Faction in American Politics: The House of Representatives, 1789–1801* (Westport, Conn., 1973), 85–89; Murray R. Benedict, *Farm*

Policies of the United States, 1790–1950: A Study of Their Origins and Development (New York, 1953), 12–15.

57. Gerald Stourzh, *Alexander Hamilton and the Idea of Republican Government* (Stanford, 1970), 192–93.

58. Jackson Turner Main, "Government by the People: The American Revolution and the Democratization of the Legislatures," *William and Mary Quarterly* 23 (July 1966): 391–407; John Shy, "The American Revolution: The Military Conflict Considered as a Revolutionary War," in *Essays on the American Revolution*, ed. Kurtz and Hutson, 21–56; Edward Countryman, "Consolidating Power in Revolutionary America: The Case of New York, 1775–1783," *Journal of Interdisciplinary History* 6 (Spring 1976): 645–77.

59. Jon C. Teaford, *The Municipal Revolution in America: Origins of Modern Urban Government, 1650–1825* (Chicago, 1975); Jackson Turner Main, *Political Parties before the Constitution* (Chapel Hill, 1973).

60. [Thomas Paine], *Dissertations on Government: The Affairs of the Bank; and Paper Money*, in *The Complete Writings of Thomas Paine*, ed. Philip S. Foner (2 vols., New York, 1945), 2:372, 399–400.

61. *Annals of the Congress*, 5 Cong., 3 sess., January 14, 1799, 2650–51.

7

Natural Rights
and Scientific Racism

✻

JAMES W. CEASER

Michael Zuckert's *The Natural Rights Republic* presents the most sustained treatment to date of Thomas Jefferson's view of nature and natural rights. No work distinguishes as clearly the different schools of interpretation of Jefferson's political thought or delves as deeply into his understanding of the first principles of politics. The book appears to have an even broader and more important purpose. Zuckert is animated by the conviction that the United States not only once was, but that it can and ought to remain, a "natural rights republic." His intention is nothing less than to revive the doctrine of natural rights as a ground for modern American political life.

Zuckert is well aware, of course, of the contemporary objections to natural rights. These range from the categorical dismissals by postmodern philosophers of any thinking that can be labeled "metaphysical," to the more targeted criticisms of communitarian and republican political theorists who contend that "rights talk" leads to a selfish and destructive individualism. Rather than responding himself to these criticisms, Zuckert turns to Thomas Jefferson and tasks him with carrying the brief for natural rights. Jefferson, we learn, was a far deeper and more systematic thinker than most have supposed. Our attention is directed less to the Declaration of Independence, which Zuckert presents as a "political" document, than to the *Notes of the State of Virginia*, a work that he calls "philosophical, if not philosophy through and through."[1] The *Notes* provides Jefferson's fullest picture of nature, from the top down and the bottom up. Far from relying on airy ghosts of lofty speculation, Jefferson builds the doctrine of natural rights starting from the concrete experience of man in the world and proceeding step by step to cover the phenomena of politics. Zuckert demythologizes our understanding of natural rights, rescuing it from the many layers of distortion that have covered it during the past century.

There is, I believe, one important omission in Zuckert's analysis. No mention is made of the passage in Query XIV in which Jefferson discusses the question of a hierarchy of the races of man and offers his "suspicion" of the inferiority of the black to the white. It is not in a spirit of criticism that I make this observation, but to join Zuckert in exploring the possibility of restoring nature as a ground of modern thought. For one thing today is clear beyond all doubt. Any project to revive natural rights that rests on Jefferson as an authority cannot go much further until something is said about this passage. Contemporary scholarship on Jefferson is filled with commentary on his views of racial hierarchy, much of which questions the sincerity of his opposition to slavery and even the fullness of his commitment to natural rights. As John Hope Franklin has remarked, "It would seem hardly likely that anyone with such pronounced views on the inferiority of blacks . . . could entertain a deeply serious belief that slaves should be emancipated."[2]

Two further points speak to the need to address this passage. The first is that, historically, it has been one of the most frequently discussed parts of the book. According to Winthrop Jordan, Jefferson's "remarks about Negroes were more widely read, in all probability, than any others until the mid-nineteenth century."[3] If one is interested not just in the text of the *Notes* but in the influence that work has had, the issue of race must be considered. The second point, which is of special interest here, relates to the connection between this passage and the theme of nature. The term "nature" appears no less than six times in this passage. Combining these references with those in the section of Query VI in which Jefferson treats the Indian and the albino, it becomes clear that nature in relation to the races of man figures as one of the principal themes of the entire work.

This essay will explore the relationship between Jefferson's views of natural rights and his views of racial hierarchy. Jefferson, it will be seen, was drawing in the *Notes* on two distinct conceptions of nature that derived from two different sciences. "Nature" as this term is used in natural rights discourse refers to the characteristics of human nature. The science employed is psychology, which served as the foundation of the doctrine of natural rights beginning with Thomas Hobbes and John Locke. By contrast, when Jefferson uses "nature" in his discussions of race, he is referring to the hereditary distribution of various attributes among different groups of human beings. The science that treated this question was known in Jefferson's time as "natural history," and its chief progenitors were Linnaeus and Buffon. Jefferson's theoretical attempt in the *Notes* was to try to incorporate elements of natural history into social science and to harmonize its categories of nature with those derived from natural rights. This new and supposedly broader social science was the basis for Jefferson's recommendation to establish political regimes that recognize natural rights and that employ race as a fundamental criterion for defining the make-up of political communities.

In keeping with Zuckert's concern for the fate of natural rights, some kind of assessment of Jefferson's social science is called for. Jefferson's effort to combine natural history and natural rights, I will argue, deviated from the position of most proponents of natural rights; it was a deviation, moreover, that was known to undermine the political science that supports modern natural rights republics. To save the doctrine of natural rights for our times, accordingly, it must be decoupled from Jefferson's social science and restored to a position inside of political science. The doctrine of natural rights in alliance with political science—not the doctrine of natural rights by itself—will be seen to provide the best support for viable modern republics.

I

The relationship of natural rights to natural history (or biology) has been a major theme of political thought over the past two centuries. Jefferson, if not exactly the originator of the philosophical treatment of this theme, has surely been one of the central figures. A survey of a few of the "schools" of interpretation of Jefferson's views on this question will help indicate the theoretical questions at issue in his passage on race.

Charles White and the Science of Racial Difference

One of the first to discuss Jefferson's thought on race from a scientific perspective was the British physician Charles White, a pioneer of phrenology. In his book *An Account of the Regular Gradation in Man* (1799), White sought to prove a gradation among human types by contrasting whites and negroes, the races that most accounts of natural history had argued set the limits of man.[4] White examined the question by surveying epidemiological evidence and by investigating anatomical features, above all the cranium, where he tries to establish a connection between physical attributes and "moral" attributes, i.e., attributes of intelligence, imagination, and temperament. The craniums of the whites were larger, he argued, which he took to indicate that their brains and mental capacities were greater: "Whether it proceeds from a difference in quantity or from some other source, there seems to be a difference in the original capacity of the different tribes of mankind."[5]

Without direct evidence of his own on this last point, White turned to Jefferson's *Notes* as his main support. Although he could have relied on other, and better-known, sources from the field of natural history—almost all of the major natural historians had asserted in some fashion a hierarchy of the races—White preferred Jefferson's account because it was based on direct and fairly extensive observation. It was also conducted by someone who proclaimed his fidelity to the most advanced methods of empirical natural science.[6] As Jefferson himself states in the *Notes*: "A patient pursuit of facts, and cautious combination and comparison of them, is the drudgery to which man is subjected by his Maker, if he wishes to attain sure knowledge."[7]

White pursued the basic line of inquiry of natural history, asking what were the major groups of man, what was the status or character of these groups, and what were the causes of the differences. These questions, which had been raised sporadically in classical and medieval times, became an object of concentrated study in the fifteenth and sixteenth centuries as a result of the great explorations and the discovery of the New World. These events brought Europeans into contact with many new and different peoples, including reports of man-like beings of monstrous size or with tails. The existence of men in the New World in particular posed the theological problem of whether such peoples, separated from the rest of mankind, could have descended from Adam and Eve. By the eighteenth century a more scientific approach to these questions, based on empirical observation and inquiry into natural causes, had been adopted. A threshold in this science was reached when Linnaeus applied to man the same method of systematization and classification that he employed for plants and animals. Classification was the key of Linnaeus's monumental *Systema Naturae*. "For if the name be lost," he wrote at the outset, "the knowledge of the object is lost also; and without these, the student will seek in vain for the means to investigate the hidden treasures of nature."[8] Linnaeus divided man into some six different subtypes ("varieties"), which included the names of Homo Sapiens Europaeus (the White), Homo Sapiens Africanus (the Black), and Homo Sapiens Americanus (the Indian).

These efforts at classification had a circular character to them. Groups or types were recognized inductively by their general morphological characteristics. A variable or set of variables was then specified (such as skin color or hair, etc.) that was supposed to decide scientifically the criteria for establishing difference. This variable was then applied deductively, with types now determined by scientific criteria. The point of departure in this analysis was a set of physical attributes, but it was also assumed that the groups had distinctive "moral" attributes as well, as was the case with animals. As Jefferson put this point in the *Notes*: "there are varieties in the race of man, distinguished by their powers both of body and mind. I believe there are, as I see to be the case in the races of other animals."[9]

Focusing on the major controversy of natural history of his day, Charles White asked whether the types of man derived originally from the same line with the differences resulting from the operation of the environment and historical separation; or whether they came from distinct and separate biological origin. These two positions were known as monogenesis and polygenesis, terms that had a theological as well as natural scientific meaning. Monogenesis in its theological sense referred to the view that mankind was one, having descended from Adam and Eve. In natural scientific accounts, it meant the descent of mankind from one pair or, in a slight variant, from a single mold or prototype.[10] The different types that grew up (referred to as "varieties") resulted from complex interactions of peoples with their environment. Since all developed from the same origin, there was a degree of fluidity among the varieties.

Polygenesis designated the idea of multiple origins of man. All types were said to be man, but the types did not originate from exactly the same source or mold. To distinguish their position from that of monogenesis, many of these thinkers spoke of the different "species" of man. Polygenesis was actually a theory developed first within theology in the mid-seventeenth century by Issac de La Peyrère to account for men in the New World, but it was soon firmly rejected by the Catholic Church.[11] Its unorthodoxy was touted by some bolder souls, Charles White among them, as proof of their freethinking and scientific ways.

"Species" is a term with a prescientific meaning, referring to a class of beings that are recognized by common sense perception to be somehow essentially of the same kind. (In Latin, species means the "look" of a thing.) This prescientific meaning was supported by analyses of two kinds of questions: a "what is" question, in which for man his essence was defined as the being endowed with speech or reason or a soul, and a "from whence" question, in which the origin of man was sought. By a fateful decision the word "species" was included as a key term inside of natural history, where it designated the basic type and was defined, supposedly, in a rigorous and neutral way. (In fact, modern science has given many different definitions to the term, and its precise scientific meaning even today remains a matter of controversy.[12]) But scientific debate over the meaning of the term could never be fully separated from its prescientific meanings. Technical scientific meanings spilled over into moral and political discourse, and moral and political discourse spilled over into "pure" science.

Those who spoke of man as consisting of different species generally wanted to put more stress on the fundamentalness of the difference, while those who spoke of differences as attaining the level of varieties generally wanted to put less stress on the difference.

It is important, however, not to attribute the modern monogenetic view—that "color is only skin deep"—to most eighteenth-century proponents of monogenesis. These scientists generally placed great emphasis on the differentness of the varieties, which no longer were accounted for by *current* circumstances only, but were carried forward by hereditary. Most also spoke of a hierarchy among these varieties. Thus Buffon, a leading proponent of monogenesis, described what Jefferson called an "afflicting picture" of the American Indian, whom Jefferson defended as probably being "formed in mind as well as in body on the same module with the Homo sapiens Europaeus."[13] The difference and hierarchy among varieties for Buffon was a product of environmental influences and of separate histories. The nonwhite races were seen as a degeneration or a falling away from the most fully-developed type, which was the white European.

If the varieties of men differ so greatly, it may be asked what is the practical distinction between monogenesis and polygenesis. What seems to be important, after all, is not the question of origin, but that of how deep and enduring the differences among men had become. Some thinkers, indeed, would shortly make exactly this point, and nineteenth-century polygenetic thinking tended to downplay somewhat the whole debate about origins.[14] But the question of origins seems nevertheless to be one that people cannot entirely ignore. And it seems also to supply a residual explanatory power. On the premise of monogenesis, it was possible to hope for a progressive solution to racial differences whereby mankind, which was originally one, might become one again. What had been caused by environment might be altered by a change of environment. Varieties now lower on the scale might catch up if placed in a more favorable setting. Thus in some passages Buffon suggests that after a certain number of generations the Indian might be transformed. On the premise of polygenesis, the different species of men are seen as permanently different because of a difference in their constitution from the beginning. No amount of environmental change could—or perhaps should—eliminate all of these differences; they are products of nature and—Charles White argued—their "dignity" should be respected.

Monogenesis was the dominant position in natural history in the eighteenth century, which meant that there was a basic harmony between science and a progressive politics of universalism. Polygenesis, whose advocates included Voltaire and Lord Kames, was the minority position. But by the third decade of the nineteenth century the situation was reversed, and a modified form of polygenesis became the leading scientific view both in Europe and in America. Charles White was an important figure in this transition. So too was Thomas Jefferson, at least as White and others at the time interpreted him—and, incidentally, as many interpret him today.[15] In fact, however, Jefferson never strictly took sides in this debate and deliberately left the matter of origins undecided: "I advance it therefore as a suspicion only, that the blacks, whether originally a distinct race, or made distinct by time and circumstances, are inferior to the whites in the endowments both of body and mind. It is not against experience to suppose, that different species of the same genus, or varieties of the same species, may possess different qualifications."[16] Jefferson seemed to be pointing the way to making the criterion of real difference, rather than origin, the basis for classification.

Charles White professed to be interested in pure science only, not politics. At the end of his book he nevertheless raised a political question. Opponents of the slave trade, he reports, charged that his position "tending to establish that the Africans are of an inferior species" would, "whatever truth there may be in the opinion," prove harmful to the cause of eliminating the slave trade; they therefore wanted his work to "be repressed until its publicity could not influence the question of abolition."[17] The mere fact of raising this criticism was itself a sign of a developing crisis within the progressive strain of the Enlightenment. Progressives were now worried that conclusions from the study of natural history—indeed the very process of conducting scientific research—threatened the progressive project. They wanted this science simply to go away, much as Nathan Glazer in his review of *The Bell Curve* wished that current scientific research on racial differences would go away: "Why should we be talking about this at all? For this kind of truth one can ask, what good will come of it?"[18]

White responded to this plea for censorship by proclaiming that he had no hidden political motive in conducting his research and that the slave trade in his view was "indefensible on any hypothesis." As differences in capacity among individuals within the same race did not justify slavery, so they could not logically justify it among different groups of men, especially as there was considerable overlap in capacity among individuals: "Negroes are, at least, equal to thousands of Europeans in capacities and responsibility; and ought therefore to be entitled to freedom and protection. Laws ought not to allow greater freedom to a Shakespeare or a Milton, a Locke or a Newton, than to men of inferior capacities."[19]

White spoke here like a pure natural scientist without directly engaging the argument that the effect of his position would be to undermine support for natural rights. The closest he comes to a response on this point was to repeat the general Enlightenment defense of science on behalf of his own position. A society cannot rest on error or lies, and an enlightened populace will be able to handle any truth without it producing any dire consequences.

Samuel Stanhope Smith and the Environmentalist Thesis

An early reply to White's argument was offered by Dr. Samuel Stanhope Smith, the president of Princeton University, in his book *An Essay on the Causes and Variety of Complexion and Figure in the Human Species*. Smith, with Benjamin Rush, was one of the leading spokesmen for the position of monogenesis in America. His book, published first in 1801, was based on a lecture he had presented much earlier before the American Philosophical Society in 1787.[20] There is therefore reason to suppose that Jefferson had been his original target. Jefferson, who figures prominently in the book, is identified as the "philosopher" who maintains the essential distinction between the white and black and the one on whose "authority" Charles White had built his case for a permanent difference in intelligence between the races.[21]

Smith's argument for monogenesis proceeded on three levels: religion, philosophy, and natural science. All of these, he maintained, supported the position of the unity of the human species. Smith was writing out of a sense of impending intellectual crisis. Not only did natural science seem to be pulling away from theology, but also a new gap had emerged between two fields of knowledge previously thought to be in harmony: empirical science and Enlightenment philosophy.[22] Consistent with the view of the American Protestant Enlightenment, Smith sought to rebuild a common front among all three.

The discussion of natural science occupies by far the largest part of the work. Smith was a full-fledged proponent of the environmentalist thesis, but he claimed to have refined that thesis by expanding the conception of environment to include the "influence of the state of society [on] the varieties of mankind," i.e., the influence of culture on biology.[23] People living in different climates and stages of civilization develop different needs; they therefore favor different attributes, which are increasingly selected. Along the way, too, people develop different ideas of beauty of the human form, and these physical attributes likewise are selected. Thus cultural factors, by influencing both needed and preferred attributes, in turn influence biological qualities, both physical and moral.

Smith concluded—like Buffon—that there were notable differences among the varieties of man and that there was a clear hierarchy, with the white race possessing the superior attributes of both beauty and intelligence. Here, again, one might ask about the practical difference between Smith and Charles White or Thomas Jefferson. The answer turns on the possibilities and limits of change. Alter the environment, Smith argues, and one will see a rapid change of all attributes, if not within one generation, then at any rate over a few. Heredity is not separable from environment or nurture—a view that has been winning increasing favor among many modern researchers.[24] Monogenesis figures here as an important guide to Smith's outlook, opening the possibility that differentiating hereditary factors that have developed will recede when men are placed under the same circumstances and that man's common, original constitution will reassert itself. By contrast, polygenesis, by contending that men were originally different, lends credence to the view that groups of men will remain different permanently, even when subject to the same environment. The question of origin thus influences what is considered to be with or against the grain, i.e, natural.

Smith's theory claimed that the changes that would occur would be both moral and *physical* and that these two changes would take place at roughly the same time. It has been the white race that has been in possession of freedom and has had the opportunity to exercise reason in civilized societies. Provide blacks the same opportunities in the same environment and they will rapidly develop and display the same powers of reason and imagination. They will also become more like whites physically, without miscegenation. Smith cited instances of freed black persons developing physical characteristics redolent of whites. And he conducted his own observations of the black students at Princeton, where he found the same process at work.[25]

Smith closed his book with what he called a philosophic argument, where "philosophy" is a mode of thought that includes the conscious development of categories with a view to promoting a beneficial effect. If humans are *not* conceived as being essentially of one kind, he argues, the possibility of a universal moral science and a universal human nature or psychology will be thrown into doubt. If "species" is the word we use to designate that essential oneness, then philosophy must suppose that we are all of one species: "But destroy this unity [in man] and no certain and universal principles of human nature remain. . . . The principles and rules which a philosopher might derive from the study of his own nature could not be applied with certainty to regulate the conduct of other men, and other nations, who might be a totally different species."[26]

Samuel Stanhope Smith was seeking not just to refute the biological propositions of Charles White and Thomas Jefferson, but to ground the cause of progressive politics and natural rights on a biological proposition of his own: on the idea of the progressive disappearance of all aspects of difference. If man was truly one biologically, there is no reason in the end that there should be any traces left of race at all. Such was the logical conclusion of an environmentalist monogenesis. The problem that emerged for these proponents of monogenesis was that their scientific arguments, which possessed many insights and strengths, was at odds with the observed facts on the disappearance of race as a physical attribute. Their position became subject to ridicule and with it the suspicion grew that their whole scientific position had been built to serve a preconceived political end. Real science, it was said, was polygenesis, and more and more it came to carry the day.

The American Ethnological School: The New Polygenicists

Near the end of the passage on racial hierarchy in Query XIV of the *Notes*, Jefferson makes a plea to American scientists to take advantage of their unique situation and establish a school of natural history to investigate the varieties of man: "To our reproach it must be said, that though for a century we have had under our eyes the races of black and red men, they have never yet been viewed by us as subjects of natural history." Consistent with this advice, a group of American scholars founded a scientific discipline in the first part of the nineteenth century under the name of "ethnology." The new name was intended by its leaders to signal a break with the dominant monogenetic view within natural history. Ethnology promoted polygenesis, which fit with the trend that was developing within European thought as well.

The American school was notable not only for its emphasis on the different origins and ranks of man, but also for its strongly social and political orientation. The stated purpose of ethnology, according to the lead author of the huge American ethnological compendium, *Types of Mankind*, was "to investigate the mental and physical differences of mankind" and to "deduce from these investigations principles of human guidance in all the important relations of social existence."[27] Almost all the ethnologists accepted the idea that an interbreeding of the races would result in an averaging of human qualities, and most therefore concluded that racial intermixing was to be avoided. The chief political question in America, however, was slavery. Although a few within the group, such as the famous Harvard professor of natural history, Louis Agassiz, opposed slavery, the most active organizers of the new science militated openly in its favor. A measure of the degree of the influence they finally were able to exercise is illustrated in a speech given by Alexander Stephens, vice president of the Confederacy, in 1861, in which Stephens based the regime on the "truths" of this science. The American founding, he claimed, "rested upon the assumption of the equality of the races. This was an error. . . . Our new government is founded upon exactly the opposite idea; its cornerstone rests upon the great truth that the negro is not the equal of the white man; that slavery—subordination to the superior race—is his natural and normal condition."[28]

For Stephens and most of the ethnologists, the supposed fact of racial inequality was taken to vitiate any claim of natural rights. Although Jefferson's influence is readily apparent in some of their discussions of racial hierarchy, they generally avoided referring to him directly—no doubt because of his opposition to slavery and his advocacy of natural rights. But in the volume *Cotton Is King*, a work defending slavery that was published in 1860, two of the authors turn to Jefferson's views in the *Notes*, which had just recently been publicized again by being cited in Henry Randall's 1857 biography of Thomas Jefferson.[29] Having invoked Jefferson as an authority, these authors had to square this part of his thought with the Declaration's statement that "all men are created equal." The two positions, it was argued, would indeed be in stark contradiction if "all men" meant persons of all races. But Jefferson's real views are to be found in the *Notes*, and the Declaration could therefore have only been referring to those of the white race.

Moving from the fact of racial inequality to the claim that slavery is justified or natural is, one would think, a critical step requiring much argument. But it is a remarkable political fact (and one I will comment on later) that this gap did not need to be filled in public discourse. Some ethnologists, to be sure, saw the need to make the connection by referring to "natural" in one of its three primary senses: something that is a deep and original fact (as in a natural species or natural cause); what living beings choose spontaneously or by inclination; and what fulfills or is fitting for living beings. The main argument for slavery referred to natural in the sense of what was good or fitting. The vast difference in capacity between the two races, it was said, meant that whites alone could rule, while blacks, being unable to govern themselves, needed to be ruled for their own good. Some ethnologists argued for the naturalness of slavery by combining the sense of a deep fact with what is fitting. If two races happen to be fated to live together, slavery indirectly becomes necessary or natural as the best way to prevent an intermixing of the races. A mixing of two different species would produce a hybrid that—as occurred with other hybrids in nature—might be unable to assure its biological replacement over the long run; or it would produce an averaging of qualities that pulled down the higher race, which was not good or fitting.

Finally, there is one ethnologist, S. A. Cartwright—one who proclaimed himself to be a true follower of Jefferson's call to "study the races under our eye"—who from the point of view of a proponent of slavery sensed a weakness in these arguments. All sought to make the case for the naturalness by relying on a sense of natural that contained a teleological element of what was fitting or good for man. Cartwright understood, however, that the strongest and most evident sense of natural to the modern mind was that which refers to what living beings choose by inclination. Following the logic of this insight, he produced what he considered to be the most powerful argument for slavery. In an article entitled "Of Ethnology: Slavery in the Light of Ethnology," Cartwright argues that "the obedience of the Nirgitian to the Caucasian is spontaneous because it is normal for the weaker to yield to the stronger." On the basis of this reasoning, he comes to the conclusion that there is no slavery, properly speaking, in America because "subordination of the inferior to the superior is a normal and not an enforced condition."[30] Only where there is subjugation of an equal by artifice or force is there slavery, but there is no such thing in the United States because equals are on a perfect equality.

Establishment Historians of the Twentieth Century

Many historians who wrote in the middle part of this century and who devoted large parts of their careers to the study of Thomas Jefferson took a very different view of the passage on racial hierarchy. It needs to be said, of course, that the period in which they produced their work was one in which most scholars were trying to come to terms with the legacies of Jim Crow and segregation and the horrors of Nazism. The prevailing view in much anthropology and biology was to deny any notion of hereditary group differences outside of physical features and to insist that group differences that existed were wholly the result of nurture. Whether this climate of opinion affected the judgment of the historians cannot be known for certain. But what is clear is that many of them approached Jefferson's passage on race gingerly, seemingly aware of the depth of feeling that it could provoke and the damage it posed to Jefferson's reputation. The position they argued was almost the mirror image of that of the ethnologists. It was to insist that Jefferson's natural rights and anti-slavery position somehow compensated for any other views he held about race. The underlying ideas seemed to be that if one were genuinely opposed in principle to slavery, then one could not hold—or hold seriously—to a view of inequality of the races.

To make this argument these historians advanced a number of points. First, some cited Jefferson's views on Indians, where he argues that any backwardness to be found was due to circumstances and not nature—which corresponds exactly to the dominant twentieth-century monogenetic thesis that "color is only skin-deep."[31] The problem with this line of argument, however, is that it in no way changes Jefferson's thesis about blacks. Indeed, Jefferson claimed to use the same science to study both groups, and the policy conclusion he ultimately drew was consistent with these scientific findings: he sanctions interbreeding of the white with the Indian, but not with the black. Second, some of the historians claim that Jefferson was "ahead of his time" on issues of race and that, in the words of William Peden, "his attitude toward that of race and toward the institution of slavery was startlingly advanced for eighteenth-century Virginia."[32] This argument assumes its own conclusion by linking together views of race and slavery and making it appear as if both must be moving in tandem toward the modern view. In fact, it would be just as accurate to say that Jefferson was "ahead of his time" when he claimed that there were vast disparities among the races, because this position became the dominant view in the nineteenth century.

In yet a third argument, some historians have contended that Jefferson revised his position as expressed in the *Notes* and abandoned his views of racial inequality. While it is true that Jefferson never publicly repeated what he said in the *Notes*, there is no real evidence that he ever changed his mind. Finally, many historians rightly call attention to the fact that Jefferson offers his views tentatively and with qualifications. He makes clear that he has not proved his conclusion definitively, that it is a "conjecture" and an "opinion . . . [that] must be hazarded with great diffidence." One of the reasons he gives for this hesitation is that "it would degrade a whole race of men from the rank in the scale of beings which their Creator may perhaps have given them." This last statement demonstrates another point. Jefferson was also fully aware of the centrality of the issue he was raising and of its enormous theoretical significance.

II

This survey shows that many interpreters of Jefferson assume that because *they* think that the positions of natural rights and of a hierarchy among the races are in conflict, Jefferson must therefore have thought this as well— or that he must have been "moving" during his life to give up one or the other position. The problem with making this assumption as an interpretive strategy is that it obscures what Jefferson was trying to do. Nothing could be clearer from the text of the *Notes* than that Jefferson holds to the doctrine of natural rights *and* to the possibility (more likely the probability) of strong differences among the races. Not only this, but he is perfectly aware of what appears to be a tension between the two positions, and his whole aim is to reconcile them. Jefferson, in short, does not walk into this discussion inadvertently. He states the claims of nature as he understands them to derive from two of the most important sciences of his time, and he proceeds to try to put them together.

As Michael Zuckert has treated so well the claims of nature in natural rights thinking, here it is important only to point out the basic category to which "nature" refers in this context. The subject is "man" or the character of human nature. Nature in natural rights thinking begins with asking a "what is" question: what are the essential characteristics of human nature? Nature is concerned with propositions of *psychology*. The starting point of natural rights thinking came with Thomas Hobbes, who cites as his "first principle" that "the dispositions of men are naturally such, that unless they be restrained through fear of some coercive power, every man will distrust and dread each other." The approach that begins from psychology continues (with some changes in content) with Locke and then with Jefferson. For Jefferson, according to Zuckert, the fundamental character of human nature is the "determinative character of [man's] security-seeking. . . . All animals seek their own survival; only humans seek security, the reasonable confidence in the prospect for survival and the allaying of the anxieties arising from threats to existence."[33]

The "passion" for security is only one part of Jefferson's full account of nature. Following this passion, it turns out, does not by itself enable man to achieve the security he seeks. To realize this goal, man must make use of another quality he possesses—reason—and follow the guide of a science that reveals the propositions or laws which can produce the conditions of security. Obviously, the use of reason in this sense has not been practiced by all or even most men, but it remains a human possibility. "What transforms the claims of the passions into rights," Zuckert writes, "is the civilized figuring out of the system of mutual respect for rights."[34] Nature, then, operates or makes itself manifest in two ways: through passion or inclination, which is to say spontaneously; and through reason or a process of "figuring out," which may require the aid of science and enlightenment.

The most important function of natural rights thinking is to guide man in the discovery of the natural laws that lay the foundation for legitimate political systems. Natural rights thinking also contributes to sound political analysis by putting a spotlight on the real or deepest sources of behavior. Using Hobbes again to illustrate the point, psychology allows the analyst to understand why people in fact lock their doors at night and why nations keep troops on their borders. Contrary to the moralizing way in which many conceive of natural rights thinking today, it is based on a remarkably sober and realistic approach. Jefferson's discussions of slavery often apply this realistic kind of analysis. Where rule is not based on consent but derives from brute force, it cannot be stable. Natural rights thinking "predicts" that slaves will revolt—in particular in an age in which the doctrine of natural rights is spreading throughout the world. Establishing regimes based on rights is thus not just "right"; it is also in the long-term interest of all.

Jefferson's conception of nature inside of natural history refers to another category: the permanent distribution of different attributes and capacities among different *groups*. This conception emerges most clearly in the passage on racial hierarchy, and it is best to turn now to that passage and see the context in which this view of nature is developed. The discussion of racial hierarchy, it should be noted, occurs *inside* of the presentation of a plan to eliminate slavery in Virginia, which shows again that Jefferson was fully aware of the two different conceptions of nature that were in question. The plan surely ranks as one of the most audacious proposals of rational social engineering ever conceived. It rivals in scope (and in many ways resembles) Socrates' plan for founding a new city in the *Republic*. For Jefferson, the extreme situation of slavery justified the extreme solution he offers.

The plan has three parts: (1) *Emancipation*. The children of slaves will all be taken away from their families at an early age. A new generation, cut off from the baleful influences of slavery and brought up by the state, would be taught a variety of arts and skills needed to create a self-sustaining regime. (2) *Colonization*. The educated progeny of the slaves, after having reached the age of twenty-one for males and eighteen for females, would be sent away to a colony. (The place is not specified and would be decided at a later time.) The colony would be supplied with the wherewithal to get started and would be granted independence. (3) *Replacement of labor*. The immigration of an equal number of "white inhabitants" from around the world would be sought to compensate for the labor shortage resulting from the loss of slaves.

While this plan is offered for the state of Virginia only, Jefferson clearly intended it as a blueprint for the entire nation. And although the plan applies only to slaves, it obviously had profound implications for free blacks as well. As the foundation of the whole plan is to create a separate white nation and a separate black nation, other steps would no doubt be taken to induce free blacks to leave the United States and join the colony. This proposal for separation of the races is so dramatic that Jefferson has no choice but to make it the central focus of the discussion: "It will probably be asked, Why not retain, and incorporate the blacks into the state . . . ?" He offers two types of reasons: "political" and "physical and moral" analysis, i.e., considerations deriving from natural history.

In his political argument, Jefferson contends that a peaceful common life between the two races is impossible because of the blacks' resentment of whites for the injuries they have suffered and because of the whites' prejudice toward blacks. If left in the same place, the two races would form into antagonistic parties leading to war and the extermination of one race or the other. Because matters did not end with the utter disaster Jefferson predicted, some have questioned the sincerity and objectivity of this political analysis. Jefferson, it has been suggested, may have fit his political conclusion to support a policy of racial separation; or his natural-rights inspired analysis may have led him to overestimate the role of fear in human affairs and thus to dismiss other possible outcomes. Without dismissing these criticisms, a strong case can be made that Jefferson's political analysis, which was shared by others who held different views on racial equality, represented a sound assessment of the situation.[35]

Jefferson, accordingly, could have ended his discussion with his "political" argument. But he does not. He elects instead to leave the realm of traditional political analysis and to launch a scientific investigation of the differences between the races. The results are by now well known. Jefferson observes the black to be the equal of the white in memory, but decidedly inferior in imagination and reason (the most important of the human faculties).[36] As to the cause, he offers his "conjecture" that "[i]t is not their condition then, but nature, which has produced the distinction." The conclusion from natural history that he imports back into the political realm is that race—independent of any feelings of difference or strangeness—ought to be a criterion in determining the boundaries of political communities.

Why this step into natural history? Some have suggested a rhetorical element to this analysis because of how it functions to lend additional support to his political conclusion. As Merrill Peterson has noted, by offering this scientific theory Jefferson may have "hoped to hasten a solution—the only workable one in his opinion—to the most menacing problem of the new nation."[37] Jefferson, we know, was only too aware of the slaveholders' reluctance to give up their slaves, which leads him at one point in the *Notes* to go so far as to invoke the possibility that "supernatural interference" might punish the slaveholder. If he was willing to use a supernatural argument for political effect, might he not also have been willing to use a "scientific" one for the same purpose? Along the same lines, others have surmised that Jefferson had to deal in some way with scientific views because these views had *already* penetrated into political life and become a source of political opinion. In this reading, he could have been trying to counter the rapid-change environmentalist view that would have led to a policy based on the absurd expectations that the race problem would vanish in the next generation. Or he might have been addressing those who accepted the thesis of the inferiority of the black and who opposed slavery. This group was caught in a bind as long as it was thought that the only alternative to slavery was the incorporation of the blacks into the state as free citizens, ultimately perhaps to intermix with whites. Jefferson's plan would eliminate slavery but ensure that the black would be placed "beyond the reach of mixture" with the white.

There is no question that Jefferson's argument about racial hierarchy bolsters his political analysis about the need to separate the two races—just as, incidentally, his argument about the similarity of the Indian to the white bolsters his earlier political argument about the equality of the New World and the Old. But admitting this point does not mean that he used his scientific investigations as a mere device. Whenever a careful writer makes what is only a rhetorical argument, there are usually indications that this is the case. It is hard to find such indications here. If anything, Jefferson elevated the theoretical status of natural history inside of political affairs, and this was surely how he was understood. Jefferson elected to introduce natural history into social science in the belief that this theoretical step would improve social science, making it more comprehensive and more useful in guiding human affairs. This move was anticipated by other writers, but Jefferson was perhaps the first to elaborate scientific ideas about racial hierarchy in a work that was devoted as much to social or political matters as to "pure" science.

It is important to consider what this theoretical argument adds to the political argument in the development of political thought. Two points may be noted. First, a theoretical proposition offers an argument that is to be applied generally, outside the context of the particular case in which it might have been advanced. Once a new theoretical model is introduced, moreover, it invites further thinking along the same lines—meaning here further investigation into which racial (or ethnic) groups might form the biological basis for determining political communities. Such was the effect of Jefferson's social science, at least indirectly, on subsequent political thought in America and Europe. Second, even in the particular situation in which it is introduced, a theoretical position does more than just reinforce a political argument. A political argument is by definition contingent; it can change as circumstances change. But a theoretical argument keeps its validity even under a change of circumstances. The "value added" by Jefferson's theoretical step can be seen from the following statement by St. George Tucker, a fellow Virginian deeply involved in looking for a solution to the slave question at the time: "If it be true, as Mr. Jefferson seems to suppose, that the African are really an inferior race of mankind, will not sound policy advise their exclusion from a society in which they have not yet been admitted to participate in civil rights; and even to guard against such admission, *at any future period*, since it may eventually depreciate the whole national character."[38]

Jefferson's conclusion that natural history recommends a separation of black and white "beyond the reach of mixture" requires us to ask once again how nature operates. Posing this issue admittedly pushes the inquiry to the most extreme lengths. But it is just this kind of concrete analysis that a theory of nature, if it is not to be just idle rhetoric, is supposed to provide. Is a desire for separation something felt spontaneously, or is it the result of a rational "figuring out" with the help of science? And if it is the latter, is the end to fulfill a desire, or is it in the service of some other objective?

Jefferson proceeds in this area by suggestion and indirection without anything like the specificity that is found in his treatment of nature in natural rights thinking. Perhaps this is because he was in newer territory or because the issues go right to delicate matters of sexual attraction and breeding. So far as one can tell, however, Jefferson sees nature here as operating from a combination of spontaneous passion and of a process of rational "figuring out," one indeed that introduces certain ends not otherwise directly embodied in his political thought. There may be a repulsion, he suggests, felt by those of the higher variety at the idea of breeding with a lower one, although this does not deny a simultaneous and illicit attraction to doing the same. There is also, he tells us, a natural yearning for beauty, which works in the same direction. The most important considerations, however, relate to the fate of man's moral capacities of imagination and reason. An interbreeding of the races, he maintains, would have the effect of averaging the two; this means a lowering of the intelligence of the whites and thus the leveling of a hierarchy found in nature.[39] It is not clear, however, whether there is a spontaneous inclination in man to maintain this hierarchy.[40] Doing so, it seems, must be a result of man's figuring out its importance in the light of what science teaches us: "Will not a lover of natural history then, one who views the gradations in all the races of animals with the eye of philosophy, excuse an effort to keep those in the department of man as distinct as nature has formed them?" Those who establish societies should be concerned with promoting the "dignity and beauty" of the human race as well as liberty.[41] Jefferson, finally, seemed concerned that a black and miscegenized populace might lack the capacity to maintain a republic. While all peoples have the right to establish governments devoted to liberty, success in this enterprise is rare and depends on a populace of unusual talent.

III

In assessing Jefferson's social science there is a strong temptation today to turn immediately to a discussion of modern natural history (biology) and point out the many errors in his analysis. In the end, however, it may be asked whether biology should be granted the exclusive prerogative of deciding fundamental elements of political life. Much that is found in the biological treatment of man not only once was, but also still remains, unproven and the subject of speculation and controversy. How reasonable or prudent is it therefore to base questions of political doctrine on the shifting grounds of this science?

An alternative is to look to political science for guidance inside the political realm. Using this approach, many thinkers of the era—among them some of America's other founders and Alexis de Tocqueville—offered penetrating criticisms of the kind of social science Jefferson had developed. It was taken to task both for its method, which elevated a natural science rather than traditional political analysis to the seat of judgment in political affairs, and for its content, above all for the introduction of the new fundamental category of racial hierarchy. Together these posed a threat to the cause of promoting natural rights republics.

Let us briefly apply this approach here. If hindsight (or "experience") is better than foresight, it is wisest to begin with hindsight. And here the record of the past two centuries offers what looks like unmistakable evidence of the danger for natural rights republics of introducing a biological doctrine of racial inequality into the framework of social science. This point has been demonstrated both in the case of the United States, where this doctrine was used to defend slavery and later to justify segregation, and in Europe, where the doctrine culminated in the Nazi regime and the Final Solution. It is true, of course, that many defenders of racial hierarchy intended no such results. But the relevant consideration for political science is not the intentions of individuals; it is an analysis of the knowable and nonaccidental results of actions or theories.

Reasoning on these lines may proceed first by analyzing connections of cause and effect within a given historical context. Jefferson stated that his "two great objects" for the *Notes* were to secure "the emancipation of [the nation's] slaves" and "the settlement of their constitution on a firmer and more permanent basis."[42] He sought to solve the race problem on terms that he maintained were, under the circumstances, in the best interests of both races. But it is difficult to understand how his theoretical doctrine could have proven helpful in this regard. Even if one allows that an abstract idea of biological inequality of groups does not lead to an argument for slavery, there is this basic historical fact with which to contend: from the sixteenth century forward, the justification of slavery rested on the belief of black inferiority. How could a supposedly scientific doctrine purporting to establish *exactly* this fact be used politically in any other way but to serve this same purpose? In the case of Europe, Jefferson can be judged less harshly. When he wrote the *Notes* it was probably still too soon to have been able to foresee the specific connection of cause and effect that would produce the full explosiveness of the doctrine of racial inequality in Europe. Jefferson could not then reasonably have known that shortly thereafter, in a reaction that set in against the French Revolution and the Enlightenment, many would begin a search for an anti-universalistic ground for community, a search that would move from historical tradition to linguistic commonality and finally to race as the "strongest"—because it was the most natural and scientific—ground of difference.

The second and more important line of cause-effect reasoning focuses on the political consequences that logically flow from a certain way of thinking. On this score, Jefferson's social science posed greater problems for the cause of natural rights republics. Even those accepting his views of natural history were left with new difficulties in defending a natural rights position. The decisive theoretical element of Jeffersonian social science is its recognition of the group as a natural entity; the group has a status equal in importance and dignity to the individual as one of the two natural entities that exist in the social world. From this fact, certain political consequences follow.

1. The importance of consent and contract as the foundation of political communities is reduced or conditioned. There are natural communities that fix outer limits for determining who should be included in a community. These communities are not contingent products of accident or history that might be dealt with, albeit with great difficulty, by political means. They are instead natural entities whose integrity cannot be—or perhaps ought not to be—altered. To know what these groups are is, in part at least, a matter that is to be decided by a new kind of science.

2. The primacy of the political regime as the deepest formative influence in social life is questioned or denied. The category of the group rivals, if it does not take precedence over, the political regime. What different societies of men can accomplish is now held to be set as much by race as by the political regime. Indeed, this way of thinking would lead to the conclusion that the kind of political regime that a given group is able to choose is bounded by, though not fully explained by, the character of the group.

3. With the reason and the will of individuals subordinated in certain ways to the pre-political category of group, people are legitimated to a certain degree in thinking in a group or "tribal" way. Tribal thinking directly threatens the basic mentality that undergirds the natural rights system. Natural rights thinking is based on the idea that while great differences in important human qualities do indeed exist, these need not be acknowledged by all in specific cases and cannot be established to the satis-

faction of all. Each individual has his pride and can insist on his equality. This situation—a situation of assertable equality—is the foundation for the mental experiment that leads an individual to see, reasonably, the necessity for reciprocity. Tribal thinking backed by science changes this calculation: now the group is a factor as well as the individual, and now there is an objective and scientific determination, known and observable in advance, that establishes rank. These facts give rise to a group spirit of dominion—the antithesis of the spirit that natural rights thinking is supposed to instill. The legitimation of this spirit probably helps explain why so many could accept without further argument the rightness of slavery when the very same principle that might be used to justify it—for example, a difference in intelligence between groups—was not considered satisfactory in justifying slavery between two individuals.

Reasons of this kind led those practicing political science at the time to try to put distance between the doctrines of political science and the various theories emanating from natural history. This effort at maintaining distance applied not just to biological speculations favoring polygenesis but in some measure to those that supported monogenesis as well—for example, speculative notions about the disappearance of race. The practitioners of political science had no wish to hold their discipline hostage to the theories from another science. It was not that political science denied the possibility of group differences of some kind. Common sense, indeed, suggests these might well exist. But the origin, character, and significance of these differences had not been settled by natural history. Political science meanwhile had its own methods, techniques, and evidentiary sources to deal with these issues, and it had its own purposes as well.

Political science as a discipline seeks to offer guidance about how to promote societies that can best secure the advantage of man and then how to secure the advantage of these societies. By the late eighteenth century the leading practitioners of political science in America had decided in favor of the model of constitutional government. To promote this system, most had turned to natural rights as a doctrine that could supply a solid and logical ground for justifying the basic elements of this regime. At the same time, they were well aware that no doctrine of this kind could comprise the whole of political science. It was for political science to determine how that doctrine itself was to be employed and what other considerations and supports were needed to sustain natural rights regimes.

For dealing with the questions of who could be included in a society and what was possible for different societies to achieve, political science found in natural rights doctrine an effective ground for asserting a reasonable conception of the unity of the mankind. This unity was determined in the answer to a "what is" question about man's common psychological nature.

This common nature—that man's constitution resists any idea of rank so great as to give another an unconditional title to rule—is what helps define the species. In Locke's words, there is "nothing more evident than that creatures of the same species and rank, promiscuously born to all the same advantages of Nature, and the use of the same faculties, should also be equal one amongst another, without subordination or subjection."[43] This statement neither confirms nor denies the possibility of the existence of differences among groups. But whatever such differences might be, they are not primary and do not foreclose the possibility of a political community being constructed through the consent of any number of individuals. Again, this possibility does not preclude one from taking into account political and prudential considerations about what forms the proper limits of particular communities.[44]

Practitioners of political science have added to natural rights doctrine certain inferential elements from man's experience that bear on this question. Where some natural historians might suppose, on the basis of their field work or their analysis of certain test scores, that they have come to definitive conclusions about the nature of differences among groups, political scientists have felt that they may offer evidence of their own from political history of the successes of different groups and of the effects of different political orders. For example, responding to one theory of racial hierarchy, Alexis de Tocqueville offered the following cautionary rejoinder: "I am sure that Julius Caesar, had he had the time, would have willingly written a book to prove that the savages he had met in Britain did not belong to the same race as the Romans, and that the latter were destined thus by nature to rule the world while the former were destined to vegetate in one of its corners."[45]

Political science obviously did not answer many questions that the research of natural history raised on race and group differences. Modern science raises similar questions today, and many demand that political science somehow resolve these matters by bringing forth a doctrine like natural rights to affirm or deny certain current scientific speculation. Although it is obviously tempting to use natural rights in this way, it is unwise to do so. Political science has assigned this doctrine a highly important function in the defense of constitutional regimes. That function is to establish a solid foundation in human reason for a society that promotes the equal rights of individuals. Efforts to use natural rights to support whatever claims for equality some think are helpful only places the doctrine in a position where it cannot be defended on the grounds of reason. Natural rights become a moral wish list, and the doctrine sacrifices any claim to objectivity. There is no longer anything natural about it.

Liberal democracies probably have a need for conceptions of equality that go beyond natural rights doctrine. Political science must therefore investigate the understandings of equality that help maintain this system and the intellectual foundations that support them. But political science is clearly not in a position to dictate what the findings of other fields must be. No one vested it with this power. Indeed in our age, where various realms of knowledge may be pursued freely, political opinions will inevitably be affected by speculations from other fields. To say this, however, does not mean that political science is helpless or without influence. It retains its mild voice of reason and can still make clear to practitioners of other disciplines the responsibilities they bear to society.

NOTES

1. Michael P. Zuckert, *The Natural Rights Republic* (Notre Dame, Ind.: University of Notre Dame Press, 1996), 58.

2. John Hope Franklin, *Racial Equality in America* (Chicago: University of Chicago Press, 1976), 19. For an account which documents Jefferson's record in dealing with the question of slavery, see Paul Finkelman, "Jefferson and Slavery," in *Jeffersonian Legacies*, ed. Peter Onuf (Charlottesville: University of Virginia Press, 1993), 181–221.

3. Winthrop D. Jordan, *The White Man's Burden* (New York: Oxford University Press, 1974), 165.

4. Charles White, *An Account of the Regular Gradation in Man* (London, printed for C. Dilly, 1799). The book derives from a paper read in 1795 in Manchester.

5. Ibid., 65.

6. Jefferson's basic description of the black was in line with what was said by most students of natural history in the eighteenth century, including Linnaeus, Buffon, Voltaire, Kames, Blumenbach, and some of the authors of the Encyclopédie, not to mention the historical accounts of Edward Long.

7. Jefferson, *Notes on the State of Virginia*, in *The Portable Thomas Jefferson*, ed. Merrill Peterson (New York: Penguin, 1975), Query VI, 101.

8. Karl Linnaeus, *Systema Naturae* (Wilhelmi de Groot, 1735), 1:3.

9. Jefferson, *Notes*, Query VI, 101.

10. The French word that Buffon used here was "moule," which Jefferson rendered in English as "module."

11. On Issac de La Peyrère, see Leo Strauss, *Spinoza's Critique of Religion* (Chicago: University of Chicago Press, 1997), 64, and Léon Poliakov, *Le Mythe Aryen* (Paris: Calmann-Lévy, 1971), 153.

12. See Ernst Mayr, *The Growth of Biological Thought* (Cambridge: Belknap Press, 1982).

13. Jefferson, *Notes*, 94, 98–99.

14. According to Samuel Morton and Josiah Nott, a species may be defined as "a type, or organic form, that is permanent; or which has remained unchanged under the opposite climatic influence for ages. The Arab, the Egyptian, and the Negro; the greyhound, the turnspit, and the common wild dog . . . may be cited as examples" (*Types of Mankind* [Philadelphia: Lippincott, 1854], 375). According to Louis Agassiz, this conceptual breakthrough had revolutionized the study of man; it constituted a "true philosophical definition of species, the first to bless the world of science."

15. See Alexander Boulton, "The American Paradox: Jeffersonian Equality and Racial Science," *American Quarterly* 47, no. 3 (1995): 467–92.

16. Jefferson, *Notes*, Query XIV, 192. All further quotations from this passage can be found in Query XIV, 185–93.

17. White, *An Account of the Regular Gradation in Man*, 137. Léon Poliakov explains how, in general, the anti-slavery political position which came to dominate England in the nineteenth century slowed the emergence in that country of the newer and more advanced polygenetic thinking.

18. Nathan Glazer, "The Lying Game," *The New Republic*, October 31, 1994, p. 16.

19. White, *An Account of the Regular Gradation in Man*, 137.

20. Samuel Stanhope Smith, *An Essay on the Causes of the Variety of Complexion and Figure in the Human Species* (New Brunswick: Simpson, 1810). The final edition was published in 1810, but an earlier version appeared in 1801.

21. Smith, *An Essay*, 271, 277, 288.

22. The distinguishing of philosophy from natural science, when the two had generally been used previously as synonyms, reflects the problem that was opening up within Enlightenment thought. The empirical and positivist branch in the study of man no longer necessarily backed up the moral and political conclusions that the progressive or revolutionary side had favored.

23. Smith, *An Essay*, 7.

24. See Thomas Sowell, *Race and Culture* (New York: Basic Books, 1994), 166–68, and Rosemary Rosser, *Cognitive Development: Psychological and Biological Perspectives* (Boston: Allyn and Bacon, 1994).

25. Smith, *An Essay*, 83, 115.

26. Smith, *An Essay*, 12, 243.

27. Josiah Nott, *Types of Mankind*, 7.

28. See Harry Cleveland, *Alexander H. Stephens* (Philadelphia: National Publishing, 1866), 721.

29. E. N. Elliott, *Cotton Is King* (Augusta, Ga.: Abbot and Loomis, 1860). See Henry S. Randall, *Life of Thomas Jefferson* (Philadelphia: J. B. Lippincott, 1857), 3 vols., 1:369–70.

30. S. A. Cartwright, "Of Ethnology: Slavery in the Light of Ethnology," in *Cotton Is King*, 721–22.

31. For this position see Adrienne Koch, *The Philosophy of Thomas Jefferson* (Chicago: Quadrangle Books, 1964).

32. Thomas Jefferson, *Notes on the State of Virginia*, ed. William Peden (Chapel Hill: University of North Carolina Press, 1995), Query XIV, note 6.

33. Zuckert, *Natural Rights Republic*, 66, 69.

34. Ibid., 76.

35. Whether it would have been possible to move so many people to a new place, unless that place was a large territory of the adjacent South or Western regions, would be an important consideration. When Jefferson wrote the *Notes*, he may have had just such a region in mind. Later, however, he would suggest the Caribbean.

36. In regard to the moral sense, Jefferson does not state unequivocally that there is an equality, but he certainly dismisses the assertions of many of any great inequality: "I believe that in those of the heart she will be found to have done them justice. That disposition to theft with which they have been branded, must be ascribed to their situation, and not to any depravity of the moral sense."

37. Merrill D. Peterson, *Thomas Jefferson and the New Nation* (London: Oxford University Press), 263–64.

38. Emphasis added. Cited in Winthrop Jordan, *White Over Black* (Chapel Hill: University of North Carolina Press, 1968), 558.

39. "The improvement of the blacks in body and mind, in the first instance of their mixture with the whites, has been observed by every one, and proves that their inferiority is not the effect merely of their condition of life."

40. See Jefferson's letter to John Adams, October 28, 1813, in which Jefferson observes a certain recalcitrance in humans to the notion of breeding for perfection. This recalcitrance comes, among other things, from the mysterious attractions of our sex drive *(oestrum)* and, in modern times, from the doctrine of equal rights, which will not accord exclusive sexual privileges to the few. *Portable Thomas Jefferson*, 533–34.

41. See here also Jefferson's letter to Edward Coles, August 25, 1814, in which Jefferson writes that "their amalgamation with the other color produces a degradation to which no lover of his country, no lover of excellence in the human character can innocently assent." *Portable Thomas Jefferson*, 546.

42. Jefferson, Letter to Chastellux, June 7, 1785. *Portable Jefferson*, 386–88.

43. John Locke, *Second Treatise of Government*, parag 4.

44. This is the subject, for example, of *The Federalist* no. 2.

45. Letter of Alexis de Tocqueville, in John Lukacs, *The European Tradition and the Correspondence with Gobineau* (Gloucester, Mass.: Peter Smith, 1968), 228.

Response

᪥

Michael P. Zuckert

The seven essays in this volume demonstrate that even now there is much interest in the thoughts and doings of Thomas Jefferson. That merely confirms what is visible in many other places—the outpouring of books on Jefferson continues unabated, the "shrine" to Jefferson at Monticello attracts record numbers of visitors, movies are made about him. He is, I think it fair to say, that member of the founding generation in whom present-day Americans have retained the greatest interest. That was certainly not always so—earlier generations seem to have been more interested in George Washington and later ones, perhaps, will be more interested in James Madison. But Jefferson interests us. In the Progressive and New Deal eras, it was Jefferson, "champion of the common man," who caught the eye of the nation, Jefferson, leader of the Democratic Republican party that opposed the plutocrat Hamilton. Now, it seems, we are interested in Jefferson partly for the sake of Sally Hemings, but even more because Jefferson was the chief author of the Declaration of Independence, that inheritance from the founding era that has most resonance and appeal for us.

The seven essays in this volume also demonstrate that we have reached no more agreement on how to understand Jefferson, on what to make of him, or how to assess the value of what he said and did, than Americans of previous generations. The disagreements, as they surface in these essays, center around three issues: (1) Is Jefferson a coherent and in any sense a systematic thinker? Two of the essays (by Robert Dawidoff and Booth Fowler) emphatically answer, no. Two others (by Garrett Ward Sheldon and Joyce Appleby) just as emphatically answer, yes. At least two of the others (by Jean Yarbrough and myself) lean toward the coherence side of the continuum.

Disagreements also exist on (2), What are we to make of Jefferson on race? This is familiar territory for Jefferson, he having been deployed on both sides of American arguments about race and slavery from the very outset of the republic. Witness the extraordinarily telling fact that the leader of one side during the Civil War was named after Jefferson and the leader of the other side claimed never to have had a political idea whose source was not Jefferson. James Ceaser revisits this theme with a novel interpretation of Jefferson's race theories as put forward in *Notes on Virginia*. Finally, (3), Just what is the doctrine of rights which Jefferson so eloquently and fatefully installed in the Declaration of Independence? Yarbourgh and I face this issue directly, and most of the others at least touch on it.

Coherence

Both Dawidoff and Fowler doubt Jefferson's coherence and either explicitly or implicitly suggest I have pushed him too far toward system in my interpretation. Dawidoff, for instance, appears much less certain than I of the value of attempting "to parse" Jefferson's "thinking" and "make his views into the kind of systematic account he did not." Dawidoff, siding with the poem by Robert Frost, seems to believe that the saying about human freedom and equality itself, put in a unique place (the Declaration of Independence) and in a unique way (with the Jeffersonian stylistic elegance Dawidoff so elegantly describes in his essay), signifies more than any systematic philosophic statement might. Indeed Dawidoff affirms something like this about Jefferson in general—he "expresses ideals," he proffers "visions," he forges resonant metaphors; "his images predicted what his thinking could not resolve, and bequeathed a visionary place, not a solution." In the past Jefferson was often said to be "a bundle of contradictions"; Dawidoff has a milder version of that thesis: a "bundle of irresolutions."

I do not simply reject the wisdom of so many previous readers of Jefferson or Dawidoff's particularly felicitous expression of his variant on the older view, but I do believe, along with Sheldon, Appleby, and Yarbrough, that Jefferson's thought has more coherence and connectedness, more reasoning and analysis than he is often credited with. In particular, he can give us thoughtful guidance toward understanding those powerful affirmations Robert Frost found puzzling: human freedom and equality, and their important accompaniment, natural (or human) rights.

Having read modern sophisticates like Sanford Levinson[1] and Eva Brann,[2] I have less faith than Frost that these truths cum mysteries will necessarily always be with us. Levinson, for instance, tells us that "it is simply not open to an intellectually sophisticated modern thinker to share Jefferson's world." I have tried to make a beginning of showing that we can share Jefferson's world, and one way to do so is to follow Jefferson's reasonings so that *his* sophistication speaks to ours. At the least this constitutes my attempt for our age to understand what Frost calls Jefferson's "hard mystery."

The question of Jefferson's eclecticism, i.e., of his coherence, runs prominently through two other essays in this volume, those by Robert Booth Fowler and Garrett Ward Sheldon. Nonetheless, they respond to the charge of Jeffersonian eclecticism in altogether different ways. More harshly than Dawidoff, but somewhat along the same lines, Fowler reiterates the older view that Jefferson is eclectic and shallow, and challenges my reading as overly systematic and philosophical. Sheldon, on the other hand, reads Jefferson as someone who has made a coherent and consistent synthesis out of disparate materials.

Fowler accounts for Jefferson's eclecticism rather differently from Dawidoff, however. The Virginian is a "pragmatic Epicurean," who readily adds one or another pleasant pursuit, or kind of theory, or kind of commitment to his life without any particular difficulty or sense of conflict with other beliefs, pursuits, or commitments. "Pragmatic Epicureanism" serves in Fowler's account like a charm-bracelet on which Jefferson can string any number of things—natural rights, gardening, slavery, republicanism, good wine, and so on—without worrying overly much whether one charm "goes with" another. "This was a man for whom there were pleasures to be found everywhere in the natural and human worlds, and he reached out to enjoy a great many of them." Fowler disagrees most emphatically with the effort to read Jefferson in a relatively systematic and philosophical way, and he appeals to an allegedly broad consensus among contemporary scholars denying depth to Jefferson. Moreover, he disagrees not only with my attempt to make coherent sense of Jefferson, but also with the particular sense I do make of him. My reading, Fowler argues, gives us a "domesticated Jefferson."

I consider the last of these points most important, but a few words about Fowler's other two themes seem appropriate as well: lack of political depth and lack of consistency. Fowler quotes Jefferson's "I too am an Epicurean." He appeals to this confession in order to counter the common tendency to see a "much too political Jefferson," who is "miscast" as "a political thinker above all." If Fowler means that there is something more to Jefferson than his political activity and his political thought, then, of course, no one would be inclined to disagree. If he means that Jefferson indulged in what we might call "gracious living"—good food, fine wines, beautiful surroundings—and led a life at least partly marked by indulgence in *refined* pleasures, I think few would be inclined to disagree. To push Epicureanism much further, however, begins to draw dissent. Jefferson was surely not a literal Epicurean, not an orthodox follower of the philosophy of Epicurus, for that philosophy calls for a life far more apolitical, even anti-political than Jefferson's life was. Jefferson was surely not a literal Epicurean in his thinking about politics because none of the themes most characteristic of his political thought appear in Epicureanism. Finally, Fowler's observation that Jefferson had an "Epicurean" side to his life (in the "gracious living" sense), of course, says nothing whatever about the substance or the seriousness of the political views and commitments that he did have. Recall what Jefferson selected for his own epitaph: three consummately political activities. He did not desire to be remembered to the ages as "designer of the gardens at Monticello."

Fowler suggests it is misguided to devote "much serious philosophical attention, examination, or analysis" to Jefferson. Jefferson did not expect such treatment and he himself "displayed little interest in the self-consciously philosophical side of the Enlightenment." Anybody who has read, say, Jefferson's correspondence with John Adams should have a hard time accepting that latter claim. There is hardly a theme taken up by Enlightenment philosophy that Jefferson has not given thought to—materialism and cosmology, theology and natural history, morality and political economy. He has theories about Homeric metrics and Laplacean celestial mechanics, the former requiring substantial knowledge of Greek, the latter substantial mastery of mathematical physics.

Just how philosophical, just how coherent are Jefferson's theories? This is, of course, a matter for debate and interpretation. Clearly Jefferson was not a Hegel—he did not engage in reflections the point of which was to develop explicitly the systematic interconnections among all his thoughts. But then few are Hegels, and Jefferson, along with many other European thinkers before and since, would consider the Hegelian path one to avoid. These questions can hardly be settled in advance, even by a survey of current biographers and their opinions on the subject. I have attempted to explicate the degree of philosophic depth and consistency I find in Jefferson. The only response is to point out concrete failings in the account.

I did not claim, by the way, to have rendered Jefferson consistent in every respect, in part because my study was not of Jefferson per se, but of Jefferson so far as he can help us understand the natural rights philosophy and its political implications. Thus I think Fowler overstates my position when he says that by attending to Jefferson's audience I think it is "possible to unlock the meaning of Jefferson's thought and appreciate its fundamental consistency." My point about Jefferson's audience is more modest: I believe that he tailored what he had to say to match the views of those with whom he was speaking. He did not much believe in the value of arguing; he did believe in being amiable. Thus, when he discovered James Madison to have no sympathy with his "the earth belongs to the living" theories, he stopped talking to Madison about them. That did not stop him from broaching the subject with others. When William Short wrote him about Epicurus, he obligingly replied, "I too am an Epicurean." I am not suggesting Jefferson was a master of esoteric writing, but only that he was an uncommonly dedicated practitioner of the arts of tact and amiability. Keeping his antipathy to conflict in mind helps make some sense of apparently conflicting sentiments he voiced.

Finally, Fowler argues that "the natural rights republican image of Jefferson's thought drastically domesticates or conservatizes Jefferson," for it omits "Jefferson's radical and communitarian democratic program." Fowler points to "a host of strongly democratic ideas and measures" Jefferson supported "to ensure that government was as close to the people as possible, including public election of judges." Fowler builds his case for my having omitted this side of Jefferson by pointing to my reading of the Declaration of Independence, where, he rightly says, I do not find much "commitment to democracy or radically equal political power." But have I made very clear that the Declaration did not express Jefferson's full views on legitimate form of government; in my essay in this volume as well as in the concluding chapter of *The Natural Rights Republic*, I insisted that Jefferson drew far more democratic inferences from the natural rights philosophy than the Declaration contained. Indeed I spent much space tracing the stages by which Jefferson became ever more democratic. In that discussion I explicitly spoke of his proposal for the popular election of judges, for instance.

Fowler also seriously misapprehends my argument about Jefferson on natural rights. In an interpretation of my discussion of "self-evident truths" (not included in this volume, but available as chapter 2 in *The Natural Rights Republic*), Fowler claims that I take these "truths" to be only "what is appropriate within the practice of a given society." That is, the "truths" are no longer seen as "radical" or "universal," but merely as commitments or practices of some society. Fowler sees this as part of my "broader objective of domesticating Jefferson." I had no such "objective." I do not see Jefferson as a wild puppy requiring house-breaking. I do not say that the truths are not truths; I say that they are truths and understood to be such by Jefferson—universal truths, even "radical" truths. I do say that he did not understand these truths to be actually self-evident. Political communities which come to understand and "hold" these truths must do so (as communities) in the mode of "self-evidence," "as if" self-evident. Indeed in chapter 3 of *The Natural Rights Republic*, I tried to show how Jefferson understood and grounded these truths, that is, how he derived them philosophically. As "derived" truths, however, they are not self-evident. I was attempting to show how Jefferson dealt with the dilemmas resulting from the fact that political life in the era of the Enlightenment and beyond can and even must rest on philosophic truths (the ones summarized in the Declaration), but that whole societies of human beings are not well suited to grasping philosophic truths as such, that is, complete with the reasoning which establishes or grounds their truth.

Garrett Sheldon too is impressed with "Jefferson's eclectic political philosophy," but unlike Dawidoff and Fowler, he believes Jefferson managed to forge a coherent synthesis. This is a conclusion with which I have much sympathy, although I draw the lines of the synthesis differently from the way Sheldon does. According to Sheldon, the three chief strands out of which Jefferson constructs his synthesis are "Christian ethics, Lockean liberalism, and classical republicanism." Sheldon certainly demonstrates that an eclectic thinker capable of effecting a synthesis such as the one he attributes to Jefferson need not be confused and need not be a "bundle of contradictions," or even a "bundle of irresolutions."

Sheldon's synthesis is simple, yet remarkably powerful: Christianity supplies the moral foundation, a morality of benevolence and justice; Lockean liberalism supplies the notion of rights and therewith "the parameters of government." Yet Christianity is not at all inconsistent with Lockean liberalism, for it supplies "the ethical culture" needed for a regime aiming at Lockean liberalism. At the same time, Lockean liberalism is deeply consistent with Christianity: "Natural Rights conform to a basically Judeo-Christian worldview in his [Jefferson's] understanding of individual rights as 'the gift of God.'" The Christian and Lockean elements are both consistent with the classical republican or Aristotelian strain in Jefferson's thought, for on the one hand, the Christian ethical notion is completely compatible with the affirmation of natural sociability and public-spiritedness posited within the republican tradition, and on the other hand, Jefferson made Lockean liberalism compatible with republicanism by "adapting it to 'free and independent' colonies as well as individuals." More than that, Jefferson's "later appeal to classical republican politics . . . would enhance the preservation of fundamental rights and liberties."

Sheldon concedes there are differences "in fine points of philosophy" among these three components of the Jeffersonian synthesis, yet he draws an attractive and almost persuasive picture of a possible Jeffersonian position. It is only "almost persuasive," for two reasons: (1) despite his explicit argument in favor of the synthesis, at nearly the last moment he pulls back from his own claims about the success of the synthesis; and (2) on closer examination the synthesis he constructs succeeds as well as it does only because Jefferson has so modified two of the component parts that they no longer can be conceived as independent contributing elements of a synthesis.

Although Sheldon claims to have worked out a Jeffersonian synthesis, he finds that two of its components—the "classical republican" and the "Lockean liberal"—"contrast" with each other. I think his term "contrast" serves as a soft form of what he really means—"conflict." The theory of classical republicanism builds on natural human sociability, the moral sense, a rejection of egoism, and an understanding of the human good as the natural fulfillment of human beings in political participation." Lockean liberalism affirms natural individualism and self-interestedness, the artificiality of the political community, and the ultimate ordering of government to the securing of self-centered rights. These are differences that are more than "contrasts." It is not clear, in other words, how much Sheldon believes in his own synthesis.

The synthesis he gives us requires so much deep-going truncation of two of the partners in the synthesis that it is difficult to take at face value his description of Jefferson's political philosophy. Sheldon is surely correct to emphasize the intensely political character of Jefferson's position compared to many straight liberal positions. Jefferson's ward republics are meant to be deeply political places, encouraging abiding, deeply felt political attachments and prompting a level of active political participation our apathetic and apolitical age can barely imagine. Yet Jefferson does not project this theory as a *synthesis* of liberal and republican elements. At bottom it is a version of Lockean liberalism which happens to converge with some of the theories of the Aristotelian republican tradition. An Aristotelian republican could never say what Jefferson is famous for having said: "that government is best which governs least." An Aristotelian republican would never say what Jefferson says, that anything that can be left to the individual to do for himself should be so left. Jefferson's theory bears all the marks of the liberal theory of government as necessary evil. An Aristotelian republican would never conceptualize citizenship or the rights of participation and control as Jefferson does—as appurtenances of the citizens' status as joint makers and thus joint owners of the new "property" they have brought into being, the state. A genuine Aristotelian would never do what Jefferson does, place abstract principle of right so far above considerations of prudence.

Rather than calling Jefferson's position a synthesis of two traditions that even Sheldon realizes cannot be readily synthesized, we should interpret it as a fundamentally Lockean liberal position which has been able to assimilate some features of the classical republican tradition, features which are compatible with and in the service of the underlying liberalism of Jefferson's political thinking. Those connections come to light when one follows out carefully the actual trajectory of Jeffersonian theorizing that brings him to his ward republics.

The situation is very similar regarding the Christian component of the so-called synthesis. According to Sheldon, Jefferson appeals to Christianity so far as it contains "the ethics . . . that any civilized society requires to operate smoothly and effectively." Jefferson understood, independently of Christian revelation, what these requirements were, discerned that Jesus preached them (or many of them), and encouraged the use of Jesus' preaching as a way to inculcate this kind of ethics. Nonetheless, he also saw that Christianity—the actual inherited religion—contained much that was contrary to or at least not a part of this rational social ethic. Those elements, Sheldon concedes, Jefferson excised. These included such matters as the divinity and redemptive mission of Christ, no small loss for historical Christianity. Under these circumstances it is difficult to say that anything *distinctively* Christian enters into the Jeffersonian "synthesis." Jefferson affirmed and assimilated that part of Christianity that is independently known to be valuable for social life. Christianity can hardly be seen, then, as an equal, much less (as Sheldon implies from time to time) a senior partner in Jefferson's philosophy of politics.

Joyce Appleby reacts to the same larger scholarly debate as Sheldon, but does so in a quite different and, I think, more successful way. Sheldon accepts the terms of the ongoing scholarly controversies regarding the founding era in general and Jefferson in particular. The debate is between those who see the founding as a manifestation of classical republicanism and those who see in it Lockean liberalism. Sheldon claims, as we have seen, that Jefferson synthesized the two positions, but as we have also seen, he recognizes that the synthesis, as he formulates its original elements, cannot succeed.

Appleby more successfully proceeds by drawing an important distinction between classical and liberal republicanism. Jefferson, she emphasizes, was indeed a republican, but this does not require buying into the classical paradigm of republicanism. In one of her other important essays, "Republicanism in Old and New Contexts," for example, she points out how much in Jefferson's most abiding thinking was inconsistent with the classical, backward-looking character of the republican model and how much instead cohered with the liberal model. As she insists, Jefferson and his followers claimed to have "liberated themselves from the bondage of old systems. They recognized that theirs was a new era." They had great hopes for a future altogether different from the past. She quotes Jefferson's well-known statement to Joseph Priestley: "This whole chapter in the history of man is new."[3] He was not only not a follower of Aristotle, but he thought modern developments had "rendered useless" Aristotle's science of government. She concludes by observing that "there is little evidence . . . of a mingling of liberal and classical traditions."[4] Jefferson needs to be understood as a modern, liberal republican, quite a different animal from the classical sort. For Jefferson, the liberal or "natural rights republican," there was a seamless fit between the commitment to the social contract/natural rights political philosophy and a republican political science.

Appleby's essay in this volume is part of her effort to save Jefferson from the clutches of the classical republicans and to vindicate his consistency from the open criticisms of a Fowler, or the implicit criticism of a Sheldon. In this essay she is most concerned with the important work of Drew McCoy on Jeffersonian political economy. McCoy sees Jefferson as torn inconsistently between his classical republicanism (inherently anticommercial) and his attempt (under the prodding of various necessities) not to "disregard the new imperatives of a more modern commercial society" (quoted in Appleby). In the economic sphere as in the political sphere, Appleby insists on some distinctions the republican synthesizers overlook. They, for example, identify Alexander Hamilton with a modernist, pro-commercial, pro-economic expansion, proto-capitalist vision and read the Jefferson opposition to him as a hankering for a noncommercial, classical republican society: stable, virtuous, small, and anti-capitalist. Her alternate view, in a word, is that this is a false way of characterizing the Hamilton-Jefferson split. "The battle between the Jeffersonians and the Federalists appears not as a conflict between the patrons of agrarian self-sufficiency and the proponents of modern commerce, but rather as a struggle between two different elaborations of capitalistic development in America." Her account of the expansion of American exports of foodstuffs in the 1790s helps make clear that Jefferson's option for an agrarian America was not an option against the market, against international trade, or against capitalism.

Her demonstration that Jefferson was an agrarian, but a thoroughly commercial agrarian, with no nostalgia for the past and no lingering hopes to prevent progress or to stand against science or to resist the spread of new liberal ideas, is a great aid in clarifying the real character of Jeffersonian thinking on political economy. His views on that subject have always been among the elements most insistently seized on both by those who doubted his commitment to liberal modernity and those who doubted his consistency as a political thinker. Pegging Jefferson as a classical republican in his political economy contributes to the vision of Jeffersonian inconsistencies, for he seems to adhere to a political philosophy of a Lockean sort while promoting an anti-commercial and anti-Lockean political economy. After

Appleby's contribution reprinted here and her earlier book *Capitalism and a New Social Order*, Jefferson's political economy is no longer so available as evidence for either of these two positions.

Race: Natural History and Natural Rights

James Ceaser does not try to present an overall account of Jefferson's thinking or of his legacy, but he does forcefully raise one of the most troubling themes in recent discussions of the Virginian: his theories on race and their possible bearing on the project of a natural rights republic. Not only did his comments on race have great, and greatly deleterious, effects for the causes of liberty and equality he held dear, but his argument seems in direct conflict with his own most ringing phrase: "all men are created equal." As Ceaser says, "any project to revive natural right that rests on Jefferson as an authority cannot go much further until something is said" about Jefferson's treatment of race in *Notes on Virginia*. Ceaser has said a great deal about that subject, both in this essay and in his marvelously instructive and entertaining book, *Reconstructing America*. Nonetheless, I welcome his invitation to add something more.

Ceaser, of course, is not the first to notice the problem to which he refers, but his treatment of it is much sounder than that of most scholars who have addressed the problem heretofore. Ceaser's discussion contains two themes of very great importance and truth. First, he notices the central point as Jefferson saw it: the inequalities that he surmised to exist between the races could never justify slavery. Neither the kind of equality affirmed in the Declaration nor the universal possession of human rights is affected by any of the sorts of inequalities Jefferson's discussion of race evokes. Indeed, it is Jefferson's very security in that conviction that allows him to be so free in his discussion of racial inequality: anyone who understands the foundation of rights correctly will know that any racial inequalities are irrelevant to the question of the rightfulness of slavery. Of course, as Ceaser demonstrates, Jefferson was far too sanguine. Not everyone understood the principles of right correctly, and his racial discussions were put to mischievous uses of which he would not have approved. Ceaser is surely correct to say that Jefferson should have been more alive to the possibility, even likelihood, of misunderstanding and misuse.

Ceaser, moreover, sees clearly that Jefferson's discussion occurs in a very specific context, the defense of his proposal for emancipating and then colonizing the slaves. Jefferson emphasizes the necessity of the latter quite as much as the necessity of the former. The two races not only share an unfortunate history, which bodes ill for their future together as fellow citizens of a republic, but have natural differences, Jefferson speculates, that will reinforce and exacerbate the legacy of that history. The whites, used to ruling, will carry "deep rooted prejudices," the blacks will correspondingly nurse "ten thousand recollections . . . of the injuries they have sustained" (*Notes on Virginia*, Query XIV). In this context, "the real distinctions which nature has made will be particularly relevant," for (as Jefferson understands these "real distinctions") they will reinforce the "prejudices" and "recollections" that are the historical heritage of slavery. Perhaps Jefferson's point is that either set of circumstances alone might be overcome, thus making a biracial society possible, but the two together cannot. The natural differences would matter less for a common citizenship if there were not that history; the history could matter less if it were not reinforced by fresh lessons constantly revivifying the attitudes carried over from slavery. Jefferson's observations on race differences, then, are meant to be the ultimate support for the policy of colonization he recommends.

The structure of Jefferson's thought is this: because of natural rights and natural equality, there must be emancipation; because of racial inequality and the legacy of slavery, there must be colonization. Ceaser insists, probably rightly, that Jefferson's comments on race undermined his commitments on emancipation in the minds of his fellow citizens. And, Ceaser also insists, Jefferson could well have anticipated that effect. Given its foreseeable costs, why did Jefferson play his "race card"? Ceaser suggests that Jefferson was seduced into it by his attraction to the natural history of his day, one form of the Enlightenment philosophy (pace Fowler) to which he was generally attracted.

I want to suggest another way to understand Jefferson's disastrous foray into race theory. Particularly intriguing is the frequently remarked different style of analysis Jefferson used in speaking of the Indians compared to that he used in speaking of the blacks. In the case of the former he applied a sophisticated kind of environmentalism to explain the physical and moral traits displayed by the Indians. In the case of the blacks he went out of his way to reject the same sort of environmental explanations, and instead fastened on nature in the form of inherent racial differences. The difference in treatment accorded these two peoples demonstrates that Jefferson was not captive to any one scheme of natural historical explanation.

That fact makes one think that Jefferson's attachment to racial explanation is not best understood in the terms Ceaser proposes. It is more revealing to reason backward from the effect of his endorsement of race theory to its cause. The *effect* is the conviction that colonization was the only appropriate policy to follow; emancipation by itself would not be in the interests of either whites or blacks. That meant that emancipation, the demand of natural rights and the demand of justice, had to be deferred until the massive political and economic will to effect colonization could be mustered as well. This deferral had to govern both political and personal action. The state of Virginia would be irresponsible to emancipate without providing adequately for the freemen (which meant colonization); the individual would be irresponsible to emancipate and merely leave the newly enfranchised persons in the midst of the society that enslaved them, and in which, for both historical and natural reasons, they could not thrive.

Race theory, as the decisive ground for colonization and thus for the deferral of emancipation, offered Jefferson an avenue for dealing with what was probably the deepest and most abiding internal conflict he faced. He was an enemy to slavery on philosophic and moral grounds. None of the efforts to impugn the sincerity of his professions are convincing. He was also a slave-owner, enjoying, as Fowler points out, a style of "gracious living" built on slavery. Surely Jefferson can be blamed and even charged with hypocrisy for denouncing slavery in the abstract but relishing so much the life built on it. However, Jefferson's complex structure of thought on slavery and race served the important function for him of supplying a justification for carrying forward—without a bad conscience—a life built on the labor and wealth produced by slaves, not because race theory made slavery just or legitimate, but because it made emancipation without colonization an inappropriate response to the injustice of slavery. Race theory, in other words, allowed Jefferson to have the cake of moral and political opposition to slavery and at the same time to eat the cake earned with the sweat of his slaves' brows. Jefferson never took concrete steps toward emancipation of his own slaves, unlike many other founders. In part this followed from his ever-present debt, but that in turn was a matter of his choices—to make Monticello the most magnificent dwelling in America, for instance. Jefferson could always justify himself in terms of the alleged necessity of colonization, a necessity supported by his race theory.

Surely there were many others in Jefferson's position, so that race theory functioned, even for those who accepted natural rights and natural equality, as a device enabling them to carry on as slaveholders and beneficiaries of a slave society. But the problem lies not with natural rights theory itself nor with Jefferson's adherence to it, but with his human, all too human, attempt to continue to benefit from an institution he sincerely denounced as unjust. There is no organic or logical connection between the natural rights philosophy and the race theory to which Jefferson also appealed.[5] His adherence to the latter was an effort to reduce the conflict between his conscientious beliefs and his favored style of life; it testifies to the power of self-interest and self-justification to overwhelm even the good among us, even the well-meaning and the wise. It is not a testimony to the inherent defects of the natural rights philosophy.

Rights, Virtues, Goods

Jean Yarbrough's essay displays what her recent book, *American Virtues: Thomas Jefferson on the Character of a Free People*, demonstrated—one can learn a great deal from her about Thomas Jefferson and about the qualities of character required of a free people. Given that, I would, of course, be happier if we agreed more completely than we do about Jefferson on natural rights. Her central thesis, or at least her central response to my construal of Jefferson on rights, is contained, I think, in the following passage: "neither a structural nor a purely Lockean analysis of the Declaration is sufficient" for enabling us "to recover the true meaning and ground of our rights as Jefferson understands them." A subordinate but still significant disagreement between us emerges at the very end of her essay where she blames "Jefferson's failure to instruct Americans in the deeper meaning of the principles they shared," a failing which, she believes, "has encouraged future generations . . . to believe they are free to interpret their rights in whatever manner they wish." She wishes both to endorse Jefferson's political orientation and to endorse the criticism of "rights-talk" or "the rights-industry" that is so important a part of political rhetoric in some circles today.

Let me begin with the smaller and move to the greater point. It does not seem plausible to me to blame Jefferson for the level of discourse about rights in America (or the world) today. He had his say two hundred and more years ago, and no thinker or statesman can ensure that future generations will continue to understand him as he understood himself—not even these who write huge tomes explaining their every thought in great detail. Much "rights-talk" has been talked since his day and he cannot be responsible for the direction it has taken. It is rather for us the living to recapture and revitalize his thought (or any other thought) as we find it valuable and necessary. Yarbrough herself is engaging admirably in that very task. She has presented Jefferson's doctrine of rights so that those who follow her argument will not "believe they are free to interpret their rights in whatever manner they wish."

On the more central issue between us of the "true meaning and ground of our rights," she maintains not only that my structural approach cannot tell us what we need to know, but that I admit as much: "as Zuckert himself acknowledges more than once, the structure of the documents sheds no light on the central idea of natural rights." Although I argue in *The Natural Rights Republic* that one needs to go beyond the Declaration to understand all that we wish to about rights, in my essay in this volume I present a structural analysis of rights in the Declaration through showing the coherence the listed rights have as a system of rights, and thus shedding light on the meaning and even the ground of the rights. Yet Yarbrough and I agree that there are limits to the philosophic insight into rights one can achieve on the basis of the Declaration alone. In order to understand Jefferson better on this subject, we agree that we must have recourse to his correspondence and (I argue) his *Notes on Virginia*.

According to Yarbrough, I attribute to Jefferson a purely Lockean account of rights. For the sake of the present argument I do not think this is an important issue, for I attempt to draw Jefferson's theory of rights out of his own presentation. (Unfortunately, some of the main elements of this discussion are not contained in this volume, but in chapter 3 of *The Natural Rights Republic*). For the record, however, I would like to say that my position on the relation of Locke to Jefferson is a bit more complex than she believes. I do argue that the theory of legitimate government presented in the Declaration is Lockean so far as it goes. I do not argue that Jefferson is thoroughly Lockean in all aspects of his thinking. I agree with Yarbrough, for example, that Jefferson is both more agrarian and more republican than Locke. Moreover, I do not even argue that Jefferson's theory of rights is purely Lockean. I think Locke has a deeper and more adequate conception of the basis of rights than Jefferson does, but that was not part of my field of interest in *The Natural Rights Republic* and thus I did not explore that subject.

Attributing to me the view that Jefferson has a thoroughly Lockean doctrine of rights, Yarbrough signals her disagreement by detailing the ways in which she sees Jefferson deviating from Locke. Her catalog of these deviations is a model of clear writing and orderly thinking. She identifies three differences in the grounding of rights and she identifies three resultant differences in the character of the rights themselves.

Since my discussion of the ground of rights is not contained in this volume, I will pass over this topic very briefly. Yarbrough finds that Jefferson works with a different "political psychology" and therefore derives rights from human nature differently than Locke. She emphasizes two themes: the greater role in Jefferson of "spiritedness" or "pride in self-government" as part of the ground for the right to liberty, and the role of the moral sense in pointing us toward happiness in the exercise of the social virtues, as part of Jefferson's grounding of the right to pursuit of happiness. Yarbrough's discussion of both is most interesting, but in neither case does she show that Jefferson connects the asserted qualities of human psychology to his doctrine of rights. In chapter 3 of *The Natural Rights Republic* I tried to show how, following Jefferson's texts, natural rights are grounded more or less independently of the moral sense, although rights do ultimately lend support to the moral sense. Until Yarbrough gives a textual analysis relating these features of Jefferson's thought to the ground of natural rights, I am inclined to hold fast to the most explicit discussions Jefferson does provide of the ground of rights, which do not contain the kind of theory she attributes to Jefferson.

The central issue in the present context, however, is Yarbrough's alternative rendering of the character of Jeffersonian rights. Her important claims are three. First, she argues that Jefferson's notion of the right to liberty, grounded in "pride of self-government," culminates in a "more positive or 'republican'" view than is characteristic of Lockean liberalism. Secondly, she denies that Jefferson "ever unequivocally states that property is a natural right." Finally, she insists on a different notion of the right to pursuit of happiness than I attribute to Jefferson.

I must disagree with her statement that Jefferson nowhere unequivocally asserts a right to property, for, as I quoted in chapter 3 of *The Natural Rights Republic*, Jefferson says quite straightforwardly: "I believe that a right to property is founded in our natural wants, in the means with which we are endowed to satisfy these wants, and the right to what we acquire by these means." In her note 6, Yarbrough cites a letter where Jefferson says: "it is a moot question whether the origin of any kind of property is derived from nature at all." To call it a moot question, of course, does not imply that property is not natural, merely that whether property is natural is a debatable or discussable issue. If one reads the whole of this statement and keeps the context in mind, I think it becomes clear that Jefferson is certainly not denying that property is a natural right. The issue in play between Jefferson and his correspondent is the patent right. Some commentators had asserted "that inventors have a natural and exclusive right to their inventions, and not merely for their own lives, but inheritable to their heirs" (Peterson, 1291, Letter to DuPont). Jefferson disagreed; he generally disliked monopolies of the sort patents supply. To counter this assertion of a natural right, Jefferson said that it is a question for discussion whether there is any natural right to property, so it cannot be taken for granted there is a natural right of the extraordinary sort claimed by the commentators he cited. Thinking perhaps of a discussion of the history of property he had copied into his *Commonplace Book* forty or more years earlier from Lord Kames' *Historical Law Tracts*, Jefferson moved to settle the question of a natural right to a monopoly use of inventions with the following preliminary reflection:

> It is agreed by those who have seriously considered the subject, that no individual has, of natural right, a separate property in an acre of land, for instance. By an universal law, indeed, whatever, whether fixed or moveable, belongs to all men equally and in common, is the property for the moment of him who occupies it; but when he relinquishes the

occupation, the property goes with it (Peterson, 1291; *Commonplace Book*, entry, 559).

Jefferson does not here deny in any way a natural right to property; indeed he affirms such a right, so long as the claimant occupies or possesses. This includes a natural right to land as well as to movable goods. This natural right is limited in nature to property possessed, and a right to own land that one does not occupy, say, comes only when "social law" is added to natural right: "stable ownership is the gift of social law," but ownership simpliciter is the gift of nature, of occupation, or in Lockean terms, of labor.

Yarbrough concedes that "the pursuit of happiness remains the most elusive of the rights announced in the Declaration." She believes that this right can best be grasped by relating it to Jefferson's understanding of happiness itself; "he repeatedly insists that the core of happiness is permanent and universal: there can be no genuine happiness, without virtue." The virtues he most associates with happiness, moreover, are the "social virtues." While her discussion of happiness is instructive, I do not believe it helps us understand Jefferson's right to pursuit of happiness. In the first place, the Declaration affirms not happiness, not even a right to happiness, but a right to *pursuit* of happiness. The phrase was apparently borrowed from George Mason's Virginia Declaration of Rights, suggesting strongly that it was not an idea unique to Jefferson. Mason most likely borrowed the phrase from Locke, in whose *Essay Concerning Human Understanding* it was a central concept and intricately related to the reality and possibility of liberty. It is suggestive of a Lockean provenance that Mason and Jefferson both use the phrase "pursuit of happiness" in a context with "liberty."

In attempting to assimilate Jefferson's "right to pursuit of happiness" with his "happiness" as end product of the exercise of social virtues, Yarbrough confuses two critically different concepts of political philosophy. Happiness, as she so nicely describes it, is a good of human life, an object worthy of pursuit. But the Declaration affirms not a good, but a right. The rights embodied in the Declaration are all of the sort often called negative rights: they are a combination of moral permission and moral immunity. To possess a right to life (or as Yarbrough refines it, a right to preservation of life) means that one has moral license or permission to act in ways that will secure that preservation and that one has a rightful immunity against others acting in ways that threaten one's life. Those who violate that immunity commit a natural wrong.

The right to pursuit of happiness is thus doubly removed from Yarbrough's conception of happiness. As a right, it is an immunity and a license—to pursue happiness without interference from others, unless, of course, one's pursuit interferes with the rights of others or the needs of society. It is also a right to a pursuit—i.e., the individual search for happiness, more or less as the individual chooses. No doubt Jefferson understands that not all modes of pursuit are likely to achieve their goal, but he nonetheless affirms the right to the pursuit, not the good of happiness itself. At the end of the day Yarbrough concedes this very point: "Although the moral implications of understanding happiness in this way are profound, the impact on politics is minimal: the rights and duties connected with happiness are not the objects of governmental concern." Her conclusion to this discussion is just what I (in my Lockeanizing way) had said the right amounted to from the outset: "The Declaration . . . leaves individuals free to pursue happiness as they see fit."

Yarbrough also takes issue with my treatment of Jefferson on republicanism. She thinks that my account, "if it were true, would indeed turn the republican tradition on its head." Perhaps so, but I merely followed where Jefferson led; I think it more likely that he and not I overturned the republican tradition. Jefferson was at bottom, as Yarbrough concedes, a supporter of the modern liberal theory of legitimacy, that is, of the theory of the state as expressed in the Declaration of Independence. At the same time he was the most democratic or intensely political devotee of liberal politics up to his time. (On this Yarbrough and I, as well as Fowler, agree). It would not be surprising if Jefferson's deep republicanism had something quite unique about it, vis-à-vis both the precedent republican and Lockean traditions.

Yarbrough's and my difference arises from our differing ways of understanding how Jefferson comes to his very democratic, participatory conclusions. She traces Jefferson's affirmation of "the natural right to self-government" to an expansive (non-Lockean) notion of liberty. She and I agree that this new right is based in part on purely instrumental considerations. As she puts it: "One reason the people insist on retaining the right of self-government is because they cannot always trust their elected representation to protect their rights." We also agree that this instrumental reason does not completely capture Jefferson's idea. According to Yarbrough, Jefferson's non-instrumental commitment to a through-going republicanism "seems at least partly grounded in pride and its associated passions, the love of honor and laudable ambition, which attend the spirited, as opposed to the appetitive, dimension of human nature." "Men seek to govern themselves," she also says, "not only because it promotes their interests, but because it gratifies their pride." Her argument is thus built on a distinction within human nature between "appetitive" and "spirited" dimensions. This is a distinction I recall very vividly from Plato, especially *The Republic*, a book Jefferson contemned, but it is not one I can ever recall seeing Jefferson make. The references Yarbrough appends to these claims are thus of very great interest: her chief authority, it turns out, is not Jefferson but Harvey Mansfield, admittedly a seminal thinker, but one whose goal appears to be to present an account of modern liberal politics in categories at least in part adapted from ancient political philosophers like Plato. His theory may give a superior account of modern practice to that provided by the architects of modern practice (like Jefferson), but his account should not be confused with their self-understanding. Yarbrough also refers us to chapter 4 of her book, but in that place we see a similar kind of argument: citations once again to Mansfield, coupled this time with citations to one of his students' study of *The Federalist*. In her book she attempts to enlist Jefferson in the camp of the Platonists by highlighting his use of the term "spirit," as in the phrase "spirit of the people." She wants to read this as if it were equivalent to "spiritedness of the people" as opposed to their "appetitiveness." Examination of the instances quoted or cited in her text does not support that reading. Jefferson's most common use of "spirit" is rather like that deployed by Montesquieu in his "The Spirit of the Laws," to signify an overall characteristic quality—as in the phrase "the spirit of the age."

She disagrees with my alternate account of Jefferson's "right to self-government," an account resting on the admittedly paradoxical claim that Jefferson conceived this right as deriving from "his assimilation of the public sphere entirely to the theory of private property." I traced this notion to Jefferson's assertion that society is "an acquisition" of man "which he has a right to regulate and control, jointly indeed with all those who have concurred in the procurement." Jefferson's language here is unmistakably the language of property—"acquisition" and "procurement." Society is "acquired" through being made, in the manner described in the Declaration of Independence. As a making and an acquisition, the men who have made it (all who "consent" to it, not just the original makers) own it, so to speak. They have the "right to regulate and control" it, "jointly" with their co-procurers, or co-owners, or fellow citizens. Their rights in it are similar to their rights in some more standard kind of joint property or joint enterprise.

They have a right to control the state (i.e., a right to republican self-government) not only because that will better serve their interests, but because the state belongs to them, each and every one of them. The state is a product of the human power to create property and thus embodies, expresses, and reflects the human quality of being a rights bearer and, to a degree, a rights creator. The state is thereby a token of human dignity, and the right of republican self-government thus embodies a demand of human dignity itself. Hence Jefferson concludes, although not in the Declaration, not only that the natural rights philosophy implies republicanism as the preferred form of government, but also that there is a right to such government. I do not, as Yarbrough suggests, criticize Jefferson for insisting on this right. I did wish to call attention to the important shift this signaled from previous views and to indicate that it has been a mixed blessing. I also concede what Yarbrough does: that Jefferson recognized that not all, perhaps not any, political societies would be able to live up to these abstract requirements of natural right. He displays a certain flexibility, it is true, but it is also true that the one standard of legitimacy hovers above all the imperfect regimes. This is an especially tense matter, because Jefferson, like late-twentieth-century Americans, does not merely posit republican self-government as the most desirable or best regime, but as *the* legitimate regime, the regime to which all human beings have a right. He thus renders all actual regimes not only less than "ideal," but more or less illegitimate. I consider this a problematic idea that has much to do with Jefferson's frequently noted "interest" in, if not intoxication with, revolution.

Jefferson's commitment to natural rights republicanism may lead in problematic directions, but these problems, like so much else in his thinking, remain our problems, because they derive from his commitments, which remain for the most part our commitments. Most Americans can still thrill to his last written words, attempting to capture the global significance of the American Revolution and its statement of purpose, the Declaration of Independence:

> May it be to the world, what I believe it will be . . . the signal of arousing men to burst the chains under which . . . ignorance and superstition had persuaded them to bind themselves, and to assume the blessing and security of self-government. . . . All eyes are opened or opening to the rights of man. The general spread of the light of science has already laid open to every view the palpable truth, that the mass of mankind has not been born with saddles on their backs, nor a favored few booted and spurred, ready to ride them legitimately by the grace of God. These are grounds of hope for others. For ourselves, let the annual return of this day [the Fourth of July] forever refresh our recollections of these rights, and an undiminished devotion to them.

We remain interested in Jefferson more than two hundred and fifty years after his birth because he, even more than the holiday centered around the most famous text he wrote, "refreshes our recollection" of both our greatest hopes for and our deepest disappointments in America. That, I think, is ultimately the meaning of the controversies about him to which the essays in this volume bear strong witness.

NOTES

1. Sanford Levinson, "Self-Evident Truth in the Declaration of Independence," *Texas Law Review* 57 (1979): 858. "[To] believe in Jefferson's Declaration of Independence [today] . . . would require a leap of faith indeed."

2. Eva Brann, "Concerning the Declaration of Independence," *The College* (of St. John's College) 28 (1973): 13.

3. Joyce Appleby, "Republicanism in Old and New Contexts," in her *Liberalism and Republicanism in the Historical Imagination* (Cambridge, Mass.: Harvard University Press, 1992), 23.

4. Ibid., 24.

5. For a contrary view, see, e.g., Herbert J. Storing, "Slavery and the Moral Foundations of the American Republic," in *Toward a More Perfect Union*, ed. Joseph Bessette (Washington, D.C.: AEI Press, 1995), 142–44.

Contributors

✽

Joyce Oldham Appleby is a professor of history at the University of California at Los Angeles. A recent president of the American Historical Association, she has written extensively on economic and political thought. Her numerous books include *Capitalism and a New Social Order: The Republican Vision of the 1790s* (New York University Press, 1984), *Economic Thought and Ideology in Seventeenth Century England* (Princeton University Press, 1978), and *Liberalism and Republicanism in the Historical Imagination* (Harvard University Press, 1992).

James W. Ceaser is a professor of government and foreign affairs at the University of Virginia. He is author of a number of books, including *Presidential Selection: Theory and Development* (Princeton University Press, 1979), *Liberal Democracy and Political Science* (Johns Hopkins University Press, 1990), and *Reconstructing America: The Symbol of America in Modern Thought* (Yale University Press, 1997).

Robert Dawidoff is a professor of history at the Claremont Graduate University. Among his books are *The Education of John Randolph* (W. W. Norton, 1979) and *The Genteel Tradition and the Sacred Rage: High Culture v. Democracy in Adams, James, and Santayana* (University of North Carolina Press, 1992).

Thomas S. Engeman is an associate professor of political science at Loyola University Chicago. He is co-author of *Amoral America*

(Hoover Institution Press, 1975) and co-editor of *The Federalist Concordance* (University of Chicago Press, 1988). He has written several studies of the American Founding, Abraham Lincoln, and American literature.

ROBERT BOOTH FOWLER is a professor of political science at the University of Wisconsin, Madison. His numerous books include *Religion and Politics in America* (American Theological Literary Association, 1985), *Unconventional Partners: Religion and Liberal Culture in the United States* (W. B. Eerdmans, 1989), *The Dance with Community: The Contemporary Debate in American Political Thought* (University Press of Kansas, 1991), and *The Greening of Protestant Thought* (University of North Carolina Press, 1995).

GARRETT WARD SHELDON is the John Morton Beaty professor of political and social science at Clinch Valley College of the University of Virginia. He is the author of a number of books, including *The Political Philosophy of Thomas Jefferson* (Johns Hopkins University Press, 1991), *What Would Jefferson Say?* (Berkley Pub. Group, 1998), and *The Political Philosophy of James Madison* (Johns Hopkins University Press, forthcoming).

JEAN YARBROUGH is a professor of government at Bowdoin College. She is the author of *American Virtues: Thomas Jefferson on the Character of a Free People* (University Press of Kansas, 1998) and a variety of important studies of the American Founding.

MICHAEL P. ZUCKERT is a professor of political science at the University of Notre Dame. His two major studies are *Natural Rights and the New Republicanism* (Princeton University Press, 1994) and *The Natural Rights Republic: Studies in the Foundation of the American Political Tradition* (Notre Dame Press, 1996).

Index